Sarah,

Nothing is by coincidence, I thank God for having the opportunity to meet you. Thank you for sharing your gift of worship in service to our family.

May you be inspired, encouraged, and be challenged in your own personal path journey through reading this book + studying God's Word.

By God's grace,

[signature]

1 Cor. 3 - 5.

May 11 - 2011

Hidden Masks *Unveiled*

HELEN
C. D. JAMIESON

CREATION
HOUSE
A STRANG COMPANY

HIDDEN MASKS UNVEILED by Helen C. D. Jamieson
Published by Creation House
A Strang Company
600 Rinehart Road
Lake Mary, Florida 32746
www.creationhouse.com

Unless otherwise noted, all Scripture quotations are from the Holy Bible, New International Version. Copyright © 1973, 1978, 1984, International Bible Society. Used by permission.

Scripture quotations marked NKJV are from the New King James Version of the Bible. Copyright © 1979, 1980, 1982 by Thomas Nelson, Inc., publishers. Used by permission.

Scripture quotations marked ESV are from *The Holy Bible: English Standard Version*, Wheaton, IL: Crossway Bibles, 2003.

Scripture quotations marked NAS are from the New American Standard Bible. Copyright © 1960, 1962, 1963, 1968, 1971, 1972, 1973, 1975, 1977 by the Lockman Foundation. Used by permission. (www.Lockman.org)

Scripture quotations marked KJV are from the King James Version of the Bible.

Design Director: Bill Johnson
Cover design by Jerry Pomales

Library of Congress Control Number: 2008929186
International Standard Book Number: 978-1-59979-395-5

First Edition

08 09 10 11 12 — 987654321
Printed in the United States of America

❧

*Dedicated to my Triune God who
loves me as I am despite my masks.*

With Heartfelt Thanks

꒱

THIS FIRST BOOK project has been one of the most challenging tasks I have ever completed. In my past work I was surrounded daily by people, but working on this book project involved extreme discipline to work alone effectively. I quickly realized that God did not leave me alone to work on it. By God's grace He had sent me many people into my life to help me throughout different stages of this project, my invaluable "Book Prayer Warriors," who had faithfully prayed for me weekly, some even for up to three years! None of you ever knew who the other prayer warriors were until now, as I want to publicly acknowledge your support. Thank you to Betty Lau, May Fong, Jennifer Mah, Pam Chan, Kulbir Johal, Sandra Lung, Wendy Toh, Winnie Ma, Linda Kiing, Linh Leung, Kathryn Chiang, Ingrid Devos, Shirley Eu, Hin and Evelyn Kwan, and Susanna Yip (in order of the weekday each committed to pray for me, starting on Sunday). There were many other friends who prayed for me. God knows and heard each of you! To my faithful fellowship, "Experiencing God Group": Thank you for praying and encouraging me through this journey.

This has been an amazing journey of learning about staying faithful and trusting God and others for support. Thank you to Pastor Tim Tze,

Joan Fong, and May Fong for inspiring me and providing encouraging insights to share with others in this book.

I am blessed to have my own brother, Chi Lam, gifted in the knowledge of God's Word and truths, to edit my work to ensure God's truths were not distorted or conveyed incorrectly. Thanks, Chi, for your faith in God's work through me. My niece, Niki, even at the age of sixteen at the time—and now eighteen—was so supportive in providing me the input I needed. Special thanks to my dear friend Wendy Toh for her endless hours of editing my manuscript for my initial submission to the publisher without losing my "conversational style" of sharing.

I want to extend a big thanks to Creation House for trusting me to partner with them in my first hardcover book. I look forward to our future partnership if God continues to use me in this way. I am so grateful for their team in their professionalism, patience, and personal attention for the entire process that is new to me. I thank Allen Quain from my initial queries and constant questions in handling my manuscript; to Virginia Maxwell for encouraging me while she was setting up the layout for my book and managing the production from beginning to end. Thanks to Jihan M. Ruano for all the administrative details. Thank you to Atalie Anderson and the team for their marketing efforts and making the title of this book better. Only God can choose the right editors, Ken Holmgren and Diana Richardson, to use their gifts in making this book flow the way it does. Thank you for making my words concise to flow seamlessly better to convey my heartfelt thoughts. Thank you, Amanda Lowell, for your support in the book cover copy. Thanks to Jerry Pomales for the book jacket design and Annette Simpson for the interior design. May God continue to use the whole team at Creation House for His glory!

I am so thrilled and encouraged by my own daughter Kayli for her continual prayer and support for me. She is my greatest supporter.

Through her own passion to write and become an author one day, she inspires me to do my best and to persevere. Kayli, thank you, sweetie. You are my inspiration. Words cannot begin to express how blessed I am by God to provide me with the most supportive husband. Bill, thank you for believing in what God is using me to do. Thank you for trusting and allowing me to share our family's most personal stories. Thank you for not giving up on me and encouraging me to "press on" for the Lord. Thank you for providing me the technical hardware so I can write when God inspires me—like my first lightweight laptop, and the biggest home monitor I have ever seen! Thank you for all the back and leg massages while I worked many long hours on this book. Thank you for taking on the role as my marketing agent; you have always been the best promoter and supporter in this book ministry. I am so thankful to God for partnering us together in this ministry. You are my lifetime partner, and I love you dearly!

There are so many people that I want to acknowledge, but I am limited in space. Special mention is required for an anonymous individual that God chose to send my way. I was on my final leg of completing the manuscript and wanted to give up. I cried out to God in prayer one night without telling anyone. By the next day, God prompted someone with an obedient heart to drop off a gospel tract and an excerpt note in an envelope on my front house mat.

As I read this small, oval, jagged, cutout excerpt, I started to cry, as I knew that God had answered my prayer, affirming me to complete this book for Him. I kept this excerpt by my office desk each day to read before writing to remind me of God's working in me. The excerpt from *Gideon Had a Great God* by J. Vernon McGee was as follows: "When God gets ready to do anything, He chooses the weakest thing He can get in order to make it clear that He, not the weak arm of the flesh, is doing it."

Dear friend, whoever you are, if this book makes it into your hands, I want to thank you for being obedient in God's prompting in your life to extend unconditional love to others. This book is testimony that God does choose the weak things of the world to bring glory to Himself! It is God's grace to use and equip me to do His work.

Dear Lord, I want to thank You for choosing me despite all my weaknesses to complete this book for Your glory! I pray that many hearts turn back to You as they face Your truths. Thank You for healing me through this writing process so I can live a life of freedom in You! Thank You for allowing me to boast Your name, Lord Jesus!

But God chose the foolish things of the world to shame the wise; God chose the weak things of the world to shame the strong.... Therefore, as it is written: "Let him who boasts boast in the Lord."

—1 CORINTHIANS 1:27, 31

—HELEN C. D. JAMIESON
Visit me at www.hosannahouse.ca

Contents

ॐ

SECTION I: The Unveiling of My Masks

SECTION II: The Masks We Wear

SECTION III: After We Unveil Our Masks

Foreword

⌁

There is no deep knowing of God without deep knowing of self and no deep knowing of self without deep knowing of God.
—JOHN CALVIN

Grant, Lord, that I may know myself that I may know thee.
—ST. AUGUSTINE

Among Christians, we speak much about knowing God. Indeed, that is the proper emphasis and pursuit for those who profess to follow Jesus Christ. However, as St. Augustine, Thomas à Kempis, John Calvin, and a great many others tell us, there cannot be deep knowledge of God without deep knowledge of one's self. In this, her first book, Helen Jamieson takes us onto the path of self-discovery. She points us to the way of attaining genuine self-understanding: unveiling one's own masks. She does not merely name these masks— twelve altogether—but goes on to outline how God will deliver us from them. The ultimate aim of *Hidden Masks Unveiled* is to challenge us to cast aside our meticulously crafted false self and arrive at a place of genuine self-understanding. And that will in turn lead to the revitalization of our spiritual life.

Hidden Masks Unveiled is a worthy volume for a further reason: it is the work of a devout heart. Her writing here is direct and sincere. The contents of this book have come from her deep personal experience, which she plainly and courageously shares with her readers. She writes credibly of God, for she—and this is plainly evident to me—has had a close walk with her Lord.

I count it a privilege and blessing to have known Helen for fourteen years, as a friend and as her pastor. Her courage and her desire to lead a God-honoring life have been an inspiration to me. I recommend *Hidden Masks Unveiled* unreservedly. Read it for spiritual enrichment and profit.

—TIM TZE
SENIOR PASTOR
BURNABY ALLIANCE CHURCH

Preface

ॐ

WHY WRITE A BOOK ABOUT HIDDEN MASKS UNVEILED?

It is the irony of life that in our quest for freedom we become slaves to what we do. In our quest to be free from superficial relationships and have genuine relationships, we become trapped in our "masks of pretense," controlled by the lies we create. We think we will be free when we become the person others envision us to be. Suddenly, however, we realize that we have so fooled ourselves into believing in and wearing our masks that we cannot remove them.

My quest to find physical healing led me to the real healing that I needed—spiritual healing. I have worn too many masks in my life's journey, and it has taken over twenty years for me to take some of them off. I realize that this is true not just for me, but for many others like me. We have deceived ourselves into believing that we are free because we wear our masks. On the contrary, we need to remove our masks to be truly free.

As a Chinese Canadian, I think about what a mask is in my native Cantonese tongue. It sounds like "mean-hawk," which translated literally means a "face-shell" that we wear in front of our face to cover up our real self.

The Merriam-Webster dictionary defines *mask* as: (1) a cover or partial cover for the face used for disguise; or in verb form

(1) to disguise one's true character or intentions, or (2) to form a covering for protection.

Why do we hide behind masks? It is a form of security we use to protect ourselves when we do not want people to know the real "us." We may be afraid of being hurt, or we may be convinced that others will love us more if we appear to be someone else. Although there are times when confidentiality is necessary, we must also recognize the difference between confidentiality and keeping the truth about ourselves a secret. Confidentiality maintains trust in relationships, but keeping truth a secret damages relationships. Guilt and bitterness will eventually surface, and reality will hurt others even more once it is uncovered.

What are the masks that we wear? Do we even know we wear them? Instead of allowing God to reign in our lives, we put ourselves on the throne and try to control our lives by pretending to be something we really aren't. We wear masks that are lies produced by our sinful nature and our unconfessed sin that block us from having genuine relationships.

First John 3:9 and 1 John 5:18 remind us that it is not possible for a child of God to continue in sin. We may sin, but the Holy Spirit indwelling each of us is grieved when we sin. We are convicted of our sins, and we repent and confess them to God; hence, we do not continue to sin. However, when we do not allow the Holy Spirit to reign in our lives completely, and instead control our own lives, we end up wearing masks. Each mask tends to look like the "fruit of the Spirit" we desire to emulate, but it is just that—emulation.

We will wear masks until we surrender complete control of our lives, moment by moment, to God. We cannot wear and display the fruit of the Spirit on our faces by our own ability; only the Holy Spirit can work through our hearts so that our lives will display it. Without Him we live in the endless cycles of guilt, shame, anger, anxiety, fear, lack of joy, or depression. These cycles, which are manifested from the masks we wear, are opposite of the fruit we bear when we allow God to rule in our lives. The fruit of the Spirit is love, joy, peace, patience, longsuffering, kindness, goodness, faithfulness, gentleness, and self-control (Gal. 5:22–23, NKJV).

God is calling us to acknowledge the truth He has revealed to us about our masks and to confess and repent of our pretenses. As He delivers us, we will no longer hide behind our masks. He will set us free from the endless cycles of despair, and we will begin to walk with new hearts and develop people relationships to their fullest. We will embrace the most priceless relationship of all, a genuine and joyfully intimate relationship with God!

When I first started writing down all the masks I was wearing, I named each mask as if it were evil. I was going to give each chapter names such as "the mask of pride", "the mask of sadness", and "the mask of deception." However, it occurred to me they were not the masks I actually had on; sadly, they were what I was feeling deep inside. The masks that I really had on were the masks of pretenses that I was trying to wear as a façade.

To my horror, I discovered that my "mask of perfection" was really covering up my self pride. My "mask of strength" was hiding my weaknesses. What a fake I was when my "mask of honesty" was really covering up lies. I was so ashamed. But God, by His grace, allowed me to realize that He has promised deliverance from each of the "truths" I was trying to hide. For my "mask of perfection," God gave me His *grace*; for my "mask of strength," He gave me *power through the Holy Spirit*; for my "mask of honesty," He showed me His *truth* and offered me *freedom*. God reminded me to take my veil off, "No more hiding, Helen, take it off."

But whenever anyone turns to the Lord, the veil is taken away. Now the Lord is the Spirit, and where the Spirit of the Lord is, there is freedom.

—2 CORINTHIANS 3:16–17

Introduction

ॐ

But by the grace of God I am what I am....yet
not I, but the grace of God that was with me.
—1 Corinthians 15:10

My Recurring Dream

I woke up startled. I had just had the same strange, recurring dream.

> *I am in a sheepfold with many sheep, and I see a wolf digging*
> *a hole outside the fence. I move toward the hole, curious and*
> *compelled to go into this hole underneath the fence. Before*
> *I enter the hole, I feel a sudden yank on my neck and am*
> *pulled back by the crook of the shepherd's staff. The jerk is*
> *so hard that it wakes me up.*

This time, however, the dream had started the same but ended differently:

> *I see other sheep going into the same hole I had wanted to*
> *go into. I am compelled to warn them not to go in, and I try*
> *to warn them.*

Before I discovered what would happen, I woke up. Troubled, I asked God to reveal the meaning of my dreams, and He spoke to me through the Holy Spirit and His Word that morning. God depicts us as sheep, which are not too smart and need to be led by a shepherd. That shepherd is Jesus Christ. The wolf is Satan. The hole is anything that would tempt our desire to be led away from Christ.

God showed me that He wanted to use me to warn my fellow believers in Christ about the dangers ahead. In the end times we may become complacent in our relationship with the Lord, because we are safe in the fold. We take God for granted. We may minister and serve, but that is not what God really wants; He wants our hearts. We forget that the Shepherd says His sheep will know His voice and will follow Him. (See John 10:4). When we are complacent in our relationship with the Lord, we can forget our Lord's voice and be deceived by the enemy. Even though our salvation is secure, we can still be enticed by the enemy who will lead us out of safety and away from our Shepherd's protection.

> At that time many will turn away from the faith and will betray and hate each other, and many false prophets will appear and deceive many people. Because of the increase of wickedness, the love of most will grow cold, but he who stands firm to the end will be saved.
> —MATTHEW 24:10–13

Strangely enough, when I finally committed myself to writing this book that God had placed in my heart and shared my recurring dream with others, I stopped having the dream.

IT'S NOT ABOUT ME

When I received the call to write this book, I felt like Gideon in Judges 6. I asked God to affirm me many times—to speak very clearly to my heart and from His Word to ensure that this was what He wanted me to do. I do not claim to have extra special spiritual insight. I believe that when each of us truly seeks to hear God's voice, He will direct our paths. We will each be given spiritual insight from God when we surrender to Him and seek Him. The Word of God is living breathing truth that can be used by God to speak to us in our present circumstances. God uses His Word and many writers and people to speak to our hearts. I hope He is speaking to you.

In this book, I will share my personal testimony and experiences to encourage us as we traverse the deep valleys of this life journey to press on, because we have the hope that our living God and Savior is here to deliver us. All that I share in this book is written to give honor and glory to God—nothing more, nothing less. All credit goes to Him alone. My intention is only to encourage, not to condemn or to judge. My prayer is that God will use this book to restore others to Him for real healing and bring Him the glory that He alone deserves.

I will share medical information, not to provide medical advice to anyone, but only to give you a better understanding of what I went through and to encourage you to seek help where you need it. Please see a medical professional if you have any health concerns. I believe that if you educate yourself and seek help, God will provide the help you need, whether it be medical and/or spiritual. For spiritual help, I recommend that you share your concerns with your local pastor and fellowship group.

This book begins with the story of my own personal struggles and the way God revealed to me the masks I had to remove. Each chapter begins with a scripture that embodies its main context. At the end of each chapter, an insightful challenge will focus specifically on the masks that need to be exposed in your life. It is my prayer that this personal application will lead you to stop, reflect, and answer each question truthfully about yourself. I pray that God will move your heart to repent of any sin that may be blocking and preventing you from a more intimate relationship with Him. The scripture at the end of each chapter reflects the promise of God's full deliverance and offers hope.

I am cautious about sharing my private journal excerpts, but I realize that God has given me personal healing through it. As I share with you what I have personally experienced, I encourage you to do the same for others. We all have our own stories to share. Everyone experiences pain, guilt, shame, and brokenness differently, and we will never truly understand another's pain. However, as we learn from others, we gain a better perspective and understand that we are not alone in this journey. We have a living God, who is our heavenly Father and intends His best for each of us. Because of this, we can encourage each other by sharing how God's grace has delivered us.

Section III in this book is entitled "After We Unveil Our Masks." It is about spiritual warfare because we cannot ignore the fact we are in the midst of a spiritual battlefield. Appendix 1 is "A Summary of Truth about Unveiling Masks," which includes God's deliverance for each one. Appendix 2, "A Guide for Unveiling Masks," is a study guide suitable both for individuals and small groups. "Suggested Prayers for Seeking God" is found in Appendix 3. I have provided a glossary of medical terminology in Appendix 4, and a bibliography of recommended books and notes at the end. It is my hope that you will gain extra insight from this material.

THE TRUTH SETS YOU FREE

Sometimes it takes a major circumstance to break us down to where we finally realize how much we really are hiding. That is what happened to me. In addition to being my confessional, this book is also intended to encourage others to confess and admit that they, too, wear masks. God our Father sees right through our masks, and He, by His truth, has deliverance for each of us if we truly desire it.

If you are complacent and have lost the joy in your relationship with God and with others, perhaps you are hiding behind masks that block you from the truth. Are you ready to explore the many faces of the masks unveiled in the following pages and see truth revealed in yourself?

I am praying that you will encounter a life-changing experience as God uses this book to speak to your heart. Allow Jesus Christ, who is the real Truth, to reveal any lies and sins that you are trying to protect and hide from others and from God. When you make a conscious decision to surrender to God's will, any masks you may be wearing will be revealed. The Holy Spirit will convict you of your sins and enable you through Christ's strength to confess and repent, to make a commitment to give up those sins. God is always ready and willing to forgive a genuinely repentant heart.

As you make a conscious choice to be Christ-centered not self-centered, you will learn how to live a renewed and restored life in Christ. When you have an abundant and joyful relationship with God, you will be able to extend the same in all your earthly relationships with others.

Do you yearn to have a genuine and joyfully intimate relationship with God and with others? Allow God to unveil the masks that you may be wearing and discover how the truth will set you free. We are set free when we *take off all our masks* and become who we are truly meant to be.

> If you hold to my teaching, you are really my disciples. Then you will know the truth, and the truth will set you free.
> —Jesus (John 8:31–32, emphasis added)

SECTION I

The Unveiling of My Masks

1

Crying Out to God

WHO AM I?

I cried out to God for help; I cried out to God to hear me.
When I was in distress, I sought the Lord; at night I stretched
out untiring hands and my soul refused to be comforted.

—PSALM 77:1–2

WHERE AM I? Am I still in my bedroom? What happened?" As
I awoke to these confused thoughts, I struggled to look at
the clock. With aching eyes that seemed to be sealed tight, I read a
blurry 11:00 a.m. I glanced over quickly to see if Bill was still lying
beside me. He wasn't, for I was in the guest room of our house. I was
so tired that I did not want to get up. And then I remembered that
I had passed out from crying. "God," I acknowledged, "this is real,
isn't it?" Oh, how I wished it was just a nightmare, but it was not. It
was very real.

The night before I had, once again, spun out of control into one
of my raging fits. I did not want my daughter and husband to see
me like this, so I ran into the guest room to be alone. Wailing, filled
with shame, guilt, and despair, I had cried out to God wanting to
give up and asking Him to take me home. "Lord, why am I feeling
like this?"

I was so ashamed because I did not know why I felt such rage,
anger, bitterness, and deep sadness in my heart. I felt so overwhelmed

and burdened. If little things went wrong, it seemed that they would set me off in a pattern of becoming so upset and angry that I exploded and took my anger out on those closest to me. Unfortunately, my target was mainly Bill, my dearest husband, who tried his best to please me. He took me to all my favorite places to shop and eat, and he bought me things that he thought would make me happy. I felt terrible about treating him so badly, but I could neither explain my anger nor express how I really felt.

Because of the deep sadness and despair inside me, I was simply not happy. I felt that I had lost my purpose in life. I felt unworthy to be the mother of my lovely daughter who loved Jesus and had a heart of love and affection for me. I could not bear to be with my family because I did not want them to see me like this. I felt empty. How was it possible? I had the Lord on my side. I had accepted Jesus into my life just over twenty years before, and He had been my rock and comforter. What had happened?

I kept questioning God, "Why am I feeling like this, Lord?" I was one who shared the gospel with others and said that peace and joy would come to those who receive Jesus Christ in their lives. I repeated the promise that they would have the hope of knowing that they are saved and would spend eternity with God in heaven one day. But where was my hope now? I knew that something was seriously wrong with me. I was so ashamed, but I could not tell anyone. Each week I went to church with a mask on, pretending to be positive and happy. How could I share the pain I was feeling? How was it possible that I could feel like ending my life again, as I had when I was a teenager?

Earlier that year I had cried out to God in prayer, when I felt my energy being sapped as I served others and when I had no joy but only bitterness. I had asked the Lord to draw me closer to Him as I felt my spirit drying up to the bones and my physical health deteriorating, paralleling my spiritual health. I wanted to experience the same passion and love I had for Jesus when I first accepted Him as my savior. I did not know that God would answer me by taking me back to when I was seventeen, when I was planning to take my life and realized that I had to fully surrender to God for Him to truly work in me.

I was no longer the same person as the girl who cried out to God in surrender. Rather, over time, I had been wearing different masks to cover up who I really was. Now I wondered, "Who am I?" I had to go back in time to remember what had changed me.

THE DAY MY LIFE CHANGED FOREVER

At age fifteen in early March 1982, on a day that I knew was going to be physically hectic, my life changed forever. I was down with a cold but still made it to the morning cheerleading practice. After a light lunch, I rushed off first for intramural badminton, and then for badminton again in Physical Education class. I remembered jumping up to slam the birdie to my partner when I felt a sharp ache in my lower back. I ignored the achy feeling and continued with the rest of my afternoon classes.

By late afternoon I felt a tingling sensation in my left leg. It was as if I had needles poking through it and my leg was "asleep." I shook it off, thinking that I was just tired from the day. Later, however, in Biology class, the same achy dull pain began to creep up my right leg. I massaged my legs thinking that I was simply tired from the day's activities.

After class I walked home with my girlfriend who wanted to play basketball at a courtyard near my house. We took longer than our usual thirty minute walk because I was so sluggish. By the time we reached the courtyard, I was so exhausted that I just sat and watched. After an hour, I was so tired that I asked my girlfriend to walk me home. I lounged on the living room sofa until my mother called me for dinner. It was then that I discovered I couldn't move my legs. In fact I couldn't move from my waist down!

I cried out and told my mom I couldn't move. Thinking that I was just tired from the day, she asked my brother and sister to put me in a hot bath to soak my strained legs. Thinking that I could undress myself after I could move my legs again, my siblings put me in the tub with my clothes on. My sister tried to make the experience more fun by adding bubble bath, but after a 30-minute soak I still couldn't move. My sister had to cut my favorite Rainbow jeans apart to get me out of my wet clothes.

My father called our family doctor who immediately suggested that we call for an ambulance. I was rushed to the Vancouver Emergency Hospital, where I was tested and thought to have slipped a disc in my spinal cord. Then I was transferred overnight to the Children's Spinal Cord Unit at Shaughnessy Hospital.

I remember being sandwiched in a metal contraption and not being able to move. When I arrived at the Spinal Cord Unit, I was flipped over like a pancake and my back was examined and my legs poked. The doctors determined that I had contracted an unknown type of viral infection and prepared to drain some fluid from my spinal cord. They brought me to the operating table, tapped into my spinal cord (the T10–T11 area) and removed the fluid trapped inside. Since they did not know why or how I was infected, I had to remain in the hospital for further tests and monitoring.

The first week was exciting, and I was happy to have an excuse to get out of school. I was naïve and did not understand the seriousness of my condition. A month before a man with similar symptoms had died instantly after an infection spread to his heart. I did not know this until much later when my mom told me the doctors had warned her that I possibly had only 24 hours to live. After hearing this, she stayed at the hospital the whole night and prayed for me.

By the second week, I still could not move from my waist down but

I could feel sensation and touch. While that was a good sign, I still needed more tests, and it was still unknown what would happen to me. The novelty of staying at the hospital wore off and was replaced with the fear of the unknown. Over a two-month period, specialists were flown in to examine me and conduct research on me. I felt like a guinea pig as the doctors poked and tested and discussed me. After many tests, they still had no definitive answer on what I had contracted.

FEAR AND DESPERATION

I wrote in my diary almost every day when I was in the hospital. It was my friend to whom I vented my frustrations, worries, and fears. The doctor told me the dreaded words that I should prepare my heart to accept the possibility that I may never walk again. I never believed the doctor, or maybe I just did not want to admit the possibility to myself. Instead, I secretly determined that I was going to "will" myself better. I tried every day to move my toes, feet, legs—anything. My dad faithfully came daily to massage and rub Chinese ointment on my legs to keep the blood flowing.

In response to the questions surrounding my future, my dad was prepared to make arrangements for our family to move to another housing area better equipped to handle wheelchairs. I was really touched by my dad's love but very scared. Our family situation and finances were not the best. We were already living in government-subsidized project homes in Chinatown Eastside—a poverty area known for "Asian gangs." Six family members squeezed in a home under 900 square feet with constantly infested rodents and bugs we could not keep out; I was living a "ghetto life." How much worse could our living situation get? Actually, I was afraid of the possibility that we couldn't move the whole family because of the lack of funds or that I might have to move into a specialized paraplegic center for children and teens.

I became desperate. Even though I didn't know God actually existed, I made a secret pact with Him. I told Him that if He gave me another chance and allowed me to walk again, I would put my trust in Him. *God, are You there?* I cried. *If You are real, can You prove to me that You are real by making me walk again? If You do make me walk, I promise to devote my life serving You and others. I'll become a nun, OK?*

Miracle Morning

One wonderful morning, it happened. I felt my left big toe move! I called to my dad who was nearby, and he was astonished and excited when he saw my toe move. He quickly called for the doctor, who examined me and said that it was a miracle. I was ordered to physiotherapy for rehabilitation.

I was fortunate to be transferred to the GF Strong Rehabilitation Center, which had a long waiting list of disabled patients around British Columbia. My daily schedule included both physiotherapy and occupational training to help me adapt to and live with my condition. I engaged in rigorous activities such as weight training for both upper and lower extremities, swimming pool training, in which the buoyancy of the water gives one easier movement, and maneuvering in and out of a wheelchair.

Coupled with the Center's schedule, the Vancouver School Board was kind enough to send a personal tutor to help me keep up with the classes I was missing. It was like going to boot camp for the weak: a full schedule from 8:30 a.m. to 4:30 p.m. Monday to Friday with no visitors allowed except during lunch, after the program, and on weekends. I was emotionally and physically drained. Oh how I longed for the weekend just to rest!

The specialist wanted me to adapt well to my wheelchair because there was no guarantee that I would ever walk normally again. This was very difficult for me to hear, and the novelty of doing wheelies with my wheelchair wore off as reality set in. All my dreams of any physical-based career—such as becoming a physical education coach, a dance coach, or a recreational leader—were shattered. I was ignorant of the fact that I could still pursue those dreams even if I were disabled.

"TRANS WHAT?"

Three months after I contracted my mysterious ailment, the specialists finally provided a diagnosis: transverse myelitis (TM) viral disease, an uncommon but not rare neurological syndrome caused by inflammation of the spinal cord. Myelitis is a nonspecific term for inflammation of the spinal cord. Transverse refers to involvement across one level of the spinal cord.[1]

Apparently one who has a poor immune system is more susceptible to contracting a viral infection. The day I contracted the infection, I was already sick with the flu. My body was already weak, and I was too stubborn to notice that I was weak and too busy to take time to eat and rest.

The doctors tried to comfort me by saying I was fortunate that it was not multiple sclerosis (MS)—a disease similar to TM but one with a history of returning and inflicting more serious results to the patient. Deep down, I still was not sure if they had diagnosed me correctly.

ABLE TO WALK

My goal was to attend my sister's high school graduation in late June that year. I was determined to train hard to walk with leg braces and qualify for a weekend outpatient status. I didn't know then that it was God who gave me the strength to be able go to my sister's graduation. Even though my face was bloated from my reaction to my daily medication and I was strapped in leg braces, I was so happy to be out and about in the world again. I was especially glad to be able to witness my sister's graduation.

Over the summer months, I trained even harder and was rewarded when most of the strength in my legs came back. The exception was the back muscle in my left leg, which would not respond to any strength training. It was determined that I would never regain strength there and I would not be able to run or do anything that required physical strength from both my legs. Also, I would not feel sensation, such as temperature change, in certain areas and some numbness would always be present in my legs.

A person's muscle and nerve strength level is determined by a 5-point scale, with 5 being normal. I had a 5 for strength in my right leg but only a 2 in my left leg. I was also diagnosed with a 2.5 or less for sensation normality from my waist down. Despite this, I was happy to be able to walk independently first with crutches and then with a cane.

I was treated as an outpatient for another year at GF Strong Rehabilitation Center. It was difficult to go back to school with my cane in hand, limping down the hallways, and having difficulty climbing the stairs. The hardest part was the humbling recognition that I was not all that I had been before. Prior to the disease, I was physically and socially involved in many activities (such as gymnastics, dancing, cheerleading, badminton, track and field, long distance running, skating, and hockey). I had felt like I was on top of the world, but that was no longer true.

Like so many others, once I regained my ability and strength to walk again, I forgot my pact with God. He did His part and answered my prayers, but I forgot mine. My weaker left leg and the abnormality of sensations in my legs seemed to be left behind as a reminder to me of my breach of contract. However, I did not begin to realize God's amazing plans for me until much later.

A Gospel Hall Outreach Event

Two years after I contracted the viral infection, my oldest brother, Gee, apologized to me for not treating me better and told me that he loved me. This was quite the shocker coming from a brother who was seven years older than me and had not really been open to me. He explained how he had accepted Jesus Christ as his personal Savior and how Jesus had changed his ways. I remember thinking my brother had turned into one of those "Jesus freaks." He tried to convince me to attend an outreach meeting with him and to find Jesus myself. I of course said, "No way.... been there, done that.... none of this religious stuff for me, please."

A short time later, my second brother, Chi, who had been kicked out of high school twice and almost joined a Chinese gang, also came and told me how his life was changed because he had asked Jesus to come into his life and change him. "Whoa!" I wondered. My two brothers, who were polar opposites, both believed in the same thing? What happened? Was this a brainwashing scheme? I was determined to find out!

I was eventually coaxed into attending a gospel hall outreach event. As I entered a house for the service, I was totally surprised because there was nothing fancy about the inside. A small pulpit was at the front of the room, and folded chairs were in place. I was immediately drawn by the friendliness of the people.

A gentleman shared about Jesus Christ and what He did for sinners. As he pointed at the audience, I felt like he was pointing and talking to me! My heart beat so rapidly when he asked the question, "Do you know where you are going if you die tonight?" I was a little afraid, but kept it to myself. My brothers asked me what I thought of the event, and I said something along the line of "It was an interesting experience." I did not know that God would later use the message I had heard to speak to me.

THE NIGHT GOD CHANGED MY LIFE

My world fell apart around me in the fall semester of my twelfth grade year. Many people would have been surprised because I was positive and popular in my senior year. By all appearances, I was a happy teen, dating one of the most popular, athletic, and well-dressed guys in the class, being a class representative, and being involved in a lot of social activities. No one knew how unhappy and disturbed I truly was inside.

With high school coming to an end, it seemed that everyone but me knew where they were heading. I had a plan before I contracted the viral infection, but that had disabled me, and I started to feel sorry for myself. I was dating my high school boyfriend because I felt obligated to date him. He was the only sincere and persistent male friend who had visited me in the hospital. I felt that no one else would want a disabled person like me, so I dated him to feel like I was normal and to fit in with others. I was devastated when he ended our relationship. My whole world crumbled, and I felt even more worthless and meaningless.

Lacking direction and purpose and fearing that I would get stuck living "the ghetto life," I no longer wanted to live. I cannot recall how long I thought about ending my life, but on the night of October 26, 1983, I decided to act on my death plan. First I cleaned my room and wrote a note to my family to explain my actions and to leave all my possessions to my sister. After considering other options such as overdosing on pills and jumping off the roof, I decided to use our Chinese kitchen knife to cut my wrist vein and end my life. I did not pause to consider how my death would affect my family members and friends. I was too selfish, too absorbed in my own pain. All I wanted was to end my life—and quickly.

At the moment I was going to cut my wrist, my head suddenly started spinning and memories from the night of the gospel meeting came back to me. I recalled hearing the man say, "Do you know where you are going if you die tonight? You will die and go to hell without Jesus Christ. Hell is portrayed in the Bible as a place of torment and weeping and gnashing of teeth."

"Yikes!" I thought. "I'm in a terrible state right now, but what if everything I've heard is true? What if the things my brothers have shared with me are all true?"

And that was when I dropped to my knees, sobbing deeply, and prayed: *Jesus, if You are really real, if You did die for my sins and You are truly alive; then help me to believe in You. Change my heart and change what I am going through right now. Please, God, take away all my problems right now.*

I scrambled to look for the tract my brothers had given me and flipped to the back where the prayer of repentance was. I read it over and over until a deep peace filled me as I had never felt before. My huge weight of anxiety and burden was lifted from me. The room was still and quiet. I was amazed and scared at the same time. I put everything away and told no one what I had intended to do that night or what had happened to me. I kept it to myself for a few days. Each night I would take the gospel tract and pray the same prayer to ensure that I had repented, was saved by Jesus, and would inherit His promised eternal life.

The next weekend, one of my brothers approached me and, as always, asked me to receive Jesus into my life before it was too late. For the first time I responded, "I did...a few days ago!" With much excitement, I told both my brothers what I had done. They were ecstatic with my decision, and one of them gave me my first Bible that same week.

It was amazing how almost everything I had worried about became insignificant when I finally surrendered them to the living God. I no longer cared about not having a boyfriend. I was surprised when he came back and asked me for another chance to date me. Another surprise was that God inspired me to prepare for a new vocation in accounting. I attended Simon Fraser University and six years later obtained instead a business degree in marketing and organizational behavior.

I was beginning to learn that our plans for the future are directed and guided by our living God. I served Him faithfully, giving all my extra time to Him and, at every opportunity, sharing His good news with everyone who crossed my path.

An Insightful Challenge

Were you ever in such despair that you cried out desperately for God to save you? Did He answer right away? What have you learned from it? Are you in despair now? Cry out to God and release it to Him. God is always faithful, and He answers our cries for help. It does not matter how many times we cry to Him, He is full of compassion and will always deliver us through.

> And when they cried out to you again, you heard from heaven, and in your compassion you delivered them time after time.
>
> —Nehemiah 9:28

2

Coming Out of Hiding

I will not die but live, and will
proclaim what the Lord has done.
—Psalm 118:17

WHAT HAPPENED TO me—the girl I just described, the girl who was so passionate in her life with God? I had so much joy in serving God and loving others. Twenty years later, I felt like I was re-living my past. I was living a life of pretense, shielding the truth from my siblings, parents, and all my friends. I was struggling with physical and spiritual depression, and for many years tried to keep it a secret from Bill and my doctor.

I don't think Bill knew how serious my condition was until I broke down and told him that I wanted to leave home. I explained that I did not deserve to have him as my husband, nor was I in the right condition to take care of our daughter Kayli. My relationship with God was slipping and my heart was complacent. I felt that I had lost my first love and the joy I had in Him. Desiring a more intimate relationship with God, I cried, *Please do not forsake me or leave me, Lord!*

DR. JEKYLL AND MRS. HYDE

I had known that there was something very wrong with me for a very long time, but I did not want to admit it. Whenever something did not go according to my plan, it would trigger intense emotional outbursts from my mouth. My mind would feel as if it was being spun into a big dark hole and my stomach would knot and tighten up into a huge ball. My chest and throat would be so tight that I couldn't breathe.

The more I tried to fight this condition, the worse it seemed to be. It was as if I was out of control and turning into a monster. I would experience fits of anger that were expressed not by profanity but by screams of pain like "*aaaaaaaaaargh!*" I struggled deep down because I knew this was so wrong, and I started crying—crying to the extent that I would use at least half a box of Kleenex. I would sob so much with intense pain that I would choke on my own tears and saliva. It usually didn't stop until I passed out because I was worn out from my own crying.

My thoughts about myself were negative: how unworthy I was, how useless I was, what a hypocrite I was, what a lousy wife I was, what a terrible mother I was. I felt like the female version of Dr. Jekyll and Mr. Hyde. I was normal some days and a scary monster other days. One day I would be so happy, enjoying life, and the next day I would be in deep rage or be filled with sadness. I felt so guilty and ashamed, and I was so tired, so very tired of what was happening to me. As I cried out to the Lord, I asked Him to *take me home.* I had grown so tired of life, so tired of the journey.

I thought I was happy and had purpose in worshiping and serving the true living God who had saved me. I was involved in different ministries, both inside and outside the local church. I had started a women's ministry, the FAB (Friendship Arts 'n Crafts Bible Insight) Ladies Group, over five years before. It was going well, and the attendance was doubling. I was proud because I was doing something for the Lord, and it was bearing fruit. I had just started a new Bible ministry, JAM (Jesus and Me), a discipleship Bible study program to know Jesus and the relationship we are designed to have with Him.

How ironic was it that I was the one struggling with my relationship with Him.

But I could not tell anyone about my problems. Sure, I would share a few snippets here and there with some close friends and family, but never the whole truth of my condition and the depth of my sadness and confusion. Why was I not open enough to tell others? I had always thought I was an open book and encouraged all my relationships to be honest and transparent. Now God was showing me otherwise. I had masks on, and I couldn't take them off.

I was afraid to share with my Christian brothers and sisters because I was concerned that I would over burden them with my problems when they had their own. And I was too ashamed to admit my weaknesses. I couldn't share with my non-Christian friends for fear of damaging the Lord's name with my weakness and leading them to think God was weak and not real. The more I covered up and withheld the truth from others, the more I deceived myself. I was lying to others and to myself. I kept telling myself that surely I could get myself out of this mess because I had counseled so many others with their problems. I didn't know how wrong I really was.

God Takes a Deeper Look

For the Lord sees not as man sees: man looks on the outward appearance, but the Lord looks on the heart.
—1 Samuel 16:7, esv

Holding secrets inside me has always been a part of my make-up, and that made it even more difficult to remove my shroud of lies. As I grew up, I knew that my parents kept many secrets hidden from our family and I accepted their secretiveness. Being married to a senior executive only fueled my ability to keep secrets and withhold the truth. Sadly, if you keep something inside long enough and tell enough different stories, you'll eventually end up believing your own lies.

I don't know how many masks I have donned over the years. They seemed to creep up slowly. With every attempt to hide the real me, each mask seemed to blend in and over another until it became natural to keep them on all the time. The scary part is that I did not even know I was wearing these masks and when I did, I was afraid to take them off. They had become a part of me.

All my life I learned and believed the lie that everything will be fine if you tell people only what they want to hear. People want to hear about good things; they don't like hearing about bad things. They don't know how to react when they hear bad things; they don't know how to deal with another's vulnerability or even their own. Yet you and I both need sympathy. And when people respond to our bad news, they may do it out of motivation of love and compassion rather than pity. The question is: can we lay aside our tendency to be independent and accept gifts of compassion from others?

Although I tried to hide my struggles from everyone, I couldn't hide from God. And when my world collapsed on me again, I was not strong enough to put on another mask. I felt so trapped in my own problems. As I tried to deal with them on my own, I felt that God was silent when I cried out to Him. I would discover later how wrong I was. He was there all along, trying to talk to me, but I was too busy moping and too distracted to hear Him.

SURRENDER LEADS TO RELIEF

Come near to God and he will come near to you.

—JAMES 4:8

As God lovingly probed my heart, I came to the place of submission to Him and prayed, *Lord, I give up. I give you full complete reign in my life*. When I started to hear Him speak clearly, my broken heart slowly began to become whole, complete and renewed by God. God gave me a heart that was willing to yield to my sovereign Lord's promptings, and I felt alive again! God healed me in His right timing.

God did not reveal every awful sin to me at once, or I would have been too overwhelmed to deal with them. Instead He drew me to His throne of grace to surrender myself at His feet and allow Him to slowly reveal what I needed to do to have a closer relationship with Him. He showed me each sin and mask that was blocking the Holy Spirit's work in me. One by one, each time I took off a mask, God gave me time to realize it, accept it, confess it, and renounce it. I sought His help to deal with each mask I wore, and I allowed Him to take control in each area I uncovered. I released myself, with all my sins and weaknesses, to Him.

Through my act of release and surrender to Christ, I received relief from every sin that had been holding me down. I came to realize what it really means to deny myself daily (see Luke 9:23) so Christ can work in me. I praise God for Jesus Christ's finished work on Calvary's cross—He conquered death through His Resurrection! He is alive and is sitting at the right hand of God in the heavenly realms, ready to welcome me home one day! And He enables me to live before Him without masks, free to love and serve Him and others.

AN INSIGHTFUL CHALLENGE

Have you ever felt the way I have? Do you, like me, try to present a bold front? Do you wear a different mask each time you see someone? When you go to your local church, do you put on one kind of mask to talk to your fellow believers? How about when you go out with your non-believing friends, or when you are sharing your faith with others? Does another mask come on? Do you hide the truth of what you are actually feeling inside for fear of how people will react when they discover the real you?

It's interesting that we put on yet another mask when we are with our family members and when we come before God. We forget that God knows what we are really like; we can't fool God, for He knows who we are. Perhaps that's why some of us are afraid to spend quiet time with Him. We might be afraid of what He will tell us and that He will reveal how vulnerable and weak we are. But that's exactly where He wants to take us.

Perhaps the following acronym for *RELIEF* will help you open your heart to God and receive His provision of wholeness:

- **R**ealize that sin is blocking your relationship from God; identify it and confess it.

- **E**mbrace God's truth that He loves you and has already forgiven you.

- **L**earn what led you to your sin and renounce any unholy thing God shows you.

- **I**nvite God to take control of your heart.

- **E**ngage God in your life every moment of every day.

- **F**ully surrender your life to God and release it to Him.

God wants us to come before Him with honesty, naked and without masks, so that we can depend on Him for everything. Sometimes it takes a broken heart for us to truly learn this. However, the freedom He gives and intimacy we enjoy with Him will give us the true security and satisfaction we cannot find anywhere else.

> I sought the Lord, and he answered me and delivered me from all my fears.
>
> —Psalm 34:4, esv

SECTION II

THE MASKS WE WEAR

3

The Mask of Wellness

*It is not the healthy who need a doctor, but the sick. I have
not come to call the righteous, but sinners to repentance.*
—LUKE 5:31–32

I FIND IT INTERESTING that I had to suffer physical problems
before I realized something else was wrong. If I had not been on
a quest to find physical healing, I would not have been led to the
healing that I really needed—spiritual healing. I would not have been
open to receive God's revelation of all the masks I was wearing.

We humans are creatures of habit. We are selfish, and we only look
to God for help when we need Him for something that it is beyond
our control. I was reminded of this again in my dad's recent illness
when he faced the possibility of death. God takes us through uncontrollable circumstances beyond our own physical ability so that we
will put our faith in Him, surrender our will to Him, and allow Him
to be in control. My dad is much more open to hear the gospel and
what God has to say because he is desperately searching for a cure.
Just like with me, it's not the physical cure he needs. What he really
needs is the spiritual cure available in Christ Jesus.

As I have looked back at my struggles with physical suffering,
mainly related to my back and legs, I have always felt that there was a
reason for my infirmities. I have felt like the Apostle Paul, who wrote

to the church in Corinth and said that the thorn in his flesh was "to keep me from being conceited" (2 Cor. 12:7). Paul also testified that "when I am weak, then I am strong" (2 Cor. 12:10). And I have long kept 2 Corinthians 12:9 in my head to remind myself that God's grace is sufficient for me and His "power is made perfect in weakness."

The following list of physical suffering related to my legs alone, reminds me of how much I have had opportunity to look to God for His grace and strength:

- transverse myelitis viral disease

- acupuncture treatment for pain and for the healing of my legs

- a car accident that affected my strong right leg when I was a university student

- arthroscopic surgery on my right knee

- arthritis that developed from my surgery

- restless leg syndrome that developed from pregnancy

- acupuncture treatment for my restless leg syndrome and the inflammation of my joints

- my most recent burn injury on the side of my right knee

(See Appendix 4 for a glossary of medical terminology.)

Because my left leg was rendered untreatable by the doctors, I received acupuncture treatment for it in hopes that it would stimulate my dead nerves and muscle. Thus, as I lived with the disability and weakness of my left leg, I had to get used to being poked on my back and legs with thin 3–4 inch pin-like needles. During that time, when I was a university student, I was a passenger in a car that was involved in an accident. My right leg, which was my stronger leg, slammed into the side of the car, and my whole right kneecap shifted out of alignment.

I found myself in the hospital again, sharing the whole story of my experience with TM so that the specialists could understand the reason for my extreme pain. I had to undergo arthroscopic surgery to realign my kneecap, despite the disapproval of my acupuncturist who warned that future arthritic pain would occur because of it. To allow my knee to heal, I hobbled on crutches again for a month after my surgery. I had to deal with the loss of my stronger right leg.

Sure enough, ten years later I found myself with extreme inflammation pain near my right knee joint each time it was about to rain. It rains 80 percent of the time where I live in Vancouver, British Columbia, so I am reminded of my pain quite often. Arthritis developed in my joints, and it was exasperated by restless leg syndrome (RLS), a new condition the doctors diagnosed after I gave birth to my daughter in 1998. Unfortunately, this unexpected RLS condition overshadowed my joy in the blessing of having my miracle child—I was not expected to have children due to remnant paralysis from my past viral disease. Women may experience leg muscle spasms during pregnancy, but the spasms tend to disappear after they give birth. However, I continued to experience muscle spasms and twitching after the birth of Kayli, and the pain was more pronounced when I was sleeping.

After undergoing tests, it was determined that during my pregnancy the weight of the baby and the changes to my body irritated the scar tissue from my previous infection to the spinal cord. Because of the blockage of electrical currents that run through my body and past the scar tissue, my leg has uncontrollable spasms and feels like it is inflamed with pain. I was put on Clonazepam pills to relieve the spasms, and I am still on the same medication for the past ten years now.

Temporary Relief, Permanent Results

By spring 2005, my restless leg syndrome condition, coupled with my inflammation of the joints, made my pain unbearable on my stronger right leg. Acupuncture treatment had worked to minimize my pain before, and even though it was only temporary relief, it had allowed me to function more normally. My acupuncturist had retired, and I was thankful my friend Jenny found me another reputable acupuncturist. In my first meeting with the acupuncturist, I was so happy to discover that he had been in practice for thirty-seven years and even wrote the medical column in my dad's newspaper, the *Chinese Times*! Because he knew my dad, I felt comfortable to trust in him. And I learned that if the reputation of someone encourages our trust in that person, how much more should we trust our living God, the One who has the best reputation for healing!

Following are my summarized journal excerpts for my initial acupuncture treatments:

Treatment 1: Painful first treatment. Dr. Wong said it should only take one or two treatments to help me take my pain away. He used up to ten needles, burned some stuff on my back and knee. He attached mini black and red plugs to the needles. I felt like a giant battery pack, with the positive and negative electrodes attached to a machine to increase its voltage. My right leg was jumping for this whole treatment. . . . I felt very stiff afterwards, but also relaxed.

Treatment 2: Ten to twelve needles were inserted. . . . God gave me opportunity to share with Dr. Wong that I was a follower of Jesus Christ. He had asked me what type of music I was listening to on my MP3. I didn't know how to say gospel music in Cantonese, so I told him I was listening to Bible music. Dr. Wong only speaks Chinese and very little English. I am learning that it is by God's grace I can communicate with him each time. My whole leg is even more painful after the treatment today. The next two days I was in major pain.

Treatment 3: I shared about my pain with the acupuncturist today and gave him some Chinese tracts. God gave me opportunity to share the full gospel with him. I thanked the Holy Spirit. I felt His prompting. It is so strange to share to gospel with someone when all these needles are poked in my back and legs and my body is twisted. What a reminder how God can use us in any circumstance. Dr. Wong had thought I only needed two treatments, but I'm beginning to understand why God is allowing me to continue with further treatments—to share more about Christ with him.

Treatment 4: We shared about the tracts he read, Dr. Wong said he wanted something more substantial to read. God has orchestrated everything available to reach Dr. Wong. My brother Chi had some Chinese writings of Chinese characters relating to the Bible. It was well suited for Dr. Wong as he collects Chinese painted writings.

Treatment 5: OK, I'm getting better, but my leg still hurts after a week. Dr. Wong inserted the needles in my head while he was talking to me. He said he wanted to stimulate some areas in my brain for my leg to react better for the treatments. I felt like a television with two needles as antennas on my head! I am not looking forward to going

*twice a week, but I do look forward to how God will be
using me to share with Dr. Wong.*

After about twenty-five treatments with the acupuncturist, most of
the pain went away in my right leg. However, I realized that God had
another purpose for me to receive help from Dr. Wong. Through the
power of the Holy Spirit and with my broken Cantonese, I was able
to share and introduce him to Jesus. I am still in touch with him,
and have recently discovered that he is attending a nearby Chinese
Missionary Alliance Church. I know that God can turn Dr. Wong's
heart toward Himself.

God not only gave me temporary relief for my pain, but more
importantly, He used me to share the good news of Christ with
Dr. Wong. I was given the opportunity to plant seeds that God will
nourish for His kingdom. Temporary relief for me, but permanent
results for Dr. Wong. It was worth it.

STRUGGLING WITH THE
SYMPTOMS OF DEPRESSION

During my treatments with my acupuncturist, I prayed that I would
not trust in man but in God to heal.

As I learn to live in chronic pain, I am encouraged to exercise
this trust by Christ's words in 2 Corinthians 12:9, "My grace is
sufficient for you, for my power is made perfect in weakness." My
weakness is to show God's perfect power. No matter how much pain
and suffering I have, God knows exactly what I am going through.
I need to remember this when I find myself asking God to remove
my physical pain with the anthem, "Pain, pain, go away, please come
back another day."

And in my response of trust toward God, I have learned to recognize a deep inner emotional anguish that has affected me more than

any physical pain I have encountered. For the longest time I did not face the fact that I was going through spiritual depression; I had too much pride to admit it. I had counseled many friends who were going through their own pain and depression, but I never knew that it was I who needed the positive counsel.

I was so stubborn that I didn't even talk to anyone about what I was going through until an incident during which my daughter Kayli got sick could not keep anything down. I took her to the doctor, and after explaining Kayli's condition, the doctor spoke to me in a manner that seemed rude to me. I held my upset feelings in only until I got home, but then I started to cry and I couldn't stop. When I returned to my doctor to tell her how upset I was about the way she had treated me, she said that she was not going to apologize. I started to cry right there in her office, and told her that I had these uncontrollable crying fits over little things all the time.

My doctor said that it was possible that I was going through post-partum depression even though Kayli was two and half years old! She said that it was not uncommon for women to experience what I was going through, especially for me as a career woman who then made a decision to stay home. She reminded me that she had warned me about this a few years back and had suggested that I do something meaningful for myself, even if it meant going back to work part-time. It was a difficult choice since I was trying to listen to the advice of others to stay at home to support my daughter. However, deep inside I was struggling with significance and worth—I did not understand my real worth as a mother and wife to my family.

After much discussion and prayer with Bill, I felt that God opened the door for me to take a managerial position at a local chocolate manufacturer. Everything seemed to be fine until I discovered that when I came home from work, I was still not happy and was becoming negative again. It was as if God answered my prayers by allowing me to be laid off from the job after only four months because the company could no longer subsidize the new division I was managing, when the unionized staff went on strike. Soon after that God gave me another full-time management opportunity with a telecommunications company. This kept me busy for a year, until I discovered that I was even more negative and could not shake off the deep sadness within.

I was very involved in church ministries and served wherever there was a need (e.g., children's nursery, teaching adult Sunday school class, directing and choreographing the Christmas programs, hosting bi-weekly fellowship meetings and the women's outreach ministry). I was trying so hard to seek meaning and do more for God, but it still did not seem to be enough. I was trying to do more in hopes of preoccupying my negative thoughts and behavior, but it did not work. I was feeling more negative, and it made me miserable. I became overwhelmed with feelings of guilt and was even more ashamed of sharing my unhappy, negative feelings with anyone.

LOOKING FOR THE SOURCE OF MY MOOD SWINGS

When I went through my wild mood swings, I thought quite natu-rally that it must be a medical problem. There was *no way* I could be responsible for feeling and acting out the way I was. Rather, it must be an external problem that I couldn't control.

In my research to find the source of my mood swings, I read an article by a journalist who wrote that she was perimenopausal at age thirty-one and menopausal at age forty-two. I thought that perhaps I was in a perimenopausal stage because I seemed to be exhibiting the symptoms of moodiness, extreme mood swings, hot flashes, late night sweats, and irregular period cycles. My doctor was skeptical about this, but she took blood tests. When the tests came back negative, I was very upset. It was as if I wanted the doctor to discover that something was wrong with me!

Then I thought my problems might be a side effect from Clonazepam, the medication I had been taking for five years to treat my restless leg syndrome. When I read more closely about the medication, I noted that it was used to treat patients with epilepsy, schizophrenia, and other similar conditions. After I once again talked to my doctor and expressed my concerns to her, she determined that it was not possible to attribute my mood swings to the medication that I was on.

I was still determined to find out what was going on with me, and deep down I was worried that I had extreme signs of depression. Since my husband, Bill, was travelling more for his work, we made the decision for me to leave my managerial role with the telecommunications company. To my dismay, after I left my full-time position the world collapsed around me even more because I felt like I didn't have any self-worth. I measured my self-worth on what I did to bring financial means into the family, not on what I was already doing as a wife, mother, daughter, and friend.

Bill thought that taking time to rest would help me, but I knew I needed something else. After I dropped my daughter off at school, I would go home and crawl into bed until my body demanded food. I would then muster enough energy to quickly make something that was usually unhealthy and eat it before I crawled back into bed and slept until it was time to get Kayli from school. This routine would drag on day after day until something would happen to set me off into a fit of rage or sadness. Then I would rant and cry to Bill about what a terrible wife and mother I was and list every single negative quality about myself.

Our marriage was slowly going down the drain, and I had no feeling of intimacy toward Bill. Although I longed to be near him, I would not express any initiative toward him because I did not feel worthy. I was in my own private negative world and no one would know it as I kept a happy façade to the public. I couldn't understand why I could not focus on the blessings of everything I had—a loving husband, charming daughter, beautiful home, financial security, many friends and so much more. I was desperate to change, and I would prostrate myself before God, crying and pleading for Him to change my circumstance. I clung to God's promises that He would not allow me to endure beyond what I could handle.

As I lived in this darkness, I felt very complacent in my relationship with God. I didn't know that sin was blocking my relationship with Him and that the actual problem was me! Even though I was crying out to Him, I was crying only to ask Him to change my circumstances. I was spinning out of control, trying unsuccessfully to control everything. All the while, God wanted to let me know that He was in control and that I needed to personally surrender to His control.

SEARCHING FOR HELP

I researched depression on the Internet and found a Web site that listed questions to help me determine if I was struggling with depression. After scoring a perfect ten on the questionnaire and confirming that I was at a high risk for depression, I went back to my doctor. I explained how I was feeling that I wanted to take my own life and that I was afraid that I would feel the same way I did when I almost took my life at the age of seventeen. It was determined that I had long believed so many lies to cover up the real me and I needed to be set free by telling the truth.

My doctor said that we could try to treat my problem with antidepressants, but she was against it because I was still on Clonazepam. Instead, she prescribed communication therapy—opening up to people and revealing my secrets. It was difficult for me to reveal my secret lies. I was a child of God, someone who was supposed to be an "ambassador for Christ" (2 Cor. 5:20). What kind of ambassador has a lack of integrity by lying to others about who they really are? What would people think of me when they learned the truth about me? I decided to hold the truth in, deal with my problem on my own, and perhaps seek a Christian counselor to deal with my personal issues. However, this response only made things worse.

I finally broke down and shared my problem with depression in a conversation with a very close friend who had not yet received Christ as her personal Savior. As we sat in my kitchen late one night, she told me that she had experiences similar to mine, although they were not as extreme. She recommended that I check my serotonin levels, which could affect my mood swings.

After I shared so openly with her, I confessed to her that I had been afraid to do so because I did not want to damage Jesus' name or reputation. She responded by saying that she was glad I was not perfect, but human after all. I learned a valuable lesson that night. Through my imperfection, Christ can shine even more brightly; it is He who stands out, not me. That was the beginning of many life lessons.

When I went back to the doctor and asked her to do a test to check my serotonin levels, she said there was no such thing. She remained firm in her prescription of communication therapy over antidepressants, which, she said, just cover up the symptoms to buy time for people to deal with their real problems without hurting themselves. She again recommended that I talk things out with others. I realize now that God was using her to put me in a situation where I had no choice but to tell others the truth so I could become truly free.

A WEEK ALONE WITH GOD

As my depression became more and more severe, I decided to go away for a week alone with God. I needed a personal retreat where I could be free from all distractions to seek the Lord's help and hear His voice in my life again. This was when God taught me lessons about spiritual depression and revealed all the ugly masks I was wearing.

God showed me that spiritual depression is in a category all its own. You know you are struggling with spiritual depression when your spirit is dry and feels down, when you are burned out and ready to collapse, when you have no joy in serving, when your spirit seems far away from God and you have no excitement for the Lord. Your heart is complacent and your love for Him has taken a backseat to everything else.

How does this happen? It may creep up slowly for some of us because we start serving God with our own strength. We neglect to feed on God's Word and be filled with the Holy Spirit. We put ourselves on the throne, rather than allowing Christ to rule in our lives. We let our own will take control rather than allowing God's will to lead us. We slowly don masks that block us from having an intimate relationship with God.

During my weeklong retreat—what I call my "healing retreat"—one of God's greatest eye-opening lessons and amazingly the simplest remedy for my depression was learning about my spiritual diet. I discovered that taking quality time to feed myself spiritually is an absolute necessity. Just as I am learning to eat a healthier diet physically, I have to do the same spiritually. I have to feed daily on the Bible—the Word of God—to receive spiritual nourishment. I learned that I shouldn't eat spiritual food just for the sake of eating it, but also for the purpose of eating it properly.

I had been reading my Bible and doing my daily devotions only because I felt that it was something I had to do because it was expected of me. Even my personal study of God's Word had no depth, because I felt that my study and research for my Sunday school or Bible lessons was sufficient for my daily walk with God. I didn't realize that I wasn't taking the time to feed myself and allow the Holy Spirit to speak personally to me about what God wanted *me* to hear.

God reminded me that just as it is with my physical diet, if I skip breakfast and cram junk food into me, my body will not receive the nutrients I need to stay strong. If I just read the Bible and do my devotions only for the sake of doing them, I will not be feeding properly on the Word of God. Because my heart had not really been involved in my study of God's Word and because I was easily distracted, my spiritual health was deteriorating.

As I started to feed my spiritual being properly and also surrender my will to God, I felt my spirit lift. I received a sense of new strength and direction from God. Yielding and obeying the Holy Spirit involved my confession and repentance for every secret mask I was wearing.

My time away with God led me to form a habit that I yearned to practice daily when I returned home. My quality downtime with God allowed me to hear His remedy for my physical and spiritual health. One morning I was meditating and praying to God about my need for motivation to do my physical workouts again. God answered by showing me 1 Corinthians 6:19–20 and reminding me, "Do you not know that your body is a temple of the Holy Spirit, who is in you, whom you have received from God? You are not your own; you were bought at a price. Therefore honor God with your body."

The next thing I knew, despite my physical limitations, I was jumping up and dancing and it felt great! And the next day I started to listen to my worship music again, and danced to the music as if my whole body was worshiping God! It was amazing. I was building a daily exercise routine centered on God, and I was motivated to do it because it was my worship to the Lord. I was to sacrifice and give my whole heart, soul, and body to worship Him. I was to keep my body, the temple of God, healthy for the Holy Spirit to indwell.

How is your spiritual diet? What is your heart's motive to feed yourself spiritually? Do you read the Bible and do daily devotions as just another chore that you feel that you are required to do, or because that is what people expect you to do? Or do you personally yearn for time in God's presence so you can be closer to Him?

Do you show signs of spiritual depression? Is your heart complacent about your relationship with God? Or do you still have the same excitement you had for Jesus when you asked Him to come into your life? Do you daily surrender yourself to the Holy Spirit and yield to Him to do His will? Ask God to show you everything that is blocking you from enjoying an intimate relationship with Him. Confess and surrender to God and let Him rule again in your life.

The Danger of Self-diagnosis

After my week alone with God, I began to share the truth about myself with others. I changed my diet, started a daily exercise regimen, and began taking vitamins and herbal supplements. Most importantly, I had a daily meditation and quiet time with the Lord. I was progressing quite well in my natural treatments. But when I had another episode of uncontrollable rage, I thought something else was wrong with me and I started searching the Internet for more help again.

One of my problems is that I can almost be labeled as a hypochondriac—someone who worries excessively about their health despite reassurance and medical evidence to the contrary.[1] The more I read about violent mood swings, the more misled I became. I started to believe that the things I read were true of me. I felt that I had bipolar disorder and I was so adamant about it that my doctor finally referred me to the hospital psychiatrist for a second opinion.

The psychiatrist's medical assessment was that I had no symptoms of any major disorder. She said I had the type of personality that would lead me to think and act as if I had bipolar disorder (e.g., ambitious, driven, perfectionistic). Because of my personality, I was prone to anxiety attacks, and may have been experiencing mild forms of depression due to my self-ambition and own high expectations.

Her report to my doctor was, "I think this woman has mild generalized anxiety disorder, and two years ago she had some very mild depressive symptoms, but I do not really think she has ever met the full criteria for a depressive episode, nor do I think she is at high risk to ever develop one."

I was relieved when I read my full medical assessment. It made sense that I have mild Generalized Anxiety Disorder (GAD). The National Institute of Mental Health says:

> People with GAD have a tendency to go through the day with exaggerated worry and tension, even though there is little or nothing to provoke it....People with GAD can't seem to get rid of their concerns, even though they usually realize that their anxiety is more intense than the situation warrants. They can't relax, startle easily, and have difficulty concentrating. Often they have trouble falling asleep or staying asleep. Physical symptoms that often accompany the anxiety include fatigue, headaches, muscle tension, muscle aches, difficulty swallowing, trembling, twitching, irritability, sweating, nausea, lightheadedness, having to go to the bathroom frequently, feeling out of breath, and hot flashes.[2]

These were the symptoms I had been experiencing along with my mild depression. At least now I know what I really have, and I can be vigilant in treating it properly.

I learned a lesson from this experience: my own self-diagnosis could have paved the way for self-destruction. If you believe something long enough without looking into the facts, it becomes a reality in your life. I was playing into the hands of the enemy, and I am glad that God enabled me to be open and honest enough to ask for help and prayer to see the truth.

Have you ever gone through something like this? You want an answer to your problem so desperately that you believe whatever remotely makes sense. It may not make complete sense, but it's good enough to satisfy you. The longer you keep telling yourself it's true, the more the misconception becomes a reality. It is so important that we heed the warning of God's Word to test the spirits and ask God for a discerning heart about all things.

God Is Our Ultimate Physician

In my journey to find healing, I read many books. I was so thirsty for knowledge that I must have read a book every week. Two key books that God used to open my eyes were John Eldredge's *Waking up the Dead* and Sheila Walsh's *A Broken Heart No One Sees*. Both books reminded me that Satan, our enemy, attacks us spiritually and that God calls us to fight in the spiritual battle that is raging. They led me to equip myself for the battle rather than remain a wounded soldier. (Read more about this in Section III, "After We Unveil Our Masks.")

God gave me time to search my heart, and I realized that I am responsible for my actions. He showed me each area that I needed to surrender to Him before *real healing* could begin and that I have to do my part to receive His healing. I need to confess my sins and repent before God as I battle with selfish motives. If I do not surrender to God, the enemy takes advantage of my weaknesses and I am not strong enough to resist him.

As I learned about my health issues, I discovered that I suffered from a combination of physiological, psychological, and spiritual depression. Because of my anxiety disorder, I know that I have to constantly trust and cling to God's promises. I can cast all my anxiety on him because He cares for me (1 Pet. 5:7). The key word is *all*. Part of my difficulty is learning how to surrender *all* my anxiety to Him. I tend to hold back and let my own will take control and deal with my problems. As I learn to release and surrender every anxiety that comes along, God fills me with His peace and real healing begins.

We are on a life-long journey of daily surrendering to God. We need to be led by the Spirit as we battle with our inner self and the enemy's tactics. We should surrender ourselves to God to be led by Him not just daily, but *every moment* of our lives. I have learned that as soon as we let our guard down, it is so easy for the enemy to penetrate us again and mislead us with our own misconceptions. Yet, as Jesus healed the blind man so "that the work of God might be displayed" (John 9:3), God can use our weaknesses to bring glory to Himself.

As I finalize this book, I am entering into my fifth month of healing from a deep burn and infection on the side of my right knee. Surprisingly, the burn injury was caused by the electric heating pad (even though it has a 20 minute automatic shut off) that I use to control my muscle spasms before I go to sleep at night. Because I had to dress and bandage the burn on my stronger right leg, I was forced to walk on my weaker left leg and rely on my cane to help me walk. Since I have not been walking as much, my right leg needs to be rehabilitated and restored to its original strength.

I am grateful that God has refined me to the point where I realize that He is in total control and has a purpose for all of this. Since I have been walking with my cane all the time over the past five months, many people have asked what happened to me. In response, I have shared my testimony of how God has worked in my life. Those who do not know about my underlying disability—I suffer the effects of TM and therefore cannot feel sensations such as temperature change in certain areas in my legs—have wondered why I could not feel the heat burning my leg. God has given me the opportunity and the courage to tell how He has given me the strength to move forward in Him.

It would never have occurred to me that my physical disability would be used to glorify God. However, by God's grace I no longer accept the enemy's lies and do not feel ashamed of my physical ailments. I realize that God can use me in the midst of my pain to encourage others. My testimony and experiences with pain give glory to God because I live to share the hope that God provides for those who are struggling. I am able to be a true witness for God, the greatest physician we could ever have.

In my search for a physical cure, God led me to a renewed spiritual healing. He healed my spiritual condition, which was more important than my physical healing. The psalmist testified, "It was good for me to be afflicted so that I might learn your decrees" (Ps. 119:71). If it is not God's will to heal us physically now, we can ask for His strength to understand His will and for endurance to go through our suffering. We can trust that God is sovereign and claim His promises. Many times our hearts need to be healed, and God alone is our ultimate physician in all things.

An Insightful Challenge

Do you have health problems that you are trying to handle on your own? Do you put on the mask of wellness and pretend that you are stronger than you really are? Are you struggling to find out what is wrong in your life? Are you searching only for answers, or are you seeking the help you really need? Do you know that God will use your circumstances and the physical afflictions you cannot understand to help others? Our internal pain aggravates our external pain. Turn to God, our ultimate physician, for healing. He has been my healer and He will be yours too.

And the God of all grace, who called you to his eternal glory in Christ, after you have suffered a little while, will himself restore you and make you strong, firm and steadfast.

—1 PETER 5:10

4

The Mask of Honesty

*For there is nothing hidden that will not be
disclosed, and nothing concealed that will not
be known or brought out into the open.*
—LUKE 8:17

WHEN I WENT on my healing retreat, God orchestrated everything for me to have time alone with Him. My sister and her
husband were at Calgary for a wedding and their house was located
near some great beaches I wanted to visit. I was able to house-sit
for them and also have a place where I could rest. During these five
precious days, God revealed so much to me. When I finally took the
time to listen to God—to refocus, renew, replenish, and rest at the
Lord's feet—He spoke volumes to my heart.

The first day of that week I wrote in my journal about God as a
third person. However, as my heart began to break, I began to write
directly to Him in the first person. I sensed a new peace all over.
As God revealed all that I was designed to be, He showed me the
good, the bad, and the ugly. It was good for me to see the ugly, to
break down and realize my need to come back to His saving grace
and unfailing love.

During my retreat and in the subsequent year and a half, God
revealed to me one by one each of the masks I had been wearing.

I felt His gentle reminder that each of us may have on these masks, and it is time for us to be real with each other so we can truly live the life He wants us to live. God wants us to live a life of truth and freedom in Him. He wants me to live in Him, and I intend to do just that so that I can proclaim to everyone what God has done for me (see Ps. 118:17), and tell others what He can do for them.

It's Hard to Be Real

How can we be real with each other? The following excerpt from my daily journal to God shows how I have struggled with this:

I think what led me to finally admit and share with my family about what I was going through was the incident that happened that Tuesday, Sept 7th. It was the first day of school for Kayli. Everything was great that morning. It was a nice warm day, and we ended up getting invited to our new neighbor's place for lunch so that her daughter could play with Kayli. I couldn't stay that long as I had a date with a good friend who was visiting.

Lily, my neighbor was gracious enough to offer that Kayli stay to play with her daughter so I could have some quality time with my friend. I accepted the kind offer, but before I could spend any time with my girlfriend, I had an unexpected call from my mom on my cell phone. She informed me that there had been a fire in the complex right behind them just a half hour before. Nothing was damaged at their place and they were fine. Good.

I later discovered that my parent's place ended up having water damage from the water the firemen used to douse the fire in the neighboring complex. All I really remembered was trying to reach all my family for help but no one was available, I was calm at the time, but became stressed when my mother and father started grumbling and complaining. Eventually I was able to locate my brother-in-law Herb, my brother Chi, and my husband who came to the rescue.

Three huge fans were drying my parents' place, so I offered to have them stay with me the next four days. Although I loved my parents, their constant demands wore me down that whole week and even made me bitter as I felt that I was left to take sole responsibility for them. Without this incident, I would not have blown my top off and finally admitted to the others that I cannot do it alone any longer. I cannot shelter everyone around me, I need to let go of my chief's hat.

I am like the cat that climbs up the tree, higher, and higher. If the cat has enough boldness to climb the tree so high, why can't it come back down on its own? Just inch down slowly you silly cat! When the cat finally reaches to the top and realizes that there are no more branches to climb up, it finally meows for help. Up comes the nice fireman on the ladder to save the day.

I have struggled all of my life to prove myself to others, but for what? To gain popularity? To gain approval? I don't know yet, but I am definitely out there on the limb, trying to reach for the higher branch each time. Finally I've reached my last branch, and I cannot go up anymore and I cannot come down. Silly me....now what? I have no choice, I finally cry out....but unlike the happy familiar story, I don't see the fireman who comes and saves me.

Yet, my heavenly Father, knows what's best for me, He waits and waits because He wants me to ask for help. He has already surrounded me with help that is always available for the asking. He surrounds me with a treasure of family and friends I have helped along the way. I am too foolish. I have too much pride. I cannot let them know that I have cornered myself up on the tree. Can I not climb down, inch by inch backwards on my own, to safety? I have learned the hard way; I cannot do it alone.

I am so glad that God has never forgotten me. Rather, He has heard my endless cries for help and deliverance. As He revealed truth to me, I was surprised to discover all the ugliness trapped inside me. I had so much to confess before I could be free again. I wrote about this in the journal I kept on my healing retreat:

Lord, I just want to unload and confess some of my burdens on you. It seems like ever since I was afflicted with my disease when I was fifteen, it left a scar in my heart. The scar is my pretense that everything is fine. I know that I've struggled with the fact of not telling a lot of people the truth about me. I don't know why. When a lot of my Christian friends find out what happened to me, they are amazed at me and say how strong I am, and that they can't tell anything is wrong.

However, I struggle with the idea of sharing this. I am not sure why, maybe it's because I am still ashamed of not being "normal" per se, I don't know. I just know that through the years, I've said some little white lies about myself when people ask me why I'm limping and all. I have said that I sprained my leg or I change the subject and walk off in a different way or I refer to my arthritis problem from the car accident. I never mention my infection. Is it because I'm afraid of what people think and that they will treat me differently? I yearn to be treated normally, and I guess I need to confess to be accepted as a whole person.

Throughout my childhood and into my adulthood, I've always strived to do my best, and to feel accepted. But, Lord, You have broken me down, and the shame that I felt was that I could not live up to other's expectations—especially my own. I did not realize that this is exactly what I need to come before You—to be broken down. I am not perfect. I need a Savior. Lord, help me to share this with others. I don't want to shatter people's dreams about me, but, Lord, I know I need to tell them the truth, or the mask I'm wearing would be permanent and I could never take it off. Lord, teach me and show me the way.

LESSONS FROM SPIDERMAN 2

Once you tune your heart with God's heart, you can learn from everything that is around you. It can be the scenes you see daily: the air you breathe, the people around you, and even the movies you watch. When my niece, Niki, and I watched *Spiderman 2* together, it was enjoyable to see all the cool special effects. I did not even think anything about the movie's plot except that the truth will set you free. However, during my quiet time with God the next day, my mind and heart wandered back to the movie, and I was so amazed to sense God speaking to my heart about it.

As I was praying, God reminded me of the scene where Peter Parker was losing his Spiderman powers and he couldn't understand why. He was in love with his best friend, but he could not tell her. He thought he would endanger her because he was Spiderman and if his enemies found out they would go after her. Thus, he decided to not pursue a love relationship and be a fulltime saving hero instead. However, he learned that when he suppressed love in his heart, he became sick.

Peter had been heavily burdened the last two years since he discovered his special gift was to serve and protect all of New York City.

He was overwhelmed because there were too many crimes for him to handle, and he disappointed many of his friends because he was not there for them. He was so tired from fighting crime, but he literally pushed himself until one day he started to lose his powers.

When Peter went to the doctor, he shared his dream of being Spiderman and the fact that he was losing his powers. He kept slipping and falling when he was climbing up walls. The witty and compassionate doctor told him that perhaps this person having these dreams of losing the powers of Spiderman was not meant to be Spiderman and that not having a sense of real identity is the hardest thing in one's life.

The concept opened Peter's eyes. He began to deal with his past and discovered why he had chosen to be Spiderman and why he had given up and sacrificed his love relationship. He recalled a dream in which he was speaking with his uncle and was told that if one is given a special gift of intelligence, one must use it to serve mankind and that sometimes sacrifices are necessary.

Confused and doubting his existence and purpose, Peter knew that he had a conscious choice to make. He chose to give up being Spiderman and decided to pursue his other dreams, not realizing until later that he was making a mistake. He was gifted to be Spiderman and help others.

God opened my eyes to see the message in this movie. I was like Peter Parker! I felt discouraged like Peter, and I wanted to be by myself and give up my title as "God's princess." Yet I knew I could not run away from what He has gifted me to do, to serve others by counseling them in times of need. God has called me to serve and that includes building my relationship with Him, my husband, my daughter, and my family and friends. Even when I try to run away from God's purpose in my life, He will bring me back to His plan for me.

MORE LESSONS FROM SPIDERMAN

When Peter Parker was searching for the reason he chose to become a crime fighter, he discovered that he was doing it out of guilt related to his deceased uncle. In a flashback scene, Peter told his uncle that he wanted to go to the library to study and his uncle drove him there. However, Peter only pretended to go to the library. He actually went to a place nearby to wrestle, so he could win money to buy a nice car that would impress his best friend and cause her to like him.

When he did win, the ring owner would not give him his money. Later, the wrestling place was robbed and the robber fled. Peter saw the robber and had the opportunity to stop him, but because he wanted to seek revenge for the people who cheated him out of his money, he did not bother to help. That same robber wanted a car for a runaway. It just so happened that Peter's uncle was sitting in his car, and the robber stabbed and killed him to steal the car. Peter suffered from guilt about this all these years. He then tried to redeem himself by doing what his uncle wanted him to do.

I had so much baggage to release to God. I realized that all my efforts to serve and please people were attempts to redeem myself, not just to God but to others. God knew my past hurts and failures, and there was nothing I could do to save myself; God saved me by His grace.

At the end of the movie, Peter's best friend decided not to marry their other friend. She came back to Peter and told him that if he loved her, then he should respect her enough to allow her to make her own decision whether or not to take risks. This reminded me of my own fears. I suppressed the truth from the people around me. Yet, if I truly valued their friendship, I should speak the truth and not shelter them or be afraid of what they would think.

Worse yet, I think I'm protecting them when I conceal the truth. I should respect others and think of them more highly. I should trust that they can make their own decisions and even help me. The best friend told Peter that he should let someone save him. That is so true for me. It is time that I let others into my life and help me.

At one point in the movie, Spiderman's mask accidentally came off as he finished saving a train full of people. They all saw Peter Parker's real face without the mask. He was petrified when his identity was revealed and was worried about his future. Two young children and the rest of the passengers reassured him, that he didn't need to worry because his secret was safe and they wouldn't reveal his identity. Peter felt reassured, and the passengers courageously gathered together to protect Spiderman when the enemy came to attack them again.

This was a wonderful reminder that if I take off my own mask, it is OK to trust others. They will gather around to help me when the enemy attacks me. This affirmation from God came at the perfect time when I was struggling whether to share truthfully with the FAB Ladies Group and my other friends. God spoke a strong reassurance to my heart, "It's OK to tell the truth Helen; the truth shall set you free." (See John 8:32.)

When Peter Parker made the decision to come back as Spiderman, he tried so hard on his own. However, he couldn't because he was worn out. This reminded me that when I try to do things on my own strength, I will burn out. I need to be daily empowered and renewed by the Holy Spirit to do the things God has planned for me. "'Not by might nor by power, but by my Spirit,' says the LORD Almighty" (Zech. 4:6).

TRUTH AND FREEDOM IN CHRIST

Even if we try to hide our sin and guilt from others, eventually the truth will come out. If we commit sinful acts, our conscience often gets the best of us and we eventually want to confess and tell the truth to be relieved of our guilt. Perhaps this is what Jesus meant when He told us that nothing will be hidden. We may think we can get away with something, but God sees everything; in the end, He will judge us all. (See Luke 12:1–3.)

God convicted me to confess my sin of living a life of hypocrisy. After twenty-five years of holding in the shame and guilt of not embracing my physical disability, I realized that it had led me into the web of lies in other parts of my life. I was finally able to share the truth about my physical and spiritual condition with my family and friends. First, I took steps to accept my disability and depression. I bought a medic scooter, got a disability pass, was fitted for orthotic shoes, focused on healthy eating, exercised daily, took herbal supplements and daily vitamins, and weaned myself off caffeine, coffee, and refined sugar. I committed the first portion of my morning to spending time with God. Without God, I could not be honest.

I realized that I had to be honest with myself first, before I could be honest with others. God rewarded my honesty and at last, I was set free from the burdens I had been carrying. Only God can convict our deceptive hearts to repent and tell the truth. When we embrace and share the truth, others can see that God is truly working in us. (See John 3:20–21.)

What did Christ mean when He said, "I am the way and the truth and the life. No one comes to the Father except through me" (John 14:6)? Jesus is the only way to God because we will never be able to meet God on our own. Our sins block us from entering into His holy presence. We try our best to reach God, but it will never be good enough. Jesus is the *truth* because He alone is perfect and His testimony on earth—His life, death and resurrection—shows that God's love for us is real. Jesus is *life* because without Him we would live a life devoid of purpose and meaning.

We were never meant to hide in our sins and keep the shame and guilt to ourselves. Jesus wants to set us free. Jesus Christ died and bore our penalty of sins upon Himself so that we can be set free, if we trust and surrender to Him. He wants us to live a free and abundant life in Him. (See John 10:10.)

Jesus reveals the real truth about us. We need to acknowledge the truth He has revealed about our masks and confess and repent of our pretenses. We will no longer hide behind our masks when He delivers us from our pretenses. He will set us free from the endless cycles of guilt, shame, anger, anxiety, fear, lack of joy, and depression. We will begin to walk with new hearts and develop human relationships to their fullest. And we will embrace the most priceless relationship of all, a genuine and joyfully intimate relationship with God!

AN INSIGHTFUL CHALLENGE

Are you wearing the "honesty mask" and yet burdened with the real truth about yourself? Do you feel that you have to make up more lies to conceal the lies that you have hidden? Do you feel trapped? Surrender your mask to God and ask Him to lead you to someone you can share your burdens with. When you confess your hidden lies to others, it starts the process of identifying people who love you for who you really are.

When your lies disappear, your burdens will feel lighter. Jesus wants you to live a life of truth in Him. Allow Christ to unveil your compounded lies, then confess and repent of them all. When you live all your relationships with honesty and integrity, you will experience a clear conscience and a life of freedom from guilt. The truth does set you free.

> But whoever lives by the truth comes into the light, so that it may be seen plainly that what he has done has been done through God.
>
> —JOHN 3:21

5

The Mask of Perfection

God opposes the proud but gives grace to the humble.
—JAMES 4:6

WE ALL STRIVE for perfection. Because the measure of our success is based on how well we do things, we tend to do our best not just for ourselves, but because we are seeking the affirmation of others. We are proud of what we do through our own abilities. Society recognizes this and rewards those who have the ability to accomplish things well. We literally work ourselves to exhaustion trying to prove to the world that we are perfect in what we do. We don't like failure, and we don't like to admit that we have made mistakes.

For the committed Christian, striving for perfection may become more intense. A new society—our circle of church friends—forms around us, and suddenly it seems that the bar has been raised a little bit higher. We now have a new standard, God's standard, and to reach it requires a new way of thinking and acting. We are supposed to live a wonderful new life in Christ, a wonderful victorious life. We may strive to live that way, but we don't.

Yet, our pride makes us believe that we can reach God's standard. We get sucked into believing that lie and living with the fear of being discovered imperfect, both by our non-believing friends or, worse yet, our circle of believing friends. We are all fallible creatures, yet we will not allow ourselves to admit it because we are supposed to be changed persons. Holding onto the mask of perfection and subjecting ourselves to pride block us from God's love and prevents Him from working in us.

THE PROBLEM OF PRIDE

I was a very independent child. At the age of eight I started to earn my own wages. I worked in a small wooden makeshift booth selling lottery tickets in front of a bakery in Chinatown. I was so proud when I made my 10 to 25 cents for each lottery ticket I sold! I would save my earnings and surprise my family by bringing home a small bag of plums or apples. My mom would be so proud of me, and I felt great. It was the beginning of a series of events that would lead me to work to please others to gain affirmation and to gain more independence. I became self-reliant and proud.

My stubborn old nature lured me to take matters into my own hands when I knew something was wrong. Rather than tell anyone else, I kept it to myself. I was the type of person who felt that if anything was to get done, I'd better do it myself. My dad was like that. He was the editor-in-chief for the *Chinese Times*, a local Chinese newspaper, and I was always proud of him because he took so much pride in his work. He loved his work; he lived and breathed it. I didn't realize until now that his pride is part of his downfall. Unless he puts away his pride, he will never see the grace of God in his life. He turns ninety-four this year, and I am still praying for his salvation.

My dad basically self-medicates himself because he believes that he knows more than the doctors. When I was about eleven years old, his pride nearly cost him his life. My dad was complaining that he had bad stomach pains, but he would not see the doctor even though my mother urged him to do so. One day he was in too much pain to eat with us in the kitchen. When we took some food to him in his room, we discovered to our horror that his stomach had bloated so much that he looked like he was pregnant!

My mother immediately called our family doctor and then the emergency ambulance. The paramedics came and took my dad in to receive treatment, and we learned later that my dad had a gallstone broken inside him. If he had not received treatment within four hours he would have died! God had mercy on our family even when we did not know Him.

When I came to know the Lord, I realized that I did not just inherit pride uniquely from my father. I also have pride instilled in me because Adam and Eve sinned and all future generations have inherited sin with all of its ugly traits including pride, greed, lust, and selfishness. Romans 5:12 teaches, "Therefore, just as sin entered the world through one man, and death through sin, and in this way death came to all men, because all sinned."

Praise God for His grace! Because Jesus Christ was obedient to God's plan, He died on the cross for our sins, so we can inherit Christ's righteousness. No matter how much we try, we cannot enter heaven without Christ in our lives. Romans 5:18–19 explains, "Consequently, just as the result of one trespass was condemnation for all men, so also the result of one act of righteousness was justification that brings life for all men. For just as through the disobedience of the one man the many were made sinners, so also through the obedience of the one man the many will be made righteous."

Throughout history, the downfall of many men and women has been their pride and their quest for perfection and success. Pride has been my key problem. I thought that my ability was better than others, and I also had a need to be in control. I also feared what people might think of me and needed the affirmation of others to make me feel secure. I have a tendency to promote myself and affirm myself. I'm glad that God revealed my pride to me so I could repent and surrender it to Him. "To fear the LORD is to hate evil; I hate *pride* and arrogance, evil behavior and perverse speech" (Prov. 8:13, emphasis added).

THE PROBLEM OF TRYING TO CONTROL

I become defensive when I am called a control freak. Why is planning meticulously and having an organized day considered a negative thing? The term *freak* sounds like such a strong word for someone who is capable of doing multiple tasks in an organized and efficient manner. As I consider these thoughts, I recognize that being a control freak is linked in with the mask of perfection. Part of being in control of things stems from trying to be perfect and making everything work out just right. If you cannot maintain control of a situation, it's hard to make things perfect.

Control freaks tend to fall harder and be disappointed more frequently. That's because we set our standard so high that it's difficult to reach it. We set ourselves up for failure. We also plan everything in great detail, hoping that it will all work out perfectly with no problems. We try to have everything under control. The problem is that in reality, we can't have everything under control. You might think we would learn this when we fall, but because of the old nature in ourselves, we just pick ourselves up and set the bar up again.

One thing I keep learning is that I may not be able to control all my circumstances, but I can control my attitude and trust that God is in control. God reminds me of this every now and then when I forget that He is the One who is in control and not me. A recent example of this was when I planned and prepared for my daughter's school field trip. She and her schoolmates were to go to a wonderful beach for a number of pre-planned activities. My husband Bill took the day off from work to surprise our daughter by going to enjoy the gorgeous sunny day with her. The night before I had everything ready for her: suntan lotion, cap, pail and shovel, disposable camera, sandals, t-shirt and a light jacket, and a packed lunch with extra juice and nutritious snacks.

The next day, because Bill was going on the field trip, I slept in. By the time I woke up, I remembered that I had forgotten to pack her shorts as she was wearing her Capri pants for the hike that was planned. I frantically called my husband, hoping that he had not yet left from the school. Fortunately he was still nearby and drove home to pick up the shorts. When he mentioned that it was clouding over and it might rain, I quickly grabbed Kayli's rain jacket and passed it to him. That morning, it poured with rain.

I prayed continuously and asked God to protect them all and give them an enjoyable experience even though things were not going according to plan. I was worried about the teacher who was a perfectionist like me. She had painstakingly planned and organized every detail of the activities she wanted the children to enjoy on the field trip. She had even driven to the beach the week before to ensure that all the trail routes and home activities were mapped out. The rain changed everything.

When my husband and daughter returned from their wet soggy trip, they reported that they had a good time. Despite the craziness of it all and the unplanned rain, my husband had a great learning experience in addition to making good memories with our daughter. I was happy to hear from my daughter that the children named him the "warming parent." The children were cold, shivering, and wet, and he volunteered to take them into the lodging area to dry out and warm up. One of the owners of the lodge thought Bill was one of the teachers because of the loving way he was caring for the children.

God blessed my husband for his servanthood that day, and I was blessed with another lesson in yielding control of unplanned circumstances to God. Despite the sudden change in the weather, I recognized that God is in control of everything. He controls the weather, and He knows what's best. He makes everything turn out for the better even though we may not understand.

IMPERFECT, BUT SAVED BY GRACE

We cannot reach God by anything we do. Our bridge to God is His grace and the righteousness of Christ that was imputed to us when He died on the cross for us. During my healing retreat, I went shopping in the neighborhood where I was staying. Later, I wrote the following in my journal:

> I read a little write-up that was placed near Mexican glass pottery at a Mexican d'arte store. It was a quote from a Mexican poet that read something like: Better to be imperfect and graceful than to be perfect and graceless. Wow, another lesson learned. That's for me. Right, Lord? I cannot be perfect. I'm not perfect. Only you are perfect. But why am I aiming for such perfection? If I do this out of wrong motives, I lose your grace. I know I should do my best for you but I should recognize that I am not perfect or I would not need a Savior. I am imperfect, but I am saved by grace. "For all have sinned and fall short of the glory of God, being justified as a gift by His grace through the redemption which is in Christ Jesus" (Rom. 3:23–24, NAS).
>
> I am also reminded from Ephesians 2:8–9, "For by grace you have been saved through faith; and that not of yourselves, it is the gift of God; not as a result of works, so that no one may boast" (NAS).
>
> Lord, I am also reminded in Ephesians 2:10, "For we are His workmanship, created in Christ Jesus for good works, which God prepared beforehand so that we would walk in them" (NAS). I know, Lord, that there is nothing I can do to

earn my salvation, but I do desire to show my love for You by doing all these works in service for You to gain approval from You. Lord, I know that You don't need me to prove anything; You just want to be called upon and relied upon because You love me and want me to trust in You. Lord forgive me when I get so caught up in doing these things, I think I'm doing it for You, but really I'm doing it for me. Help me, Lord, to do the things that are the part that I should do and not to worry about the things I should not.

TRYING TO LOOK PERFECT

We try to look perfect for people. We want the approval of others, and we reflect this in the way we clean our homes for guests. We become like a mad maid, scrambling to clean up and put things away so that the place will appear orderly and clean. We don't want people to know that we are messy, unkempt, or disorderly.

Once when my friend came over with her son for a visit, my daughter was showing off her playroom library. Kayli discovered to her horror that a few stacks of books were on the ground. She was very embarrassed and apologized in her most mature seven year old manner, "Oh, I'm sorry! These shouldn't be out. I didn't know there were guests coming, or I would have put them away. Let me put these back in order." Then she quickly slotted the books in their proper place.

My girlfriend confessed that she giggled inside because she knew where Kayli's orderliness came from. It was obvious to me that Kayli mimicked my actions. I confessed to my friend that, unfortunately, it was not orderliness but the pride of trying to be neat and impressing others that she had inherited.

LEARNING TO DECLUTTER

Keeping clean and de-cluttering reminds me of an Oprah show I watched with my sister one time. The topic that day was on helping others clean their cluttered homes. I was filled with empathy for the woman who was being profiled because she really needed help internally to clean up her life. She had lived in a cluttered, extremely dirty home for two years, but she had kept it a secret because she was too ashamed to tell anyone. No one would have guessed that her home was so cluttered because she dressed so nicely and always looked so put together when she went to work as a teacher. Finally, however, she couldn't handle it anymore and she asked for help.

This woman had once been a perfectionist who wanted everything to be super tidy and in its right place. However, after her sixth divorce she fell into depression. She felt like trash and literally lived in her trash. The really sad part was not just the dirt and clutter I saw externally, but what she said and how she felt internally. Because she was so ashamed of letting anyone know about her struggles, she did not invite anyone over. The only other person who saw her house in that condition was the air conditioner repairman, and she had lied and told him that she was house sitting for a friend. She was so ashamed about lying and she had asked God to forgive her. Now she wanted to expose her secret because she wanted to help others who were going through the same thing.

My heart ached to see and hear about the clutter that was in her life. Her situation made me think of myself and reminded me of the things that I was hoarding and couldn't release. I had so much clutter in my life, and I needed to let go of it. I had said that I wanted to surrender everything to God, but I thought of the things that were piling up in my storage room and my office. A lot of them were my past work related files that I did not need to keep. Why was I keeping them? I was holding on to things that made me feel somewhat important. The keepsakes that I kept were letters and cards from family and friends and pictures of the events in my life; they reminded and affirmed me of my worth.

God motivated me to clean and get rid of the physical and tangible clutter in my life, so I could move on with my life internally. I needed to let go of my past, and live in the present. It started with me confessing before God all the secrets and lies I had hidden from my family and friends. I was just like the lady on the show; I looked so clean and put together in front of others, but deep down I was really falling apart.

I was a perfectionist like the woman on the Oprah show; I too was afraid that I would collapse and break down—that I would be drowned in my own trash and clutter. God was full of mercy and grace; He allowed me to realize my need for help and enabled me to reach out to Him and others. He helped me de-clutter all the dirt that was blocking me from having a clean and honest relationship with Him and others. God reminded me that I was not alone. Just as the woman shared about herself so she could help others, I too want to share what God has done for me so I can help others.

It is ironic that we have to admit imperfection before we can receive help to be better. Pride is the core reason that many do not seek and ask for help when they need it the most. It's as if asking for help is a sign of weakness. Part of wearing the mask of perfection is to display how strong we are when we really aren't. We need help, but we're too afraid to ask; our pride stops us.

Many of us do not understand that being part of God's community is not only to serve others but also to allow others to serve us. Sometimes we get so caught up in displaying our own servant attitude that we don't realize we are allowing pride to creep in. We do not allow ourselves to be served. We forget that we were never meant to be perfect beings. We are only asked to do our best for God despite our imperfections so that His glory will be perfected in us.

GIVING CREDIT WHERE
CREDIT IS DUE

Part of trying to attain perfectionism is to ensure that others know what we are doing and to let others see what we are doing. This is very dangerous territory because it leads to boasting and puffing up our own ego. Why do we tell others all the great things we have achieved, or the wonderful things we have bought? It is all part of seeking affirmation from others to make us feel good and help us believe that we are one step closer to attaining our perfect world.

I have a problem with accepting and loving myself, but boasting allows me to be another person who I think may be more accepted. Earthly boasting is like exaggerated claims to something that makes one feel good temporarily. However, it makes only the boaster feel good about himself while it causes others to be envious. Heavenly boasting benefits both the boaster and the receiver. It gives credit where credit is due—to God, not us.

The blessings and successes we receive should give God all the glory because they not only affirm our faith, but also encourage others to trust in God's grace and faithfulness which they see in our lives. It is not what we do, but God's grace that allows us to do what we can. The apostle Paul was a great example of honouring God and giving Him all the glory in all that he did. He testified, "But by the grace of God I am what I am, and his grace to me was not without effect. No, I worked harder than all of them—yet not I, but the *grace of God* that was with me" (1 Cor. 15:10, emphasis added).

Paul also gave clear counsel for our boasting when he wrote, "Let him who boasts boast in the Lord. For it is not the one who commends himself who is approved, but the one whom the Lord commends" (2 Cor. 10:17–18).

THE HUMILITY OF CHRIST

It is so difficult to comprehend the magnitude of what Christ did for us. He came down from His royal throne, was born in a very smelly stable, walked this earth to learn about the things we go through, and suffered and died the most gruesome, cruel, and shameful death. He was stripped to his underwear—in those days this was equivalent to being naked—in front of everyone, and He taught us that nothing is too shameful or embarrassing if it is done to glorify God.

What Christ did reminds us that we must take off our masks and be totally honest with God. Jesus died for us, and we need to humble ourselves, break down our pride, admit our imperfection, and surrender our hearts to Him. God exposes all our ugliness and nakedness so that we will realize we can't do anything on our own. We need to be truly grateful for the sacrifice and gift that He gave to us—Himself. It is Christ's perfection and His love for us that teaches us what true humility is.

Reflect also on what Christ did the night He was betrayed. As He humbled himself and washed His disciples' feet, He said, "I have set you an example that you should do as I have done for you. I tell you the truth, no servant is greater than his master, nor is a messenger greater than the one who sent him" (John 13:15–16).

Jesus wanted to show His disciples a physical example of serving because that same night they were disputing among themselves about who was considered to be the greatest. Jesus had told them that "the greatest among you should be like the youngest, and the one who rules like the one who serves" (Luke 22:26), and then He reminded them that even He, their teacher, was among them "as one who serves" (Luke 22:27). Jesus taught them first, and then He showed them. He gave them an object lesson on serving others. It's not about what we say, but more importantly what we do for others.

Think about what Jesus did for us. It's hard to imagine that a heavenly king would leave His royal throne in heaven above and come to earth with a mission to die a lowly death for His servants. But Jesus Christ did just that. He made the ultimate sacrifice and gave the ultimate example for all of us. For us to be great, we need to be humbled; to be rich, we need to be poor; to be a successful leader, we need to serve others. We need to be more like Jesus, as the apostle Paul exhorted us:

> Do nothing out of selfish ambition or vain conceit, but in humility consider others better than yourselves. Each of you should look not only to your own interests, but also to the interests of others. Your attitude should be the same as that of Christ Jesus: Who, being in very nature God, did not consider equality with God something to be grasped, but made himself nothing, taking the very nature of a servant, being made in human likeness. And being found in appearance as a man, he humbled himself and became obedient to death—even death on a cross! Therefore God exalted him to the highest place and gave him the name that is above every name, that at the name of Jesus every knee should bow, in heaven and on earth and under the earth, and every tongue confess that Jesus Christ is Lord, to the glory of God the Father.
>
> —PHILIPPIANS 2:3–11

AN INSIGHTFUL CHALLENGE

Have you ever put on a mask of perfection before others? Do you need to appear perfect and present a lifestyle that looks good to others? Have you kept shortcomings and failures to yourself because you were concerned about how people might think about you or treat you? Do you want others to think that you are all put together? Do you do things to make others think you are successful? Do you strive to be perfect in everything you do and get very upset at yourself when you don't attain your goals? Have you ever boasted? Have you ever exaggerated your achievements, accomplishments, and even shopping purchases to others?

You don't have to prove anything to anyone. God loved you in your imperfection, died for you, and gave you new life in Him. Give God the glory for His grace in your life and for all His blessings to you. Surrender your pride to God and refuse to listen to the enemy's lies. Christ will give you a humble heart and glorify Himself through His work in you.

> For it is God who works in you to will and to act according to his good purpose.
>
> —PHILIPPIANS 2:13

6

The Mask of Strength

He gives strength to the weary and
increases the power of the weak.
—ISAIAH 40:29

A COMPLEX HAS BEEN defined as "a system of interrelated, emotion-charged ideas, feelings, memories, and impulses that is usually repressed and that gives rise to abnormal or pathological behavior."[1] Our complexes are usually defined and shaped by our past experiences and how we dealt with them. If we think about it, we all have had experiences that are segmented in different phases in our hearts. We remember life by these phases or time periods, which may include the loss of a loved one, an accident, a person who came into your life and changed you, a circumstance that really spoke to your heart, a disappointment or major setback in your life, or an amazing achievement.

I have at times displayed a superior complex because I was really repressing all my childhood memories and experiences. My superior complex hid my true inferior complex. Contrary to what people know about me, I started my life as a shy, quiet girl, the youngest of four children in Vancouver, Canada. I lived in a government subsidized project home in a rougher community near Chinatown, a place where you can't stay weak very long or you will fall.

For some reason, God kept me small in stature the first seventeen years of my life. I was always the shortest in my peer group and my class; but I was blessed to have my second brother Chi who took a special interest in me and trained me in the field of martial arts so I could defend myself against any one who bullied me. Prior to my viral infection, I had already put up a tough front to protect myself from being put down or bullied in my neighborhood and in my school.

To this day I am grateful that a selfless teacher in our community school took a keen interest in training a group of young shy girls, including me, and introduced us to the world of rhythmic gymnastics. My confidence grew as my abilities developed in performing and competing publicly. My dance coach, Penny Tonge, continued to support me and even had our school sponsor me in extra special summer dance lessons because my family could not afford them.

I had strong dreams of competing in the Olympics and was excited to learn that one of the training coaches for Olympic athletes was interested in coaching me. I would have to move to Toronto for the summer for part of the training, and my coach faithfully and persistently tried to convince my dad of the potential in this opportunity. However, my dreams were shattered when my dad adamantly refused to give his permission. He felt that an athlete would not be able to feed any mouths whereas an education could. This was probably the same time I started to sell lottery tickets, so I could prove that I was able to make money. As I entered my teen years, I coached other young girls and involved myself as much as possible in intramural sports.

Through many career transitions, my heart has wandered back to my childhood dreams, and I have wondered where and what would be different if I had continued to pursue my Olympic training. When I was afflicted with the viral infection, my heart became bitter toward my dad because I thought I would not have been in that predicament if I had taken a different path in life. Yet my heart turned soft when my dad faithfully came everyday to the hospital to massage my paralyzed legs. God took care of my needs even when I didn't know Him.

THE ART OF FALLING

Have you ever slipped and fallen down? Do you remember how you responded when someone asked you if you were OK? I have slipped and fallen so many times that I have perfected the art of falling. My sister says that she has not seen anyone fall more gracefully than me. This is because with my past gymnastics training in controlled falling, each time I find myself slipping or falling, I automatically slide my left foot forward and by the time I hit the ground, I end up in a "jazz split" position. You can just imagine how I look—like I'm performing the finale in a dance!

When I fall down, I quickly say I am fine just to avoid any more attention, even though I am aching all over and my pride is hurt. Why do we automatically say we are fine, when we are really in pain and it would be nice to get some help? This question is not limited to our physical falls, but also our emotional falls. We hold back our fears, worries and pains to display a mask of strength. This is more evident when we encounter a traumatic setback such as the loss of a loved one, a job, or dream. We display a front that everything is fine, but deep down we are in pain and even in anguish.

The mask of strength goes hand in hand with the mask of perfection—they are both intertwined. If we are honest with ourselves, we all fear what people will think about us. What will people think about the way we dress, how we wear our hair, the way we eat, how we keep our homes and gardens, the type of car we drive, and how we interact with others? It all boils down to impressing others so that they will affirm that we are doing fine; it's like a report card in which we try to ensure that we are making the grade as part of society. We have to meet the norms to fit in.

We Christians are not excluded from this standard, but we also have a new standard that we are expected to meet because we are believers. The secular world watches every move we make to see if we are meeting their standard of what a Christian should be, and the Christian circle does the same.

One of the greatest deceptions of the enemy is that we think we have to meet a certain standard to live up to our roles. We feel that we have to put on a mask of strength even though we are faltering inside. The truth is that we will never meet the standard that is set for us, but the great news is that God already knows that. We were never meant to put up a front that we are strong so we can gain everyone's approval. We were meant to be weak so that God's glory will be displayed in us. (See John 9:3.)

In my struggle to live as a strong, victorious, happy Christian, I was lured into believing that I had to put up a front to shield others from my pains and sorrows. There was no way I wanted anyone to know that I had not lived the joyful life I should have. I was trapped in a tangle of lies. It may have seemed like I was wearing the mask of a superiority complex, but I really had an inferior complex that I was trying to hide. I had put on a false mask of strength. When I met new individuals, they would not know my past weaknesses— especially my hidden disability; they would only see the strong front I was presenting.

When I first believed in Christ, I had the warped idea that 2 Corinthians 5:17 meant my old problems—my disability—had gone away and I had become a new person without any worries. I even struggled with the idea of sharing about my viral infection when I gave my testimony for fear that people would not understand or become close to me. I did not want others to treat me any differently or show me pity or sympathy because of my disability. Ironically, I was the one who was having my own pity party. Instead of being grateful for the life and mobility I did have, I rehearsed over and over again how unfortunate I was.

I did not realize that 2 Corinthians 5:17 really meant that we have a new and perfect standing with God in Christ and the old has to do with my past standing before God. To have new life does not mean that our physical, emotional, and even spiritual state is perfect before God. While I surrendered my old nature to Christ in the past, I have to continually do it *every day* for Him to work through me. If I would have had a more accurate understanding of this scripture at that time, I would have been more joyful in the Lord. I would have realized that my Heavenly Father sees me as already perfect in Christ and accepts me in His beloved Son.

HUMBLING EXPERIENCES

My residual paralysis and the resulting weakness in my lower left extremities left me with physical abnormalities, and, to hide this fact, I would buy clothing that fit looser and hung longer. Also, in stark contrast to my previous lack of fear, I was now afraid that I might slip and fall due to my imbalance in walking. I came to have a history of falls that caused damage and bruising to my legs. Rain and snow made me phobic. I was afraid to walk on tiled, slippery surfaces that were wet, and winters were the worst time because of the snow, slush, and ice on the pavements.

It was hard for me to tell others about my fear. I remember walking with a close shopping friend of mine and feeling so uncomfortable because she would always walk three paces ahead of me. However, to hide my vulnerability, I would never tell her how I felt until many years later when I finally decided to embrace my disability.

I have been led to believe that my limp is a sign of weakness, and as a result I feel very uncomfortable when someone is walking behind me. I also feel very inadequate because I am walking so slowly and that person has to go around me. It's similar to the way you may feel when you are driving your car at the speed limit and a car pulls up behind you and tailgates you. The car behind you continues to follow you closely, and finally when you think you can't handle it anymore, it swings over to the next lane and passes you. The driver may honk at you or give you a look as if you lack ability to drive.

Last winter I had to pick Kayli up after school one day when it was snowing. Her classroom was in the annex beside the school, at the end of a small downhill slope it becomes a nice slippery ride if you're not watching your step. As I approached the slope feeling fearful about walking in the snow, my uneasiness increased even more when another parent came up and walked behind me. I suddenly panicked and literally froze in my tracks. Then I decided to shuffle forward so I wouldn't slip and fall. As the parent behind me passed by, I confessed, "I am so phobic of walking in the snow, I have to walk slowly or I might slip and fall." It was a humbling experience; it was the first time I had not made an excuse for my inadequacy.

I had another humbling experience last summer when we purchased a medic scooter for me to ride for long distance travel. I nicknamed the scooter "Cammie" because it reminded me of a chameleon, with its coloured Velcro body parts that can be interchanged to vary the look of the scooter. Cammie can look classic and chic in champagne tone, hot and stylish in red ruby or ultra cool in metallic blue. When we took Cammie on its first long distance workout along the seawall at Stanley Park in Vancouver many people stared at me as I rode by them. I wondered what they were thinking. Were they admiring my hot new wheels, or were they wondering why a younger woman would be on a medic scooter?

At first I felt very self-conscious. However, God was gracious to me and helped me realize what was happening. For the first time, rather than staying behind and feeling left out as my husband and daughter

Rollerbladed away, I was actually there beside them. I felt the freedom of being mobile, and I experienced the joy of God embracing me as the wind blew against my body. Because I learned to humble myself, I was able to enjoy freedom that day.

The root of my problem was pride. I wanted others to treat me normally and see me as strong and successful despite my physical limitations. I did not realize that my true strength did not come from any external source. It came from faith in an internal source—Christ's strength and power at work in my life.

A PROPER RESPONSE TO WEAKNESS

Society aims for perfection; anything short of it we typecast as abnormal or weak. Because of this tendency in society, I believed that my lack of full mobility meant I could not lead a normal life. However, we are all imperfect beings. We all have disabilities—an inability to do something—and they are not limited to problems of a physical nature. Some of us may have mental and emotional disabilities. We may lack self-control or find ourselves disabled in the way we treat ourselves and others. While I may have a disability that makes it impossible for me to control my leg and run properly, someone else may be disabled in the area of uncontrolled gambling, lying, cheating, or even gossiping.

Although we may not be able to control some things related to our disabilities, we can gain control if we will view ourselves and our abilities with honesty. We may feel that we can't control what we do or say, but we can if we will surrender ourselves to God and receive the help He provides. The first step is to break down the barriers of pride and false strength and admit our inabilities and weaknesses.

> Do not think of yourself more highly than you ought, but rather think of yourself with sober judgement, in accordance with the measure of faith God has given you.
>
> —Romans 12:3

James 4:10 exhorts us, "Humble yourselves before the Lord, and he will lift you up." As we humble ourselves in surrender and submission to God, He will be able to work in our lives because we are giving Him full control. God loves us so much that He has given us the capability to choose to love Him. He will never force His love or control on us if we do not truly desire and allow Him in our lives. We are all weak, and we all need God to give us the strength we need to accomplish anything. Jesus Christ is our source of life, and apart from Him, we become weak. We are strong only in Christ.

> I am the vine; you are the branches. If a man remains in me and I in him, he will bear much fruit; apart from me you can do nothing.
>
> —John 15:5

Some may feel that they are weak, and rather than put on a mask of strength, they don a mask of weakness. Although this mask is a complete opposite of the mask of strength, it is just as deceptive. People who wear the mask of weakness *intentionally* show others how weak they are. They may claim that they are not good enough to serve, and may have many excuses to take a backseat in everything. And when adversity comes, they claim that they are too weak to defend themselves and take pride in their weakness. If they get bullied or persecuted, they do not speak up to defend a position but rather step down and say that they are humbling themselves. This is dangerous because it distorts God's purpose for us. He calls us to be meek, not weak.

In his letter to the Corinthians, Paul defended the ministry of

Christ and yet showed meekness and gentleness. "By the meekness and gentleness of Christ, I appeal to you—I, Paul, who am 'timid' when face to face with you, but 'bold' when away!" (2 Cor. 10:1). Meekness is being humble in our circumstances, knowing that our strength does not come from within ourselves, but from the power and grace of Jesus Christ. It is the realization that all our successes and achievements are accomplished by the grace of God as we submit to Christ and allow Him to direct our lives.

It is not wrong to admit our true weaknesses as God reveals them to us. However, we must guard against *intentionally* displaying our weaknesses and exploiting God's grace. Such action makes us feel too inadequate in our abilities and desirous of sympathy from the world. We want others to feel sorry for us because it makes us feel needed when we ourselves become needy—acting as if we are incapable of doing anything. The mask of weakness gives a false sense of power because we try to behave as is we can't do it ourselves. We say that we rely on God, but in our hearts we try to control our circumstances and block God from truly working in us.

LESSONS FROM ELIJAH

It never ceases to amaze me how God speaks directly to our hearts through His Word and gives us lessons to refine us when we slip and think incorrect thoughts. One morning God led me to read about the Old Testament prophet Elijah in 1 Kings 18–19. Elijah was God's chosen prophet, a very strong and faithful servant. He challenged the prophets of Baal to call on their god to send fire on the altar that had been prepared, and their cries to Baal went unanswered. Then Elijah poured water on the altar three times to soak the sacrifice and the trenches so that there could be no chance of fire starting from a spark or from dry combustion. As he prayed with faith in God, fire came down from heaven and consumed the sacrifice.

I was awestruck to learn how such a faithful powerful servant could become so afraid just a short time later when Queen Jezebel threatened to take his life. God had shown him many miracles by withholding rain for three and half years and by sending fire to burn the sacrifice and prove that He is the one true God. Yet, for fear of his enemies, Elijah fled into the desert and expressed his desire to die: "It is enough! Now, LORD, take my life, for I am no better than my fathers!" (1 Kings 19:4, NKJV). Although he trusted God and knew that He was very real in his life, Elijah felt that he had failed God, perhaps because he had become weak and afraid. I could identify with this. I had thought I was so strong in my faith, but I was so unhappy deep inside myself and was hiding the truth from everyone. I cried out many times that I just wanted to go home to God. I wished that my present life would end because I felt that I had failed God and I could not endure the pressure of serving Him. I asked God to forgive me when I felt too tired to serve Him anymore. However, I did not know that Satan was manipulating my mind to have all these negative thoughts.

My heart was pierced when I read how God sent His angel to minister to Elijah and tell him to "arise and eat, because the journey is too great for you" (1 Kings 19:7, NKJV). That was exactly what I needed. God knew my pain, and He knew that my journey ahead was too great for me. I needed to take time out for myself to replenish myself.

I thank God that He was gracious and always faithful to me. God reminded me that I had to get up and eat after I rested, like Elijah. I was tired physically and spiritually, but God strengthened me. He wanted me to get up and eat, not of physical food but of His spiritual food, the feast He has provided in His precious Word. I needed to fill my spiritual needs with His Word.

LESSONS FROM JOB

The same morning God led me to read about Elijah, He also directed me to the story of Job. A refreshing reminder of a man after God's heart, Job was full of integrity, "blameless and upright, a man who fears God and shuns evil" (Job 1:8). Yet God handed him over to Satan to be tested because God knew exactly what Job would do. When God took everything away from him, (in four separate events, God struck Job's material possessions and even his children!) Job still declared God's goodness: "Naked I came from my mother's womb, and naked I will depart. The LORD gave and the LORD has taken away" (Job 1:21). "In all this, Job did not sin by charging God with wrongdoing" (Job 1:22).

Even when God allowed Satan to administer direct physical pain to him with painful sores from head to toe, he still did not curse God. Instead, he kept silent in his suffering until seven days and seven nights had passed and then he finally spoke. He did not curse God directly, but only questioned Him for creating him and letting him suffer. He told God how he felt that he was worth nothing. (See Job 2–3.)

I felt Job's pain and knew of his anguish. When I had suffered physically, I called to God and felt the same way he did. Job cursed the day of his birth, without knowing that he was actually cursing God's creation and hence rejecting and forgetting God. He thought he was righteous and did not understand why God was making him suffer. My words mimicked Job's, "I despise my life; I would not live forever. Let me alone; my days have no meaning" (Job 7:16).

As you and I must confess, it is all about us and our meaning in life. We are so caught up in ourselves not knowing that God has a reason for everything! There is no way we can comprehend the awesomeness of God; our reasoning is limited.

Job questioned God, "What is man that you make so much of him, that you give him so much attention" (Job 7:17), and "test him every moment?" (Job 7:18, ESV). Then he asked, "Why have you made me your target? Have I become a burden to you? Why do you not pardon my offenses and forgive my sins?" (Job 7:20–21). I was deceived by the enemy and fell into the same lies as Job. I questioned God's love for me and doubted His truth.

Perhaps Job's three friends remind you of your friends who try to help and console you when you are going through hard times. They may not have the right words or actions to console you because you may have put up a strong front in the past. When you finally break down and share the truth with them, they are shocked that someone so strong can be so weak in faith. They may try to encourage you, but their words seem empty because you know deep in your heart that you were not that strong to begin with. It was a mask that you were wearing. You want help but it's not there. You know that you have to confess completely and surrender it all to God to receive real peace and comfort from the greatest counselor—God Himself.

God finally used Elihu who was just sitting by listening to Job and his three friends. Elihu didn't say anything initially because he felt that he was too young to speak and did not have enough wisdom; yet God by His Spirit compelled him to do so. Elihu gave reverence to older people: "Age should speak; advanced years should teach wisdom. But it is the spirit in a man, the breath of the Almighty, that gives him understanding. It is not only the old who are wise, not only the aged who understand what is right" (Job 32:7–9).

Elihu reminds me of how God brings help from the most unlikely of sources. Perhaps you have experienced and have received help from your neighbor, your children, someone you just met, or perhaps a complete stranger. For me it was Kayli who was only six years old at the time. I tried my best to hold in my angry emotions so she would not see me get upset, but sometimes my anger could not be contained. One day I was very upset with my husband Bill and went into my bedroom to simmer down. To my surprise Kayli came into my room and spoke in her sweetest voice, "Mommy, you should not be mad at Daddy." That broke me down. I realized that I was wrong before God and that God had sent her to calm me down and make me confess the error of my ways.

Can you remember a time when God sent someone out of the blue to speak convicting words to your heart? God always shows His love for us in the way we need it; He knows that under our tough exterior is a soft interior that needs to be reshaped according to His plan, to do new things in His strength. As I learned from Job and Elijah, God allows His passionate and strong servants to become weak so they will remember that their strength is from God. He calls us to surrender our pride and weaknesses to Him.

LEARNING TO SOAR

I have always been fascinated with birds. I learn so much from the way they fly, the way they build their homes, the way they look for their food, and the way they take care of their own. I love to see little birds move from one destination to another. They flap their wings, glide a bit to give their wings some rest, and then flap their wings some more to keep their momentum up. Eventually, however, they have to rest somewhere.

One of my favorite fascinations is to see an eagle fly. Eagles don't seem to require much effort to fly high, and they can fly higher and longer distances than other birds. This could be because they have much bigger wingspans, but they also allow the wind beneath them to carry them along and raise them to higher heights.

During my quiet time one morning, I was looking out our backyard window in great awe of God's creation. It was a beautiful sunny day; the sky was blue with white puffy clouds moving in. As I was singing about my soul longing after God, a beautiful eagle suddenly soared right in front of me and landed on one of the treetops I gaze at each morning. They never come this way, and I was so amazed. I felt such a great sense of joy because I knew that this was God affirming me with His presence as I sang to Him.

God normally revealed His presence to me by sending little birds my way, but that day He sent me something extra special—an eagle. It was as if God wanted to affirm to me that everything was going to be OK as I placed my trust in Him. Later that day I was to go to my doctor to share my concern that I might have bi-polar disorder. God wanted to remind me that He was in control and that He had anointed me with His Holy Spirit.

I had longed for the Holy Spirit to lift me up as it were on His wings, so that I could soar to higher heights for God. I did not want to fly on my own because I was getting so weary on my earthly journey. I realized that I could only go so far—and get so tired—on my own. Although I felt weak, I knew that I could be strong again because I have a great and mighty God who will enable me to do all things.

What a beautiful reminder that if we allow the Holy Spirit to work in us we can soar and do great things for God. When we try to do things in our own strength we easily become weary. But God promises that "those who hope in the LORD will renew their strength. They will soar on wings like eagles; they will run and not grow weary, they will walk and not be faint" (Isa. 40:31).

New Beginnings

I will never forget the parallel lessons that God taught my family and me last summer and the milestones we achieved because we trusted Him on a beautiful Friday evening in August. As I think back, I am so thankful that I obeyed the prompting of the Holy Spirit that it was time for me to literally step out in faith and try to run in public. It was also time for Kayli to learn how to ride her bike without training wheels. And so, I suggested that our family go to the nearby secondary school where there was a wonderful padded track.

As we talked about my idea, Kayli expressed fear about riding her bike on her own, and I encouraged her by saying that she could do it. When she responded with "I can't," I told her that if she kept telling herself that, she really couldn't. She had already failed even before she began. At that moment it was as if God was telling me the same thing. I had already failed before I even tried, because for the past twenty-five years I had listened to the enemy's lies that I could not run. I had paralyzed myself into believing that. I was trained to regain my strength to walk, but I had never tried to run after my spinal cord injury.

At the track I could see how determined Kayli was to ride her bike without training wheels, even though she had said she couldn't. She could not start riding her bike without Bill's help, but she soon began riding on her own after Bill helped her start off. My husband was running behind her only to make sure she was safe. Yet she was getting discouraged because she could not start riding her bike on her own. As I saw the potential in my daughter, I knew in my heart that this was the night she would ride on her own. She only needed encouragement.

Bill was getting tired and said he needed a rest. After a little encouragement, I was able to convince Kayli to try again, and I told her that I was going to hold her bike seat as she started to ride. I released my grip as she began riding and she did not know that I was not holding on. She only needed to know that someone was there to hold her. She had done it all on her own!

It reminded me of our life journey. We are afraid to embark on so many things, but when we know that God is right there holding onto us, we somehow become more courageous. Then God lets us go so we can learn on our own. He knows we will fall and get hurt sometimes, but that is exactly how we will learn and grow. And that is what happened the night Kayli learned to ride her bike. She fell, but she immediately picked herself up. We encouraged her to keep doing what she was doing, and in no time she was able to bike on her own. It was such a great blessing for us to watch.

I realized I had also experienced what my daughter felt that night—the security of knowing that God was holding me. It was one of the most humbling things I had felt for a long time. I needed to be confident that God was there with me. I had to surrender my pride and let Him be in control. He brought me this far, and I had to believe it and trust in Him.

While Kayli was happily riding her bike along the track, I knew it was time for me to take my first steps too. I did my stretches, prayed a short prayer to surrender my pride, took a deep breath and away I went. As I took my first stumbling steps, I thought to myself, "Rats, I forgot my iPod." If I had my MP3 player, I would be more motivated to run. I could hear my feet pounding on the track; they made a funny sound, like a "chick....book....chick....book....chick.... book" sound. My gait was uneven because my weaker left foot was trying its best to lift up and push off to run.

It was hard for me to remember how to run. I was more like "shuffle jogging." I must have looked silly as I was trying to shuffle along as I tried to jog. However, I felt that if Terry Fox could limp his way across Canada, I could limp, shuffle, and jog my way around the track. I wanted to get my heart in shape.

I remember how God had inspired me and motivated me just a few months before. I was worshiping and dancing to Him with my praises during worship and He allowed me to jog around my room. I was so happy and ecstatic to learn that I was able to do that, and now here I was, running on a real track in broad daylight, in front of the other people who were there. Yes, my right leg, took a big beating but it was worth it. It felt great to run a little and feel the wind on my cheeks. It felt great to see movement pass me as I propelled my own body forward. It felt great mostly because I did not care what people thought of me anymore. I probably looked funny, limping along the track as I tried to run, but I didn't care!

Bill was at the top bench cheering both Kayli and myself on the track that night. It was an experience I will never forget. I only ran a little and walked the rest of the lap, but my heart was filled with thankfulness and excitement as I felt the miracle of me actually running for a short time. God orchestrated it so that some friends came by unexpectedly that night to walk their brother's dog. For the first time I was able to tell them of God's goodness in my first attempt to run. It was great to be real with them, without my mask of strength.

I took Kayli back to the same track the next night. She was full of confidence from the night before and immediately rode her bike on her own. Within the hour she had biked seventeen laps around the high school track! She only fell three times, because of the bumps along the way. I forgot my MP3 player again, but I realized that God wanted me to listen to the pounding of my feet on the ground, the beating of my heart, and my heavy breathing. These were the sounds of new life, new hope, and new beginnings. God reminded me that He was right there. I sang to Him and praised Him again that evening until the beautiful sun set.

That second night, I was inspired not to give up, but to do my first full lap. When I was halfway through, I was getting tired, but I wanted to keep going. By three-quarters of the way, the upper joint of my left leg was aching, but I wanted to complete my whole lap. *Help me to finish the race before me Lord*, I prayed. As I dedicated the lap to God, I recited "I can do all things through Christ.... I can do all things through Christ!" (See Phil. 4:13.) God answered my prayer and allowed me to finish the lap! All glory went to God that night! I was so amazed by what I could do when I persevered. It reminded me that with God, all things are possible if only we step out in faith.

I am more confident to run physically now even though I still have my disability. And I am grateful for the incredible insight God has taught me. As we run the spiritual race, we will face obstacles on our pilgrimage and we will feel like giving up. We will feel that we do not have the ability to keep going, and even after we are rested, we will feel that we cannot continue the race. However, if we keep our eyes focused on Jesus and trust in His strength, we can finish the race well.

> Let us throw off everything that hinders and the sin that so easily entangles, and let us run with perseverance the race marked out for us. Let us fix our eyes on Jesus, the author and perfecter of our faith.
> —HEBREWS 12:1–2

EXPERIENCING THE POWER
OF THE HOLY SPIRIT

When God enabled me to unveil my pride, He also helped me rediscover His truth and power, a great treasure that had been hidden away. I was searching for a book in our home library when God allowed me to stumble on a Bible study guide I had never read. Written by Bill Bright, it was entitled "Moving beyond Discouragement and Defeat," and it intrigued me because I was walking on that path. The first few pages drew me to read the entire study guide that morning. I learned that it is all about the Holy Spirit and how we all need to be continuously filled with the Holy Spirit.

Somewhere along the way, I had forgotten that I needed to appropriate the filling of the Holy Spirit. I knew that the Holy Spirit lives in me, but I had never really tapped into His source of power. In one of his key statements, Bright wrote, "Just as Jesus Christ is the only one who can forgive your sins, so the Holy Spirit is the only One who can give you victory and power over your failures and weaknesses."[2]

Bright gave six steps on how to be filled with the Holy Spirit:

1. Realize that you are commanded to be filled.

2. Know that you are promised power for service when you are filled.

3. Hunger and thirst for the filling of the Holy Spirit.

4. Completely surrender to the Lordship of Christ and God's will.

5. Appropriate the filling of the Holy Spirit by faith.

6. Expect to be filled.[3]

A paragraph on the fourth step jumped out at me:

> Until this moment, the Holy Spirit has been just a "guest" in your life, for He came to live in you the moment you became a Christian. But sometimes He was locked in a small closet while you used the rest of the house for your own pleasure. Now you want Him to be more than a guest. As a matter of fact, you want to turn over the title deed of your life to Him and give Him the keys to every room. You invite the Holy Spirit into the library of your mind, the dining room or your appetites, the parlor or your relationships, the game room of your social life. You invite Him into the small hidden rooms where you have previously engaged in secret, shameful activities. All of this is past. Now, you want Him to be Master and Lord.[4]

I immediately sensed that God was showing me what had happened to my heart. I had locked it up for myself and had not given Him the key. All my masks had blocked me from the intimate relationship I was to have with Him and also from being an effective servant for Him. The Holy Spirit convicted me that moment, and I opened my heart to Him. I confessed everything that was blocking me from yielding to His will and hindering His work within me. I asked God to fill me with fullness of the Holy Spirit which He intended for me.

From that day on, when I repented and again surrendered my will to God, my heart felt so alive and excited! Having the confidence that the Holy Spirit has the freedom to work and use me for God's purposes has made a major difference in my life. It was not that I needed to receive more of the Holy Spirit, but that I needed to yield and completely surrender my will to Him.

One of the first major changes that occurred after I gave myself back to God was that I obeyed the prompting of the Holy Spirit to share the gospel in Cantonese with my mother. I still questioned God and asked, *How can it be Lord? You know my Chinese is really bad, how can I be doing this? Nevertheless, Lord, if this is Your will, I submit to You, and I know that in the right time, You will use the power of the Holy Spirit in me to work through me and grant me the right words to speak Your truth and share with her whatever You want me to say.*

It was God's grace and the conviction of the Holy Spirit that led my mother to receive Christ as her Lord and Savior in my kitchen on her eightieth birthday! I rejoice in God's grace, not only to my mother but also to affirm me in my faith to obey and submit to His will. I knew that the power of the Holy Spirit was at work to use me to communicate with my broken Cantonese and share the gospel with my mother. This was a new beginning for me in learning to allow the Holy Spirit to direct me to do God's will as I yield more of myself to Him.

Romans 12:1–2 gives each of us the challenge:

> Offer your bodies as living sacrifices, holy and pleasing to
> God—this is your spiritual act of worship. Do not conform

any longer to the pattern of this world, but be transformed by the renewing of your mind. Then you will be able to test and approve what God's will is—his good, pleasing and perfect will."

Our all important treasure is the Holy Spirit, who begins to dwell in our hearts the moment we receive Jesus into our lives. Our body is the temple of God, and we need to wholeheartedly allow Christ Jesus to reign in our bodies. Jesus has given us the Holy Spirit to empower us and to enable us to conquer all our weaknesses.

If we continue to sin, the Holy Spirit cannot be in control of our lives. Paul reminded the church of Ephesus: "Do not get drunk on wine, which leads to debauchery. Instead, be filled with the Spirit" (Eph. 5:18). It is a matter of who is in control. When you drink too much wine and are filled with alcohol, you become drunk; the wine is in control. But if you are filled with the Holy Spirit, He will be in control. Recognizing this clear, strong truth, Paul exhorted the Christians in Ephesus to continually be filled with the Spirit.

This command continues to apply to our lives today. To be filled with the Holy Spirit is not a one-time thing; it is a daily process of surrender. We need to yield to the Holy Spirit daily and allow Him to fill us daily so we can walk in the strength Christ promises us. It is not by our power or our might, but by God's Spirit that we receive His strength (Zech. 4:6).

AN INSIGHTFUL CHALLENGE

Do you wear a mask of strength because you don't want to let others know that you are vulnerable? It is much easier to show others how strong you are rather than how weak you are. Ironically, God wants to remind us of our weakness so that we can know our true source of strength is from Christ alone. Ask the Holy Spirit, promised by Jesus, to empower and fill you with His strength so you can do the things of God. Surrender and yield yourself completely to the Holy Spirit. The more you yield your will to Him, the more control He will have in your life.

I can do all things through Christ who strengthens me.
—Philippians 4:13, nkjv

7

The Mask of Busyness
and Productivity

*Seek first his kingdom and his righteousness, and
all these things will be given to you as well.*
—MATTHEW 6:33

THE WORLD RUNS on productivity. If we were meant to stay comfortable in our homes, curled up with a nice book and a cup of hot tea, how would we obtain our necessary resources? We feel guilty if we stop and smell the roses. Yet I have been guilty of getting caught up with so many businesses that I forget what my main business really should be—listening and obeying God. When we get too busy, we don't have the time to listen to God and discern if we are on track with Him.

Similarly, when we are working on a project at work, we can get so caught up in it that we don't meet with our manager to ensure that we are doing what is really expected of us. Too many times we become frustrated or discouraged because the end result is not what the other person had in mind. This can happen with anything, including work projects, business relationships, planning for a party or event, homework assignments, home chores, or ministry work and programs. If people do not stop to communicate—to listen to each other—before, during, and after a work assignment, unmet expectations will result and bring about disappointment and discouragement.

One of the great inspirations God gave me during my healing retreat was to Stop, Look, and Listen to Him. The interesting thing was that I had heard this one summer at Kayli's swimming lessons. The instructor always reminded the students right before they began their lessons that they must Stop, Look, and Listen before they entered the pool. They must stop to ensure that they were not distracted by anything. They must look to see if it was safe to enter into the pool. And they must listen to any other instructions from the instructor.

Just before I left for my retreat, I had also heard my daughter's first grade teacher give these instructions during Kayli's school birthday celebration. Because the children were all distracted and were not listening to her, the teacher reminded them to Stop, Look, and Listen. At my retreat I realized that God had been trying to tell me this. He wanted me to Stop, Look, and Listen to Him, but I had been too busy to even hear it! Now I must do it before I do anything else. The three basic words that the children were learning applied to me, too.

Stop—Stop all my busyness with too many things that are going on in my life, and just sit at His feet to rest, lest I burn out.

Look—Look and be reminded of all the blessings God had already given me, so that I don't just focus on the negative and forget that He is here for me. I need to stop and see what He has given me and recognize that He has indeed answered my prayers. If I'm caught up with the daily things of life, I cannot see the beauty of His providence for me.

Listen—Listen to what God has to say. I am so busy serving Him that I don't take time to hear what He is saying to me. I would not have suffered despair and discouragement so deeply if I had only stopped, looked, and listened. God gave me many warning signs, and He gently prompted me, but I still tried to do things my way.

CHOOSING THE BETTER THING

How many times can you remember being disappointed with a salesperson when you're shopping? Many salespeople tend to talk about the features of the product they want to sell you before they even stop to listen to what you need. As a sales and customer service trainer for many years, I often heard customers complain, "No one stopped to ask and hear what we really wanted to buy." A good salesperson will immediately acknowledge the customer and listen to the customer's needs, and look for what the customer wants. Taking time to listen is the key to satisfying the customer.

Likewise, we must take time to stop what we are doing, look to God, and listen to Him. If we don't, we cannot hear what He wants us to do. God wants to satisfy us, and we need to stop and share our needs and take time to hear His directions. Our lives will be much more gratifying if we only notice how God is blessing us.

This takes me back to the familiar story of Mary and Martha in Luke 10:38–42. I have read it many times, but as I reread it one evening, it really struck a chord in my heart. I didn't realize that I was so much like Martha. When Martha was distracted with all her preparations for Jesus, she asked Him, "Lord, do You not care that my sister has left me to do all the serving alone? Then tell her to help me" (Luke 10:40, NAS).

It reminded me that I was distracted with all my different ministries or other things that filled my day. As a result I would cry out to God, "Lord, do you not care that no one is helping me, but rather leaving me to serve alone? Stir the hearts of your people so that they will help." And when I prayed like this, God's response to me was "Helen, Helen, you are worried and bothered about so many things, but only a few things are necessary, really only one." He showed me that "Mary has chosen what is better, and it will not be taken away from her" (Luke 10:42).

I realized that I must sit at God's feet to listen to Him more, to become more preoccupied with Him. I knew that I needed to pull back on my responsibilities and put Him first on my agenda each day. I needed to let Him be involved in all the details of my daily walk, and not just get caught up in prepping and doing ministry work for Him. God wanted me to Stop, Look, and Listen to Him first.

In a conversation with Joan Fong, a close sister in the Lord and the children's director at our church, I shared what God was trying to show me about my busyness. I was so encouraged when she responded with some beautiful thoughts that God had revealed to her:

> You are right; we need to be Mary sometimes. In that partic-
> ular passage, poor Martha was badly portrayed, she looked
> like a frantic hamster, or a chronic complainer; but people
> do forget that this woman had a gift of hospitality, and a
> gift of serving, the only thing she was guilty of was failure
> to recognize the "better" thing at that moment. Last winter
> I read a book: *Having a Mary Heart in a Martha World* by
> Joanna Weaver, and it was quite inspiring.

Joan continued with her godly counsel:

> You know each one of us goes through different seasons, just
> like nature has different seasons. We go through the spring-
> time in our lives when we experience the freshness and
> newness of life, and then the summer months with all the
> hustle and bustle and the hard labor under the heat. After
> that we experience the harvest of fall when we see the fruit
> of our labor. But most of us dread the winter months—the
> stillness and coldness and lifelessness of that season really
> scares us.
>
> Yet, without the harshness of winter, we cannot experi-
> ence the new birth, or newness of spring, the time when
> we need to be renewed....I know I am babbling like a fool,

but this is experience talking. I think most of us are afraid of the stillness because we do not appear to be productive. However, it is only when we are being snowed under and going through the cold that our tulip buds can have a chance to pop out!! Yikes, I better stop while I am ahead, I am sure you are laughing your head off by now, and saying to yourself, Joan has finally fallen off her rocker!

Be still my dear sister, spring is around the corner.

I was not laughing at what Joan had written, but instead grasped onto all the simple truths God had revealed to me through her. It is so true that many of us are "afraid of the stillness, because we do not appear to be productive." This is how society and our community shape us to think. However, we need to be *shaped by God* and not by what other people think.

MAKING GOD OUR FOCUS

Have you ever rushed through a fast-food take-out so you could eat in a hurry? Compare it to a time when you had an enjoyable unrushed dining experience. Didn't the food seem much more enjoyable? God wants us to have an enjoyable and nutritional experience in our times with Him, and we have to make time for this to happen. It will replenish our spiritual lives and strengthen our resistance against the attacks of the enemy's lies and the temptation to slip back into our old comfortable ways. If we do not spend quality time with God, our hearts will wander.

It is hard to accept the fact that our lives need to slow down so we can enjoy God more. We may even feel that we can enjoy God in any situation because He is everywhere. Indeed we can enjoy God in all our circumstances. There are some mainstream Christian books that are written to cater to busy people's lifestyles. They encourage people to fit time for God into their hectic schedules and encourage those who need to slow down to spend time with God.

However, we must still ask the question: Why do we have to fit God into our schedules? Why shouldn't it be the other way around? It is a matter of the heart. Just as Jesus reminded Martha that "Mary has chosen what is better, and it will not be taken away from her" (Luke 10:42), we should put God first in our lives and then fit the rest of our schedule around God. To keep busy and think that we are doing things for God is to fall into a trap of Satan. God desires that we sit at his feet to hear Him. A dear sister once reminded me that busyness is a weapon from Satan to prevent us from doing what is truly important.

In the Sermon on the Mount, Jesus taught us to "seek first his kingdom and his righteousness, and all these things will be given to you as well" (Matt. 6:33). What did Jesus really mean by that? If you read the surrounding verses, you will notice that Jesus said we should not be concerned about what others think about us, and we should not judge others. We should look to God and ask Him for everything, and we should not worry about what He has already provided for us. God wants us to seek His kingdom and His righteousness first. Then everything, including the things we do for Him, will follow.

As Martha was scrambling around trying to please Jesus, she thought she was serving Christ well, but she was distracted with doing things for Jesus. It is so easy for us to put all our efforts into our work and even our ministry. We become distracted and forget to put God first in our lives. We find ourselves concerned with how we should look and what we should do to make us look like we are productive for God.

In God's sight the definition of productivity is that we make Him the focus of our hearts and do things for His kingdom and His righteousness. When we try to do things our way, we are seeking our own righteousness, not God's. He must be the one who orchestrates and designs all that happens in our lives. We must put Him first and then allow our schedules to fall into place as Jesus works through us.

BE STILL AND HEAR GOD

Do you remember the Old Testament story of the boy Samuel who was living in the temple with Eli the priest? First Samuel 3:1–10 tells how God spoke to Samuel three times, but he did not recognize God's voice and thought instead that Eli was calling him. The fourth time God spoke, after Eli had told Samuel that God was speaking to him, Samuel finally said, "Speak, for your servant is listening" (1 Sam. 3:10).

Do you long to know and hear God's voice? God is speaking to us, but if we are too distracted, we will miss what He has to say. At times God will have to create a circumstance or use someone to get our attention so that we will hear Him. Let us confess and surrender our distractions to God, and say, "Lord, here I am. Your servant is listening. Please speak to me." Be still and hear God in your life.

When we take time to be still, God speaks to us in many ways. For example, my journal records the following lesson I learned by observing a seagull:

> *Lord, thank You that it was not by chance I ended up spending some moments alone with You at Kits Beach tonight. I was able to see the sun that You created set on the horizon. I heard and felt You tonight Lord, thank You for that. I saw Your beauty in the waves of the sea coming in, and each folding and crashing of the water reminded me of the tides coming in and out of my life, each is good, whether I recognize it or not.*
>
> *My gaze was fixated on a seagull that was determined to catch some food from the sea. Finally a big wave came*

crashing in. "Surely," I thought, "the seagull will fly away to avoid being hit with the wave." But to my surprise, the seagull instead stuck his head right into the wave and pulled out a small fish with his beak! I saw how happy that seagull was as he ate away at his triumph, and I was proud of him.

Lord, was that another lesson for me to see? I am reminded that when I see a big wave crashing in, it's not for me to hide and flee, but to get right "into it" by faith and know that something great will come out of it. Lord, You teach me to be patient and to wait on Your own perfect timing. You will make me an effective servant for You, not of my own efforts but through faith in You. Help me to catch fish for You.

A Lesson on Being Productive and Effective

Sometimes God teaches us through the simplest things, as this journal entry shows:

Last night, I took a nice long Jacuzzi bath in my sister's home with the beautiful relaxing bath salts and soap Ellie gave me. It took me awhile to start the Jacuzzi. I kept pressing the button near the tub to no avail, and it was driving me nuts. On my last attempt I realized that I had to get out of the tub and first press the main switch on.

It's funny how I learn little lessons from God even in the small things I do.... Life is not hard, I just have to stop and think, rather than try something that wasn't meant to work. Sometimes I get so caught up in doing things that I redo the same thing over and over, and in the end it's not very productive. If I had stopped to think first, my action might have been more effective.

All I need to do is take a step of faith and reach out and press that main switch on, not just aimlessly keep pressing the button so hard (like my Jacuzzi incident). I need to stop and think and realize where my source of power is. My source of power is God.

It's amazing what we can learn from our Lord, when we actually Stop, Look, and Listen to Him! Rather than trying to do things on our own, we need to learn to walk daily by faith in God, allowing Him to guide us to be more effective for Him. When we learn to serve Him by faith, we become more effective because He is in control. When God is in control, we grow stronger in all areas of our life.

AN INSIGHTFUL CHALLENGE

Have you been so busy working and serving that you wished you had more time for God? The use of our time is actually a choice we make. God wants us to serve Him faithfully, but more importantly, He wants us to listen to His directions so we can serve Him effectively. Be still, stop, look, and listen to what God wants you to do today. We don't need to *look busy* to be effective for God. It's time for us to take off our mask of busyness and productivity and let God work through us.

Be still, and know that I am God.

—PSALM 46:10

8

The Mask of Devotion

You shall have no other gods before me.
—EXODUS 20:3

THE POPULAR REALITY show *American Idol* had the highest TV
rating of any other show this past year. Our local paper reported
that "31 million viewers watched every week in the US alone, and
another three million viewers tuned in across Canada."[1] The headings
indicated that "TV ratings show viewers worship *Idol*."[2] Not surprisingly, it tugs at our heartstrings to hear all these wonderful singers try
to fulfill their dreams for an opportunity to display their best vocals
to a world audience. Millions tune in weekly to help support potential
superstars by casting their votes for their favorite singer.

Why do we get excited for the singer who advances? Why do we
moan when the one we like is voted off? What draws us to watch this
show weekly? We follow and support reality-based shows because it
is a way we can try to fulfill our own dreams through someone else's
life. It is an expression of devotion. *Devotion* has been defined as "a
strong affection for or loyalty for something or someone."[3]

It's easy to get caught up in someone else's dreams, but what about
your dreams? What plans do you have? Ever since I was a little girl,
I had dreams of doing something big. I have often wondered why I
thought that way. Instead of doing something small, I would nearly

always do something much more complicated than I had intended. I had no idea that God was preparing me to do big things for Him. God is a big God. Is it any wonder why our dreams are big? Can He not fulfill them for us if we ask?

In all my waking hours since I surrendered my life to Jesus, I had felt that I was committed to God. I gave my allegiance and loyalty to Him, and I thought that all my plans were to fulfill His will for me. The ministries I began, my service for Him at church, and my support and time for others were all for Him. My dream of owning my own business was even custom-tailored to fit it into God's plans. I wanted to use my God-given abilities in entrepreneurship and service to help train others to make their own money; and the money I raised was to be returned to God. It sounded like a fool-proof plan to serve God with what He had given me.

However, it never occurred to me that my plans were mine and not God's. I became so obsessed and devoted to refining and retuning my business plan that I worked on it ten years and it never even got off the ground! It was never good enough—the markets would change and I would change the concept to make it work better. It was eating away at my life and distracting me from God and from my family.

As I carefully guarded the wonderful business idea I believed God had placed in my heart, He sent me an unexpected business associate who challenged me with the words, "How good is this business idea of yours when you're not doing anything about it?" It cut straight to my heart. For years I had tried to complete the plan, and time and time again obstacles and adverse circumstances would give me excuses to halt the process. The excuses included my working to make more money, my husband's disagreement with the non-profit business model, and the lack of support I felt from my friends.

I had thought that my excuses where only temporary setbacks, and when the timing was right, I would initiate my plan. I had no idea that slowly each day my dream was eating away at my heart. It was destroying and dividing my heart bit by bit. Rather than focusing on God's will for my life, I centered on my own dreams. I was holding on to them so hard, and wouldn't let anyone near them. I coveted them so deeply that they were robbing me of the joy of serving and doing anything else. My business plan became an idol to me until I ended up surrendering it to God.

When I returned home from my healing retreat, I took time to sit in the presence of God. I asked Him to reveal His plans to me and show me what was blocking my relationship with Him. When God spoke to me, I immediately denied the truth He revealed. But when He continued to remind me of what my heart was truly thinking, I became frightened. All these years I had thought that I had committed my life to pleasing God; now I realized that I was really trying to please others to make myself feel better. A mask of devotion had somehow become affixed to my face. As I re-read the journal excerpts that led me to repent of this mask, God reminded me of lessons He had taught me through Psalm 51.

How God Applied
Psalm 51 to My Life

King David wrote Psalm 51 as a prayer to God after the prophet Nathan confronted him about his sin of adultery with Bathsheba. Although I had not committed the same sin as David, God showed me that I too had sinned before Him. I had tried to do things my way and not God's way. I thought I was pleasing God, but my inner motives were to please others. It was still a part of me, and I needed to continually confess to Him that I was trying to control my own life. All sin is the same to God. Whether it is small or big in our earthly minds, God hates it all and He wants us to confess everything to Him.

I realized that Christ had already paid my debt when He died for all my sins, but should I continue to sin knowing that He had already paid the price? Shame and guilt came over me as I felt my pride arise inside me and tell me that I was better than anyone else. The Holy Spirit reminded me that Psalm 51 applied to me too. Who was I to think that I could not fall like David did when he was tempted? My efforts to puff myself up were sin. David was a mighty king who was pure and righteous before God. Yet when he was tempted, he gave into his heart's desires and sinned before God. Indeed a mighty person of faith can still fail.

As God showed me that I had given into my own selfish desires, I sought the Lord's forgiveness for my pride—for lifting myself up on my own pedestal. I felt ashamed and broken as God revealed my internal struggles of trying to remain strong and not show anyone how I really felt. I didn't want anyone to know that I was weak, not only physically but also emotionally and spiritually.

Have you ever felt the way I did? Are you are deeply struggling with your problems, and do you yearn to tell others the truth? Are you afraid to confess your need to others because it may burden them down or affect the way they act toward you? Are you afraid that your relationship will change if they know the real you? This is what I felt.

God reminded me that I was in turmoil because I had held my family and friends in high esteem to protect my relationships with them. I had turned them into devoted idols in my life. He showed me that I must not seek to please others but God alone. God's mercy and love can shine through our brokenness and weakness as He delivers us and gives us His loving grace. This is what David experienced when he cried to God for mercy:

> Have mercy on me, O God, according to your unfailing love; according to your great compassion blot out my transgressions.

Wash away all my iniquity and cleanse me from my sin.

For I know my transgressions, and my sin is always before me.

Against you, you only, have I sinned and done what is evil in your sight, so that you are proved right when you speak and justified when you judge.

Surely I was sinful at birth, sinful from the time my mother conceived me.

Surely you desire truth in the inner parts; you teach me wisdom in the inmost place.

Cleanse me with hyssop, and I will be clean; wash me, and I will be whiter than snow.

Let me hear joy and gladness; let the bones you have crushed rejoice.

Hide your face from my sins and blot out all my iniquity.

Create in me a pure heart, O God, and renew a steadfast spirit within me.

Do not cast me from your presence or take your Holy Spirit from me.

Restore to me the joy of your salvation and grant me a willing spirit, to sustain me.

Then I will teach transgressors your ways, and sinners will turn back to you.

Save me from my bloodguilt, O God, the God who saves me, and my tongue will sing of your righteousness.

O Lord, open my lips, and my mouth will declare your praise.

You do not delight in sacrifice, or I would bring it; you do not take pleasure in burnt offerings.

The sacrifices of God are a broken spirit; a broken and contrite heart, O God, you will not despise.

—PSALM 51:1–17

An Adulterous Affair
with the World

Because I had initially questioned how I could identify with King David's adulterous affair with Bathsheba, my pride blocked me from accepting the application of Psalm 51 to my life. However, the Holy Spirit pressed on my heart and clearly showed me differently when I was led to read from James 4:

> What causes fights and quarrels among you? Don't they come from your desires that battle within you? *You want something but don't get it.* You kill and covet, *but you cannot have what you want.* You quarrel and fight. *You do not have, because you do not ask God. When you ask, you do not receive, because you ask with wrong motives, that you may spend what you get on your pleasures.*
>
> *You adulterous* people, don't you know that *friendship with the world is hatred toward God?* Anyone who chooses to be a friend of the world becomes an enemy of God. Or do you think Scripture says without reason that the spirit he caused to live in us envies intensely?
>
> —James 4:1–5, emphasis added

As I read this passage, I immediately realized that I was the adulterous person identified in James 4:4! I was like King David having an adulterous affair, but with the world! I had been wooed back into the world and had loved earthly desires and pleasure. I had wrong motives in my service for God. As God spoke to me, He warned me to prepare my heart so that His life within me, as Matthew 13:1–23 describes, would not be as seed that was snatched away by the enemy or seed that failed to produce continued joy in the rocky places. He warned me to guard against the seed of His Word being choked by the worries of life and the pleasures of the world.

I recognized that I needed to prepare my heart and soul for the next six topics in my JAM ministry Bible study notes. Many hearts would be affected by what I was going to write and teach, and it was important that I do it through the power of the Holy Spirit and not on my own. If I wrote in the flesh, others would be led astray. I must be careful so that I would not be swayed and used by Satan to manipulate God's words. I needed God to equip me to fight the battle.

We can have an adulterous affair with anything that steals our time and devotion from God. It could be our work, our dreams, our hobbies, or our family. The shocking revelation I learned was that the very thing you are doing for God—your ministry for Him—may become an idol and the object of an adulterous affair. Serving and ministering to others is not bad, but Satan can tempt us to make it our sole priority so that we serve with a personal agenda.

During the same time God was speaking to me about my adulterous affair with the world, Joan Fong sent me an e-mail and shared something that immediately hit home:

> I have to be mindful that ministry does not become my idol, and rob me of my relationship with God, but believe me the line is not clear at all. Just recently, I had a wakeup call, I realized that I have been "married" to my ministry, and because of that a lot of my relationships with other people (mainly female friends) have suffered. These relationships are all God given, and at the end of the day, people, especially the members in the body, matter the most.
>
> I feel like a circus freak sometimes, riding on a unicycle and juggling all these things at the same time, I know that one of these days, something is going to crash. Learning to keep my eyes focused on the Lord has been a daily struggle and challenge as well, but I only do it one day at a time and not worry about tomorrow.

When Joan wrote about being married to the ministry, I realized that I was also married to my ministry. I was deeply involved in my ministry, and I had thought that it was for God's service. However, somewhere down the line I had lost sight of the real meaning of why I was doing it. I had become ineffective because I was not serving joyfully. I held classes, not because I wanted to share God's precious words to expand His kingdom or to help others, but because I felt that others depended upon me and I was obligated to hold the classes.

The pressure and demands of my ministry had sapped my joy. I was serving with the wrong motive, to gain the admiration of others, and I was never satisfied because I didn't really do it for God. I needed to remember that ministry is entrusted to us by God; it is not ours to use for our selfish purposes. When I made the decision to surrender my ministry to God and take a break from it, I had to be cautious because I knew that Satan could use it to discourage me from continuing to work hard and serve God. I took a year off in serving in all ministry work to pray and wait until I was led by God to serve again. I never did restart my FAB Ladies ministry, but instead God had plans for me to be directly involved in my local church's outreach ministry. Sometimes we are meant to surrender something in order for us to be used by God for other things.

It was a humbling experience—and a wakeup call—to see that I was having an *adulterous affair with the world*! I had given in to the world and its rich rewards rather than claim God's promises. I had the wrong motives in my heart, and my boasting had not been of the Lord and His will but of my own selfish ambitions. I grieved over my sin, but I also thanked God for revealing it to me so I could repent and surrender it to Him.

God's first commandment to the Israelites was "you shall no other gods before me" (Exod. 20:3). He warns us not to give our loyalty and devotion to any idols. It is difficult to admit that we have a mask of devotion on. Allow God to reveal any gods that have won the devotion of your life.

AN UNDIVIDED HEART

The human heart is a fascinating, complex organ, designed and created beautifully by God. Strong and yet so fragile, it is known to beat (expand and contract) 100,000 times in one day.[4] Studies have shown that the heart is the central source of our actions and reactions. The American Heritage dictionary gives the following definition for *heart*:[5]

> the vital center and source of one's being, emotions, and sensibilities; the repository of one's deepest and sincerest feelings and beliefs; the seat of the intellect or imagination; one's prevailing mood or current inclination

Besides being the vital organ that sustains our earthly existence, the heart is also responsible for the way we think and act. The Bible refers to the heart more than 440 times[6] and it reminds us of the heart's central responsibility, "Above all else, guard your heart, for it is the wellspring of life" (Prov. 4:23). The heart can be easily wounded if we fail to guard it. It can be easily divided, and it strays easily.

James commands us to purify our hearts because we are double-minded (James 4:8). God created our hearts special to be completely devoted to Him. Sometimes it is hard to distinguish if our loyalty is focused on love to God or on helping our families and friends. While God calls us to love one another (1 John 4:20–21), we must examine the core of our heart to see what our real motive is.

Why do we do things for others? Is it to further God's kingdom, to do His will and to give Him all the glory? Or do we strive to be at our best because we seek affirmation for ourselves? Do we honor others above God and seek to please others over Him? It is difficult for us to notice when we slowly allow our hearts to be filled with our own desires. Our only remedy is to submit to God and resist the devil (James 4:7).

One morning during my personal worship time with God, He reminded me that the idols in my life could be my family, friends, and even my love to please others. He led me to read Psalm 86:11:

> Teach me your way, O Lord, and I will walk in your truth;
> give me an undivided heart, that I may fear your name.

At the exact moment I was meditating on these words, the music from my MP3 echoed the same words in a song! I was so surprised and listened carefully as the singer sang Psalm 86:11 and repeated over and over the words of the psalm. I learned that the song was "Undivided Heart," and I truly believe that God wanted me to make Psalm 86:11 my prayer. With a compelling affirmation from His Word and from a spiritual song, God showed me that I needed to spend the time with Him, to be taught to walk in His ways, and to be true, honest, and genuine in my faith toward Him and my relationship with others.

The key words were actually at the end of Psalm 86:11, "that I may fear your name." As I thought about what it really meant to fear God, I remembered that He was the mighty, awesome God who created the world around us. He was the God who brought the plagues upon the Egyptians when Pharaoh refused to let the Israelites go, (Exodus 7–11). And He was also the God who took the lives of Ananias and Sapphira when they lied to the Holy Spirit about the gift they brought to the apostles (Acts 5:1–11). I could list a thousand reasons why I should fear God because of who He is and also because of His mighty power.

But I discovered something. Although God is all powerful, He is also all loving, merciful, and full of grace and compassion. He is my

God, my Lord, and my Father. The word *fear* in Hebrew is *yirah* and in the Old Testament context means "respect, reverence, piety."[7] This fear is not about being afraid of what God can do to me, but about being in awe of His glory and holiness. He is the King of kings and Lord of lords and He, as royalty, is worthy to receive our highest expressions of honor and our complete devotion, respect, and reverence.

We don't give God all the reverence He deserves. When our hearts grow complacent, we forget how awesome our God is. I believe that if we truly fear God, our lifestyle and the way we work and think will be completely different. If we truly believe that God is sovereign and controls every moment of our life, we will really be watching what we do. We would have undivided hearts centered on God in everything we say and do whether we are with family and friends or in the company of non-believers.

GOD IS JEALOUS FOR OUR DEVOTION

This leads me to discuss a significant attribute of God. Although we don't hear much about it, the Bible repeatedly declares that God is a jealous God (Exod. 20:5–6; 34:12–14, Deut. 4:24; Nah. 1:2–3; Ps. 78:58). *Quanna* is the Hebrew adjective translated "jealous" (only of God). Vine's Dictionary tells us that "the word refers directly to the attributes of God's justice and holiness, as He is the sole object of human worship and does not tolerate man's sin.[8]

Most of the scripture references to God's jealousy seem to describe His covenant relationship with Israel, His exclusive right to possess Israel and to claim her love and allegiance. However, throughout the New Testament it is very clear that God expects exclusive devotion from those who follow Him. After His conversion to Christ, Paul's main goal was to ban the worship of false gods—anything that we love and honor instead of God—and introduce the true and living God to others.

God places the Holy Spirit in us to direct and guide us to do His will. When we do not follow His will, we grieve the Holy Spirit, especially when we desire and covet the things of the world instead of His will. The NIV rendering of James 4:4–5 teaches, "Anyone who chooses to be a friend of the world becomes an enemy of God. Or do you think Scripture says without reason that the spirit he caused to live in us envies intensely?" In the New King James Version verse 5 says, "Or do you think that the Scripture says in vain, 'the Spirit who dwells in us yearns jealously'?"

Note the emphatic words that both versions use to describe the attribute of the Holy Spirit as He is in us. The Holy Spirit "envies intensely" and "yearns jealously." He desires to have our full devotion and love from an undivided heart. When the Bible speaks of God being jealous, it does not mean he is suspicious or fearful of being replaced by a rival as we sometimes define it. Rather, God is a jealous God and demands our exclusive loyalty because He created us. He will not put up with unfaithfulness. (See Jeremiah 13:1–11.)

It is so easy for us to be lured into believing that we have the perfect relationship with God because He has promised that He will never leave us nor forsake us (Deut. 31:6, 8). However, we take this for granted and test His boundaries for our lives by placing our loyalty and devotion elsewhere. We kid ourselves when we believe that God will not care about this. God loves us, and He demonstrated His love for us at the cross of Calvary. He has also given us the choice to return our love to Him. He does not want us to test Him or take Him for granted. He does not want us to forget Him and turn our backs on Him because we are caught up in doing other things.

God desires for us to be faithful to Him because He loves us so deeply. His jealousy is not the same as the jealousy we express as a human emotion. Rather, it is a deep love that He has committed to us, the love Romans 5:8 describes when it says that even "while we were still sinners Christ died for us." This is the greatest example of devoted love from God to us, a love that we may never truly fathom.

Is it any wonder that the Ten Commandments begin with two commandments that relate to our hearts' devotion to Him?

> You shall have no other gods before me. You shall not make for yourself an idol in the form of anything in heaven above or on the earth beneath or in the waters below. You shall not bow down to them or worship them; for I, the LORD your God, am a jealous God, punishing the children for the sin of the fathers to the third and fourth generation of those who hate me, but showing love to a thousand (generations) of those who love me and keep my commandments.
>
> —EXODUS 20:3–6

Likewise, the Lord Jesus said that the most important commandment is: "Hear, O Israel, the Lord our God, the Lord is one. Love the Lord your God with all your heart and with all your soul and with all your mind and with all your strength" (Mark 12:29–30).

We are God's beloved creation. His demands may seem overly possessive of our love, yet His anger is justified if we place our devotion and love on the things that He has created rather than Him. Jealousy seems to be such an unpleasant response, but in some situations it is the only appropriate response. A mother is jealous for her children; she will fight to never give them up or be harmed in anyway. A husband is jealous for his wife; he will not share her most intimate love with anyone else. God feels the same about His people. He is jealous for them. They belong to Him and to Him alone. He desires for us to be faithful to Him.

Our hearts should respond to the exhortation given by the writer of Hebrews: "Therefore, since we are receiving a kingdom which cannot be shaken, let us have grace, by which we may *serve* God acceptably *with reverence and godly fear*" (Heb. 12:28, NKJV, emphasis added).

Our Friends and Family
Can Be Idols

Our human nature is such that we want to be part of one or more groups. The desire to do this begins when we are children, and the pressure to do it grows through our educational experience and on into our years in the workplace. We want to be part of something bigger, and we join or stay in groups because of peer pressure and the desire for familiarity or comfort that comes when we are part of something. We experience a sense of pride when we belong to something for a long time, and loyalty is regarded as precious because it is difficult to achieve.

I fell into the category of being part of something so I would look good. I felt locked in tight with a group of girlfriends who I have been with since high school. We never missed a birthday or a special milestone, and it felt so good to tell others that I had been seeing my group of seven friends for the past twenty-five years. There is nothing wrong with having good solid friendships with those you love, but deep down I knew that something else was going on, and it bothered me. For two years in a row, every time we met, I would come home complaining to my husband and feeling very grieved in my spirit. I knew that something was wrong.

When I asked God specifically why I was feeling this way, His answer startled me—I had coveted my group of friends so dearly that it was blocking my relationship with Him and blocking the truth of what was really happening in my relationships with my friends.

The truth was that there was no real substance to our friendships. We had grown so far apart with our own separate family lives that we never really shared anything more than a time to gather and celebrate our birthdays. I never wanted to be a part of anything more with them. Even though group family trips were planned, our family would never participate. I didn't feel that we fit in and had no desire to be a part of their lives outside of our celebratory dinners. How could our families get along when we individually did not really get along?

Although I had led myself to believe that our group was so close we could share everything and encourage each other in everything, it didn't work out that way. God showed me that every time there was a birthday or Christmas get-together, I would work myself into a frenzy trying to figure out what to make for food and what cards and gifts would please the group. I was like a desperate child trying to fit in because I thought I was expected to produce a work of art or something creative to please the group. I didn't realize that my group of high school girlfriends had become idols in my heart. I sought affirmation from them over God.

God showed me that I was more fixated on pleasing my friends than pleasing Him, and He asked me to surrender them to him. However, I held onto them because I wanted to be a part of something important and my participation with my loyal friends was great for my personal social portfolio. The painful truth was that I was holding onto something that was superficial. I had been complaining that I wanted to have a closer, transparent relationship with my friends, but *it had to start with me*. I had to be open and willing to share before others would open up. Taking time to spend with them was just as important as meeting for the occasional celebration dinner.

I had to be willing to put time and effort into developing these friendships into something more meaningful. I did not have the energy or the drive to do that during my depression, and I knew it was time for me to let go. I had already confessed my heart's desires to my girlfriends and had told them that it would require commitment and time from all of us to develop a closer and more meaningful relationship. It was a painful decision to make the choice not to participate in the larger group settings, and it was equally as difficult for some of them to accept and understand. In the end, God, by His grace, allowed me rebuild closer authentic friendships individually with them as we met on dates with two or three friends together. Most recently, now almost three years since I made the difficult decision not to participate in the large gatherings, God blessed me again through my closest girlfriend May, who is also part of this high school group. She emailed me her thoughts and graciously gave me permission to include it here:

> Now in hindsight, I am affirmed and overjoyed that you had the courage to follow the Lord's plans for you. I can see how it brought you back so that you could walk close to Him again. I can see how the time allowed you to heal and revive yourself for the work ahead that He has planned for you. I can already see the fruits that you are starting to bear and the bounty that is about to be harvested. I can see how relationships that we mistakenly thought were deep—just because of the number of years together—are really just beginning and now have more of a chance to truly develop into something deeper.
>
> Your experience—and being able to go through it with you—has taught me and reassured me that I shouldn't be afraid to make hard decisions. I just need to make sure I'm listening and I'm ready to act when He calls upon me.

Praise God for using my tough decisions and experiences to encourage others.

My relationship with my family was the same. Pleasing my parents and siblings was such a priority to me, and they became my idols as I struggled desperately to be the peacemaker for the family. Even though we all knew we were a dysfunctional family, we never faced the truth. On the surface my family would act as if everything was fine, but deep down each of us had our own hidden agendas and heartaches. Family gatherings used to be painful and superficial because we gathered for the sake of my parents' happiness but cringed at what we thought of each other. We never shared our real problems with each other, and our expectations for each other were all wrong.

Just as God extended His grace for my relationship with my friends, He did the same in our dysfunctional family. It was painful to unveil our masks so our heartaches could heal, but it broke down our superficial boundaries and allowed some of us to bridge our differences and come closer to each other. God also wants to bring healing and growth in our relationship with Him. We expect and yearn for an intimate closer relationship with God, but we do not take time to be with Him. The Holy Spirit is grieved when we are superficial in our relationship with God. Even though we may go through the motions of trying to remain devoted and connected to God, He knows exactly how we feel and where our hearts really lie. God want us to be true to our faith, true to others, and true to Him.

TORN BETWEEN TWO MASTERS

The trilogy movies based on *Lord of the Rings*, J. R. R. Tolkien's novel saga, depict fantasy-themed stories with many parallelisms that relate to our Lord Jesus Christ. Many physical battles were fought in the movies, but I think the hardest battles were those that were happening in the heart of each character. Each one had to struggle with the temptation of following his own selfish desire to take the special ring to gain power for himself. I really identified with Gollum, and I asked my niece, Niki, who is a die-hard fan of *Lord of the Rings*, for some background information on him. This is what she said:

> Gollum was originally called Sméagol. This was his good self. He was what they called "river folk," not much different than a hobbit. Gollum lived an unnaturally long life as his bad self.

113

> Gollum was consumed by the ring that his friend had found and killed him for it. This ring originally was forged in secret by an evil being named Dark Lord Sauron so that he could dominate all life. This master ring was made to rule over nineteen other golden rings that had been created for each ruler in the land. This one ring had special magical powers that could only be wielded by Sauron. This master ring answered to Sauron alone. It had no other master.

The ring's transcendent power seemed to yield a darker side to anyone who desired to wear it. This reminds us of the greed for power and wealth that tears us apart from what is really important in our lives. In Matthew 6:24, Jesus warned about the danger of being caught up in the wrong type of devotion, "No one can serve two masters. Either he will hate the one and love the other, or he will be devoted to the one and despise the other. You cannot serve both God and Money."

There is nothing wrong with making money; we just need to watch our attitude toward it. However, many marriages and families are broken because spouses, siblings, and even children fight over their careers, finances, and material wealth. People work long hours to make more money and gain a better lifestyle for themselves and their families, but then they do not have time to spend with the people they love. Likewise, if our attention is so focused on making money to serve God better (or at least we try to fool our hearts into believing that), when do we have the time to spend with God and trust Him to provide for the things we need? Our hearts become divided, and we end up trusting in material wealth to give us pleasure and security.

Gollum had a "love-hate" relationship with his master, a young hobbit named Frodo who had been chosen to destroy the powerful ring. Frodo saved Gollum's life and addressed him as "Sméagol."

Because he believed there was still good in Gollum, Frodo had confidence that he would return to his true, good self as Sméagol. However, Gollum struggled with being loyal to Frodo because of his greed for the ring. Gollum called the ring "Precious," and it became his idol, the object of his obsession and of the master that controlled him.

As a physical battle raged for "Middle-Earth," Gollum also had a battle raging within himself as he toyed many times with the thought of betraying and killing his master, Frodo. His conversations within his inner self were a scary depiction of what my mind was going through when I had depressive suicidal thoughts and was struggling to learn who my real master was. I am including a short scene that shows the internal struggle within Gollum/Sméagol as it was presented in the movie *The Lord of the Rings: The Two Towers*."[9] In the following lines, Gollum's words are in italics, and Sméagol's are in regular font.

> Master's my friend...
> *You don't have any friends, nobody likes you.*
> Not listening. I'm not listening.
> *You're a liar and a thief.*
> No.
> *Murderer.*
> Sniff...sniff...Go away.
> *Go away?* (Gollum says mockingly as Sméagol begins to cry)
> I hate you...I hate you.
> *Where would you be without me? It was me. We survived because of me.*
> Not anymore.
> *What did you say?*
> Master looks after us now. We don't need you.
> *What?*
> Leave now and never come back.
> *No.*

Leave now and never come back.
Argh!... (Gollum screams)
Leave now and never come back.
(Gollum is silent—the bad side of Sméagol goes away)
We told him to go away and away he goes, Precious. Gone!
  Gone! Gone! Sméagol is free!

Sméagol was ecstatic and felt free when he thought he could control his bad self—Gollum—by telling him to leave. When God answered my prayer and revealed Satan and his demons' lies to me, I was able to use God's promises and His Word to fight against them. I felt freed from listening to the lies of the enemy.

However, I, like Sméagol, sometimes felt torn between two masters, my old self and God. When I was going through my depressive episodes, my mind was struggling with my old self, the enemy's lies, and God's truth. I thought I heard voices inside me just like Sméagol did when his bad self and his good self reasoned back and forth about what he should do. He seemed to have a double personality, and I felt like I had one too.

My mind had toyed with the thought of taking my own life. I was teetering back and forth, wondering if anyone cared for me. Did God really love me? Who was my real "master"? Did I worship "myself" or did I worship God? I was so self-centered, battling my own inner desires to do my own will rather than the will of God's.

I thank God that the Spirit in me was stronger than the enemy outside. (See 1 John 4:4.) The enemy was toying with my weakness and trying to sway my devotion and loyalty away from God, but I am so thankful that God allowed the Holy Spirit to reveal the truth to me. God reminded me of what Paul wrote to the Romans when he was also struggling to remain true to God:

For we know that the law is spiritual, but I am of the flesh, sold under sin. For I do not understand my own actions. For I do not do what I want, but I do the very thing I hate. Now if I do what I do not want, I agree with the law, that it is good. So now it is no longer I who do it, but sin that dwells within me. For I know that nothing good dwells in me, that is, in my flesh. *For I have the desire to do what is right, but not the ability to carry it out.* For I do not do the good I want, but the evil I do not want is what I keep on doing. Now if I do what I do not want, it is no longer I who do it, but sin that dwells within me. So I find it to be a law that when I want to do right, evil lies close at hand. For I delight in the law of God, in my inner being, but I see in my members another law waging war against the law of my mind and making me captive to the law of sin that dwells in my members. Wretched man that I am! Who will deliver me from this body of death? Thanks be to God through Jesus Christ our Lord! So then, I myself serve the law of God with my mind, but with my flesh I serve the law of sin.

—ROMANS 7:14–25, ESV, emphasis added

Islider, the prince who originally discovered the ring after killing Sauron in battle, could have destroyed it before Sméagol's friend found it. Unfortunately as the movie line says, "The hearts of men are easily corrupted...and the ring of power has a will of its own."[10] This is so true; when we allow the idols in our life form their own power, they become our masters and we become slaves to them. However, I have discovered that if I set my mind and heart on the things of God and allow Him to work in me, the Holy Spirit will keep my heart under His guard and enable me to be loyal to God.

In his book *The Holy Spirit*, Billy Graham wrote God's truth about the Christian's inner struggle: "We have two natures within us, both struggling for mastery. Which one will dominate us? It depends on which one we feed. If we feed our spiritual lives and allow the Holy Spirit to empower us, He will have rule over us. If we starve our spiritual natures and instead feed the old, sinful nature, the flesh will dominate."[11]

Which nature are you feeding?

> Those who live according to the sinful nature have their minds set on what that nature desires; but those who live in accordance with the Spirit have their minds set on what the Spirit desires.
>
> —ROMANS 8:5

GOD'S FAITHFULNESS

Regardless of where our loyalty lies, we can be certain that God will always remain faithful. Even though we may become distracted and place our focus on other things in life, God is faithful to draw our attention back to Him. He speaks to our broken hearts and gives us the desire to seek Him again.

> The saying is trustworthy, for: If we have died with him, we will also live with him; if we endure, we will also reign with him; if we deny him, he also will deny us; if we are faithless, he remains faithful—for he cannot deny himself.
>
> —2 TIMOTHY 2:11–13, ESV

When the people of Israel and Judah turned their backs on God and set up abominable idols that He abhorred, He forgave them and kept His promise to them.

> *I will give them one heart and one way, that they may fear me forever, for their own good and the good of their children after them. I will make with them an everlasting covenant, that I will not turn away from doing good to them. And I*

will put the fear of me in their hearts, that they may not turn from me. I will rejoice in doing them good, and I will plant them in this land in faithfulness, with all my heart and all my soul. For thus says the LORD: Just as I have brought all this great disaster upon this people, so I will bring upon them all the good that I promise them.

—JEREMIAH 32:39–42, ESV, emphasis added

God wants us to fear Him because it is for our own good. He does not want us to turn away from Him. Even though God brings *calamities* to our lives, He promises to give us *prosperity*. He wants His best for His people, and His promises will never fail. It is a glorious thing to know that our God is faithful and loyal. O how we should reciprocate the same to Him!

AN INSIGHTFUL CHALLENGE

Who is the master of your life? What is the state of your heart? Do you feel torn and divided between your devotion to God and your devotion to your family, friends, or career? Take a moment to reflect on how much quality time you spend with God. Do you desire to have a closer relationship with God but wonder what is blocking it? Pray to God and ask Him to reveal the things that are dividing your heart; surrender them to Him. Make the following verse your prayer to God:

Teach me your way, O LORD, and I will walk in your truth; give me an undivided heart, that I may fear your name.

—PSALM 86:11

9

The Mask of Patience

Count it all joy when you fall into various trials,
knowing that the testing of your faith produces
patience. But let patience have its perfect work, that
you may be perfect and complete, lacking nothing.
—JAMES 1:2–4, NKJV

HOW MANY TIMES do you remind yourself that you should have listened more before you reacted? How many times have you wished you hadn't said something because you later discovered the real facts? How many times have you blown an irritation that was really quite trivial into gigantic proportions? The Book of James, which can be summed up in three exhortations in James 1:19, speaks to these questions when it exhorts us to be "quick to listen, slow to speak and slow to become angry."

It is difficult to live by this counsel from James, and my personality is the complete opposite of it. I am *slow to listen, quick to speak, and quick to become angry.* While patience is a virtue that everyone admires, most of us just don't have enough of it. Yet when we have been fuming at a checkout line in a busy store wondering why another cash register has not been opened, we often pretend that we have patience when we finally pay the apologetic clerk.

In my past work experience as a trainer, I learned that patience is a necessity to get the work done. You cannot be a good trainer if you are not patient with your trainees. While I am always congratulated with an excellent track record of patience at work, my personal patience level suffers. I think one of the reasons I am patient as a trainer is that I expect the trainee to require time to learn. In contrast, my expectations for others in my life experiences outside work are so high that I lose my patience when they fail to meet me halfway. I need to apply the same principles I follow at work to my personal life.

I have met many parents who try hard to show patience in front of others when their children misbehave, but respond differently when they are not in a public setting. Whether we are relating to children or struggling with the many exasperating situations we face, we all try to look like we are patient when in fact we are actually very impatient and feel stressed inside. It could be at our work, where things are out of control because the reports were not done properly, the staff did not follow the instructions correctly, and we have to fix things before they get worse. In times like this, we must learn to surrender our anger and frustration to God and allow Him to work patience in us.

The Art of Listening

Communication is so important to good relationships. Not only does it involve both listening and speaking skills but it also requires a good balance of when to listen and when to speak. When I used to train people to work in customer service, I taught them about the art of listening to clients before they responded. Sometimes we have a preconceived notion of what we are going to say before we hear the full story or learn all the facts. This leads to misunderstanding and hurt feelings because those who are sharing do not feel that we are listening to them.

We can hear something, but it does not mean that we will respond to it. Listening, however, requires action on our part. How many times have you said or heard the remark, "you're not listening to me!" We have selective hearing, and we choose to hear only the things that are important to us, the things we really want to hear.

Sometimes we may feel that someone is not listening to us, and we may become easily angered. One night I was very upset at Kayli for not listening to me when I asked her to change into her pajamas. She finally complied after the fourth time when I yelled at her. That is when God used her to speak to me. "Mommy," she said, "I don't like it when you yell at me."

Of course, I made an excuse and told her, "Kayli, if you would have listened the first three times when I asked you nicely, I wouldn't have had to yell so loudly to get your attention! What should I do to help you so that I won't have to yell?"

"You can just ask me nicely," she replied.

Before I could even think, I defended myself, "But I did, and you didn't hear me. I asked you three times...and that's why the fourth time I had to yell." She promised that she would try her best to listen the first time, and I prayed to God that I wouldn't lose my patience so easily.

God taught me a lesson through this. He does not yell at me, but I know that when I do not listen to His gentle prodding and reminders, He creates a change in my life so that I will stop and listen. Of course I cry out and complain to God because I don't enjoy it, but I realize it was because I ignored Him in the first place.

Faith and patience go hand in hand. Faith involves our trust in God's good plans for us. Patience involves waiting for God's timing which may seem like an eternity. We need to trust and know that God is sovereign. If God is sovereign, it means that even if we make bad choices, He will make it work out in the end according to His plan and will. Listening to God's voice involves stillness on our part so that we can do what God wants. We have to remember that He knows what's best for us. We need to not just hear God, but also to listen to His instructions. Sometimes God sends others so we can hear Him. Listening to others intently is a key or we will miss what God is trying to teach us.

We need to balance waiting on God and trusting Him with the action of doing the work we are called to do. It is foolish to just sit back when we hear warnings and promptings and not do anything about it. We must not think that we can let God do all the work because He is in total control anyway. This reminds me of a story that was shared with me when I first became a Christian. It goes something like this:

> There was a flood warning in a small town and the people who lived there were being evacuated. Because it was a small town, all the neighbors helped each other by going from door-to-door to warn everyone to leave. One neighbor banged on the door of a devout Christian man who was still in his home. "Have you heard about the flood that is coming? Quickly grab your mementos and meet us at the corner square where a bus will take us out before we drown!"
>
> The man in the house replied, "Thank you for caring, save yourselves first. I will wait for God to provide a way out for me."
>
> Later the floodwaters overtook the man's home, and he climbed onto his rooftop. A rowboat of rescuers came by and cried out to him, "You, up there on the roof, quickly climb down to us, so we can safely row you out. The flood waters will soon be deeper!"
>
> The man again refused help and said, "Thank you for caring, save the other neighbors first. I will wait for God to provide a way out for me!"
>
> Shortly after this, the waters rose above the man's rooftop, and he climbed up and sat on the chimney top. A helicopter came and the pilot shouted to the man, "You there, good

thing we circled back to see if there were any other survivors here, quickly climb up the ladder I'll throw down to you before it's too late!"

The man rejected this emergency rescue opportunity with the words, "Thanks for caring, keep looking for other survivors. I will wait for God to provide a way out for me!"

After the helicopter left, the flood waters rose even more. The devout Christian man drowned. When he reached heaven that day, he asked God why He took his life when he still had so much service to do for Him. "God, why did you not come and save me?"

God shook His head and said, "Are you kidding? I sent your neighbor, the rescuers in the boat, and even the helicopter to come and save you. You chose to ignore them. What more do you want?"

The man in the story did not do his part to receive the help God was offering him. He should have realized that God's grace was providing all those opportunities to save him. We have to take an active part when we feel God is telling us to do so.

We hear a lot of things in society, some good and some bad. We can screen out the things we don't want to hear and choose to listen to only the good things. However, at times it is good for us to listen to things that may sound bad. For example, it is hard for many of us to hear critiques about ourselves, but such directed counsel can actually help us learn and change for the better. The Book of James teaches:

Do not merely listen to the word, and so deceive yourselves. *Do what it says.* Anyone who listens to the word but does not do what it says is like a man who looks at his face in a mirror and, after looking at himself, goes away and immediately forgets what he looks like. But the man who looks intently into the perfect law that gives freedom, and continues to do this, not forgetting what he has heard, but doing it—he will be blessed in what he does.

—JAMES 1:22–25, emphasis added

This word also applies when we hear the sermon at church. As the pastor preaches a lesson from God, our heart strings may tug because we realize that we need to change. If we fail to respond in obedience to God and later tell the pastor later how the sermon touched us, we are like the person James described in the scripture above. It is good that we can see ourselves in what the pastor has said, but we stop short if we do not do anything about it.

If we really want to change, we need to confess, surrender, and allow God to change us. We must not just listen to what has been preached by the pastor, but we must also hear God's voice and ask Him to lead us in the process of change. A process has many steps, but our first step has to be that of acknowledging our need to hear and do God's will in our lives. The first step is always the hardest, but we can be sure that God will help us to take it and then guide us further.

SPEAKING WITH A DISCERNING HEART

If we do not listen enough, we probably know what it mean to speak so much that we don't give the other person a chance to talk to us. It's humbling to discover that we talk too much and need to control our tongue. Is it any wonder that James 1:26 warns us to keep our tongue under rein? Speaking too much is part of being impatient. We tend to talk more when we can't wait long enough for the other person to finish sharing before we add our two-bits.

I was hit by a big dose of reality when my brother Chi lovingly confronted me about my problem. It was a month after I came back from my healing retreat and I was eager to share with him and my close confidantes what God was doing in my life. He told me that when I share, I go on and on. Because I don't pause, it is sometimes a draining experience for the listener.

Ouch! That was tough to hear. I had to swallow my tears as I tried to explain how I usually hold so much in and I don't have many people I trust with my deep stuff. However, he said that he noticed I tend to speak without pausing all the time. I know I can be overwhelming in my enthusiasm when I share with people, and I am trying my best to think more of the other person, so I do not dominate the conversation. I know it is part of my problem of being impatient and trying to be in control of a situation. Talking allows me to steer the subject matter to the direction I want it to go.

My brother tried to make light of the truth by saying that I had been given the *gift of gab*. Is that a blessing from God? I suppose it is, if it is used with a discerning heart of when and how long to speak words of praise, encouragement, exhortation, and love in the Spirit. I took my brother's concern very seriously and immediately asked my close confidantes if I was being a windbag and not giving them the opportunity to share. They affirmed that though I had lots to share, they were happy just to listen because they were encouraged by the stories I shared. God has blessed me with close friends who are patient with me and listen not just to my woes, but also to my stories of rejoicing in the lessons He has taught me.

It is important to note that when we do speak, we must allow the Holy Spirit to use us to speak good things. Sometimes when we are impatient, we say things that we shouldn't. Out of the same mouth, we can choose to say good things or we can choose to say damaging things. The Book of James and the letter to the Ephesians remind us to tame our tongue and ensure that everything we speak will be encouraging and not condemning.

> With the tongue we praise our Lord and Father, and with it
> we curse men, who have been made in God's likeness. Out of

the same mouth come praise and cursing. My brothers, this should not be.

—James 3:9–10

Do not let any unwholesome talk come out of your mouths, but only what is helpful for building others up according to their needs, that it may benefit those who listen.

—Ephesians 4:29

Have you ever struggled to hold your tongue from making an improper comment or a snide remark? As a parent, it's hard not to express yourself when you learn that your children are doing something they should not be doing. There are times when we should comfort and encourage our children, but we also need to warn them of danger, and discipline them when they are clearly in the wrong.

It is very hard for me to not speak up when I question the abilities of the instructors who are training my daughter. One day I struggled to hold my tongue when Kayli was at her swimming lesson. It was the third day of her lessons and my heart was feeling anxious because she was not swimming well. Kayli kept swallowing so much water and she was getting discouraged doing the back-kick because she was launching too fast and kicking too hard. I had to hold myself back from going over by the pool to give her some pointers. It was not my job, and I surrendered her to the teaching of the instructor and remembered that she was under God's protection.

Not being able to help Kayli was such a difficult lesson for me because I struggled with wanting to control the situation. I learned that I need to trust in God and know that He is in control. Just when I was going crazy and wanted to finally step in and say something, God intervened and had the swimming instructor give Kayli pointers to slow down her kicking. It was God's perfect timing. God amazes me; each time I am just about to snap or lose it all, He intercedes and helps me.

God answers our prayers in different ways. When I prayed and asked God to help me listen more to His voice and also to others, He answered me by giving me a second book project. It involves listening intently to other women share about their daily battles and then compiling their stories into a book that will encourage other women to share and be set free.

God affirmed that I was indeed listening more in one interview session I had. The woman who was sharing mentioned that she had talked all morning and had never given me a chance to speak. I confessed to her that I was overjoyed to hear that because my new goal was to listen more before I spoke. The interview was about how God had helped her, not me. These book projects, including this one, are God's way of allowing me to express myself to others without overwhelming them with my sharing. God has creative solutions for everything.

The Eruption of Mt. Saint Helens

The famous Mt. Saint Helens made headlines when it erupted in southwest Washington on May 18, 1980. Although it had been a dormant volcano, there was a possibility that it could erupt again— and it did. When I think about that, it reminds me of what I have gone through with my temperamental moods. I have been like Mt. Saint Helens, just waiting to erupt and scare everyone nearby. The only difference is that I am no saint. My anger starts with impatient feelings that fester inside me and boil over even when I try to control them. When I try to hold my anger back, my frustrations get the best of me, and I feel terrible.

A recent episode reminded me that God was listening to my desperate cry for help with my anger. Although she did not realize it, my mother was losing her hearing. As a result, she would talk very loudly in our conversations, which tested the patience of all our family, as well as her own. My mother was adamant that she was not losing her hearing, and she was concerned about the cost of a hearing aid, something she felt she did not need. However, she finally agreed to wear one after we insisted that my siblings and I would split the costs with my dad.

I spent countless hours driving my mother to see the otolaryngologist (ear, nose, and throat specialist) and the hearing aid consultant. The hardest part was the painstaking job of translating for the hearing aid consultant each time we met. I was a first generation Chinese Canadian, and my mother did not understand English at all. And in this process, my mother changed her mind three times about wanting a hearing aid.

On the day we were to go in for the final customized fitting, my mother changed her mind once again because she was concerned about the cost of the battery replacement. The moment she said that, I sensed the anger boiling up in me and quickly asked God to help me. I told her the costs were irrelevant because her health depended on it. When I said that we would pay for it, she insisted that she did not want us to. As I tried to explain, my impatience again got the better of me. I was so upset at her that I yelled at her for being so selfish.

I knew I was wrong for yelling at my mother, and I didn't want to shout at her anymore. However, I also knew that I had lost the ability to reason quietly with her. God allowed me to think of my brother Chi, and I called him quickly from my mobile phone. I was relieved when my brother answered the phone and was able to talk to my mother. Although she still disagreed, she finally caved in and said she would do it just this one last time this year. She refused to spend any more money on it the next year.

Before my mother and I went to the appointment, I talked to my brother again and briefly asked him to pray that everything would work out smoothly and that our mother would notice a significant and positive difference once she used the aid. God was merciful and answered our prayers right away. When we arrived, I told the hearing aid consultant about my dilemma with my mom and the cost of the battery replacement. To my surprise, she said although she could not change the price on the hearing aid, she could give us more batteries.

The hearing aid consultant threw in enough batteries to last a whole year. When I told my mom the great news, she was happy about it and seemed much more relaxed; she became very cooperative. I thanked God for this answer to our prayer that He would make everything right that afternoon. In two other answers to prayers, my mom learned to put the earpiece in her ear after only two tries and she noticed a significant difference in using the hearing aid. God was so good. He made a stressful day much better than I had anticipated.

When I dropped my mother off, I was able to talk to her because we were both calm by then. I learned that she had thought we had to buy a new earpiece each year, but she had never brought it up because she was just debating about the batteries earlier. Our impatience with each other had led us to misunderstand each other; but in the end, God intervened and gave us exactly what we all needed— peace of mind.

My journal entries reveal my tendency to become angry easily. Time and time again, I have cried for the Lord to control my anger. This is why I am so happy about what I wrote when God spoke to me months ago.

> *"Helen, remember to listen more intently so that you can think about what you should speak before jumping in. This will help you not to be aroused into anger. When you do speak, remember to speak only good things and not bad things. Everything that you speak or do will reflect your life*

in Christ. You will sin, Helen, if you follow your own selfish motive, and forget that I am God; but I will remind you about who I am by the Holy Spirit who lives in your heart, and you will repent and turn from your ways. Do not worry about this because I will not allow you to lose your faith in Me, you will be strong, you will know your errors and you will repent and I will forgive you."

THE PROCESS OF CHANGE

After I received Christ as my Savior, I heard countless sermons and lessons about not allowing your anger to get the best of you. I took to heart the teaching that you should forgive and make up before you go to bed, and I tried my best to be the peacemaker of my family. This changed when I got married. I had to second-guess and re-read what Ephesians really meant about not getting upset at my husband after sundown:

> Therefore each of you must put off falsehood and speak truthfully to his neighbor, for we are all members of one body. "In your anger do not sin": Do not let the sun go down while you are still angry, and do not give the devil a foothold.
> —EPHESIANS 4:25–27

The enemy would make me feel guilt and self-condemnation for sinning because I couldn't forgive and make up with my husband Bill before I went to bed. Rather than making up with Bill, I would actually run away and hide because I was afraid of what would come out of my mouth. Words hurt, and I wouldn't be able to take them back. Even if I could, the damage would have already been done. That was what I thought.

When I think about it now, it all seems funny. I believe God gave Bill to me because he had the patience to deal with me. Whatever I lacked, he had. Our first year seemed like a marriage made in heaven; we never got upset at each other and always communicated well. In our second year, things started going sideways and I found myself getting angry and running away, something that I was good at. My first impulse after a heated discussion was to grab my keys, bolt out the door, and drive off to cool down. Bill would be very upset because it was very dangerous for me to be driving in my angry condition. He was right, so I promised that I wouldn't do that anymore.

By the third and fourth years, rather than run out the door of our house, I would run downstairs to our basement to hide. By the fifth and sixth years, I would run and hide in the guest room. By the seventh and eighth years, I would actually stay in the same room and cry, although I didn't say anything. By the ninth and tenth years, I am pleased to say that I could stay in the same room and be open enough to share and pray together and work things out. As you can tell, this was not something that changed overnight. Looking back I can see how God taught me to deal with my anger issues. It is definitely a life journey we have to go through when we are dealing with a deeply rooted sin.

Perhaps you are going through something similar to what I am going through—or even worse. Be certain of this, if you are willing and want to change, God is right there with you to take you through the necessary steps to mold you and refine you. It took me almost ten years to work out my anger and relationship issues with my husband, and the process is still continuing.

THE NECESSITY OF SURRENDER

Most of my problems can be attributed to my lack of patience. For example, it seems that the more anxiety I have, the more I experience an upset stomach. I already wrote about how I wanted to take my life because things were not going according to my expectations. I now realize that the root of the problem was not just my pride and self-centeredness, but also my impatience.

As an impatient person, I understand the desire to be in control of the situations in my life. We who are impatient people feel we cannot wait for things to happen because it takes way too long. Rather than wait for things to change, we try to make things change. Sadly, this is exactly what the devil wants us to do. He gives us the lie that there is no hope or recourse unless we take matters into our own hands. It is dangerous to do things on our own because we want control so badly that we try to play God. Instead of doing this, we need to learn how to wait by surrendering control of our lives to God.

When I began writing this book and asking God to reveal each ugly mask I was wearing, He showed me that the masks we wear tend to be the qualities we desire to emulate. We wear these masks until we surrender to God's will and let His Holy Spirit work in us so that our lives will display the fruit of the Spirit. We do not have anything to prove to God. He loved us and sent Jesus to die for us even when we were rejecting Him (Rom. 5:8). God has always loved us and continues to love us, as He waits for us to come to Him. (See Ephesians 1:3–14.)

AN INSIGHTFUL CHALLENGE

Have you lost your patience by not listening enough or by cutting into conversations to get your point across? Are you easily bothered when things go wrong? Do you react in ways that you later regret? We can only be patient by understanding and accepting that God is in control of our circumstances. We cannot control the outcome of things in our lives, and we should not be frustrated or upset when it is not what we expect. Only God controls the outcome.

We cannot gain patience by trying to show that we are patient. Rather, patience is a virtue we gain through the process of being refined by the Holy Spirit. Allow the Holy Spirit to lead you in this lifetime process.

> For those who live according to the flesh set their minds on the things of the flesh, but those who live according to the Spirit, the things of the Spirit.
>
> —Romans 8:5, nkjv

10

The Mask of Gentleness
and Sweetness

But the wisdom that is from above is first pure, then
peaceable, gentle, willing to yield, full of mercy and
good fruits, without partiality and without hypocrisy.
—JAMES 3:17, NKJV

"OH, YOU ARE SO sweet, thank you so much." Don't you just love to hear that said to you when you do or say something extraordinarily nice for someone? It feels good temporarily, but then you remember the truth that deep inside you are not that sweet. You have streaks of envy and bitterness, and if you are like me, you may even have bouts of anger and rage.

We are like a sweet and sour dish; on one hand we can be sweet and gentle and on the other hand we can be sour. It's what I described in Chapter 2 as my seemingly double personality, my feeling that I was the female version of Dr. Jekyll and Mr. Hyde. But where does our sourness come from? Listen to what the Bible clearly declares:

> Who is wise and understanding among you? By his good conduct let him show his works in the meekness of wisdom. But if you have bitter jealousy and selfish ambition in your hearts, do not boast and be false to the truth. This is not the wisdom that comes down from above, but is earthly,

unspiritual, demonic. For where jealousy and selfish ambi-
tion exist, there will be disorder and every vile practice.

—JAMES 3:13–16, ESV

It is so easy to become trapped in bitterness, cynicism, and insin-
cerity. We may try to act sweet and have a gentle spirit, but deep
down we know that it is just that—an act. We probably don't recognize it, but we are all actors. We play so many different roles in our
lives that we sometimes forget which role we are playing. I have heard
that actors immerse themselves in their roles to get into the characters they portray. Sometimes when they finish on set, the lines get
blurred when they have to turn off their acting characters and return
to their real selves.

No matter how hard we try not to be conformed to a certain role,
society seems to keep shaping us back. Think of the roles that you
may play daily—a daughter, a wife, a mother, a friend, a counsellor,
a manager. Where does the role of a child of God come into play?
Jesus taught that we must come to God as children to enter into the
kingdom of heaven (Luke 18:15–16).

As little children, we can play and live freely and trust that our
Father in heaven will take care of us. We do not need to play different
parts to please others. We do not need to act sweet or gentle. We just
need to be like a child and it will come naturally. Take a moment to
think about the sweetness and gentleness of a new baby or a toddler
or a child who is playing innocently. Are we as genuine and sweet as
they are? Or do we have hidden motives?

THE DANGER OF SCHMOOZING

Have you ever heard the word *schmoozing*? My husband taught me
that word, and we define it as flattering or complimenting someone
to attain positive affirmation or results from that person. It's OK to

compliment someone, but it's not OK to "schmooze" someone to gain positive returns. Schmoozing is related to self-seeking and self-ambition for positive gain. It is fine when you are only joking and playing around with your spouse or your close friends, but it becomes a dangerous tool that aids in sin when you do it for the purpose of receiving something.

We must guard against the danger of embellishing or exaggerating our compliments and speech to gain respect or positive affirmation. You may have heard of sugar-coating, which means that you sugar coat your speech rather than speak the truth. You make your words sound sweet and nice so you won't hurt the person's feelings. We all do this occasionally. For example, when someone gives us a gift or makes us dinner, we thank them for the perfect gift (which we plan to give away) and the greatest meal we ever had (which we can actually make better). When we compliment others, we are to do it with an attitude of genuine sincerity and gratitude.

James 3 speaks very directly to the importance of our speech and our attitudes. Verses 7–8 remind us that unlike animals, which can be tamed, our tongue cannot be tamed. It is regarded as "a restless evil, full of deadly poison" (James 3:8). As verse 5 teaches, "the tongue is a small part of the body, but it makes great boasts." It is like a spark of fire that, if left unattended, "sets the whole course of [our lives] on fire" and "corrupts the whole person" (James 3:6).

We do well to listen to more of God's truth concerning our speech and our attitude.

> With the tongue we praise our Lord and Father, and with it we curse men, who have been made in God's likeness. Out of the same mouth come praise and cursing. My brothers, this should not be.
>
> —JAMES 3:9–10

> But the wisdom that comes from heaven is first of all pure;
> then peace-loving, considerate, submissive, full of mercy and
> good fruit, impartial and sincere. Peacemakers who sow in
> peace raise a harvest of righteousness.
>
> —JAMES 3:17–18

God will be faithful to guide us so that we will speak in the Spirit with honesty and gentleness for others. In one of his prayers to God, David said, "I have resolved that my mouth will not sin" (Ps. 17:3). We should think before we speak and allow the Holy Spirit to help us discern what to say. (See Proverbs 16:23.) More importantly, if we say and do everything in the name of Jesus Christ, we will not err with our own self-seeking motives.

> And whatever you do, whether in word or deed, do it all in
> the name of the Lord Jesus, giving thanks to God the Father
> through him.
>
> —COLOSSIANS 3:17

CALLED TO TRUE LOVE AND GENTLENESS

Do you know what it means to be two-faced? It is wearing a mask of gentleness and sweetness that hides the real you when you speak to someone. It is treating someone as if nothing is wrong when you may dislike that person because of a past offense. We do this because we feel that we want to protect others and promote unity and peace. Or we may feel that as Christians we should display a false expression of love no matter what. Instead of facing reality, we shield ourselves and others from it.

When we ignore the real problem and fail to address it, we foster bitterness and grudges so that they are like a balloon that becomes bigger and bigger until it fills the inside of our hearts and pops. God calls us to love others with words and deeds, but they must flow out of the sincerity of our hearts. If we are annoyed, upset, and angry, or even hate someone, we need help in learning how to forgive.

Our past experiences—what we have seen and done previously—influences our present behaviors. From my experiences with different family members, I learned how to face problems by running away, displaying external rage and even physical violence, holding anger in, pretending the pain will go away, staying strong, and pretending to be nice. Is it any wonder that I feel like I have worn too many masks in my lifetime? When one does not work, I try on another in an effort to get the result that I want.

If we are honest with ourselves, we will acknowledge that each of us wears masks at one time or another. We allowed God to reveal our masks to us before we were able to humbly accept His free gift of salvation. Now we must continue to respond to Him with a contrite heart and allow Him to work in our lives.

This is very important when God calls us to serve as a referee between people whose relationship has been broken. In a competitive group game, a referee is required to serve as an impartial person who determines if the rules have been broken and looks only at the facts to determine who is correct when a dispute breaks out. Many times the referee's role is to conciliate the parties involved and calm them down so that the game can continue. This is also true when we are referees in real life situations. We must remain impartial and aim to hear both sides of a dispute. We must speak with love and gentleness as we genuinely seek to help others forgive and make peace.

God, not man, made the rules of the "game" we know as life, and He sent His son Jesus Christ to be our ultimate conciliator and the top referee. We need to set our standards according to His standards and His plan for us to live an abundant and enjoyable life in relationship with Him. As it is in any game, people are upset when God's standards are bent or broken, and the referee is required to come in to keep the flow of His life moving. It is Jesus Christ who mediates for us so we can learn to be better referees for each other—without partiality, in true love and gentleness

MEEKNESS IS NOT WEAKNESS

Some Christians feel that being gentle in Spirit means they should be quiet so that they can keep the peace. When they see other believers outwardly sin or head toward danger, they do not say anything, but keep their views to themselves. Inwardly they are concerned for their fellow members in the Lord, but they are afraid of creating any disturbances. They keep silent rather than help others be accountable to God. This is a response of weakness, not gentleness and meekness. When we look the other way and pretend that nothing is wrong, we are not displaying the gentleness of the Spirit, but rather ignorance and the lack of sincere love.

God calls us to be accountable to each other so that together as a family we can learn and grow stronger in our faith. (See James 5:19–20.) When Paul wrote to the Galatians, he said that we should be supportive in gentleness to help those who have sinned be restored to God. Our goal is not to be judgmental but to lovingly correct others with God's truth. We need to do everything in meekness through the Holy Spirit, and we should not do anything to inflate our egos and make us appear more spiritual in front of others.

> Brothers, if anyone is caught in any transgression, you who are spiritual should restore him *in a spirit of gentleness*. Keep watch on yourself, lest you too be tempted. Bear one another's burdens, and so fulfill the law of Christ. For if anyone thinks he is something, when he is nothing, he deceives himself. But let each one test his own work, and then his reason to boast will be in himself alone and not in his neighbor. For each will have to bear his own load.
> —GALATIANS 6:1–5, ESV, emphasis added

Instead of confronting someone who is sinning, we may be tempted to ask to others to pray for that person and thus expose the problem of that brother or sister to others. We must be very careful about this. When we do not first go directly to the one who needs correction but share our views with others, it becomes slander. We need balance and wisdom from God to discern how to pray for those who need correction. (See Matthew 18:15–20.)

We express God's gentleness when we judge by the standard of His truth, not by what we feel is correct. He wants us to help others and be conciliatory so we can bring peace. Jesus Christ is our ultimate example of one who displayed a gentle, meek, and humble spirit. His real strength lay in His ability to control His temperament. He responded with gentleness, meekness, forbearance, and forgiveness to those who wronged Him. Yet He corrected and rebuked those who required it. He used God's truth to teach and correct.

When Paul wrote to the church at Corinth, he appealed to them with the example of Jesus Christ. He wanted to show the church that we can win people to God with love and a gentle spirit in Christ. And he reminded us that being meek in spirit does not mean we are to be weak.

> I, Paul, myself entreat you, by the meekness and gentleness of Christ—I who am humble when face to face with you, but bold toward you when I am away!—I beg of you that when I am present I may not have to show boldness with such confidence as I count on showing against some who suspect us of walking according to the flesh. For though we walk in the flesh, we are not waging war according to the flesh. For the weapons of our warfare are not of the flesh but have divine power to destroy strongholds. We destroy arguments and every lofty opinion raised against the knowledge of God, and take every thought captive to obey Christ, being

ready to punish every disobedience, when your obedience is complete.

—2 CORINTHIANS 10:1–6, ESV

Paul taught us that we are to share with meekness, gentleness, and love for others. We need to allow the Holy Spirit to empower us to restore people to God's family. We should not boast because it is the Holy Spirit who is working in us. At the same time, we must not be weak in our presentation of the gospel.

FORGIVING, LOVING, AND FEELING— AS GOD DOES

Part of being truly sincere is having a pure heart. This means that we, with all honesty, surrender all the bitterness and anger we may hold deep inside. It means that we forgive those who have wronged us and no longer hold a grudge against them. The act of forgiving is difficult for most of us because we tend to think that there is a condition attached to everything. This is why it is so hard for many to accept the free gift of salvation from God. It is difficult to comprehend the grace of our Lord and that He was and is willing to forgive all who turn to Him. Many still struggle to gain God's love by what they do.

Christ reminds us that we need to learn how to forgive just as the Father has forgiven us. "For if you forgive men when they sin against you, your heavenly Father will also forgive you. But if you do not forgive men their sins, your Father will not forgive your sins" (Matt. 6:14–15). We can forgive because we know that God forgives our sins, and we should therefore forgive others.

We can forgive when we trust in God's promise that He is the sovereign Judge and that vengeance belongs to Him. We can forgive because we pray that God will heal our hearts and enable us to see things His way. We can forgive because Christ, our ultimate example, prayed and asked God to "forgive them, for they do not know what they are doing" (Luke 23:34).

It may be difficult to forget what someone has done to us, especially if it involves some type of abuse or traumatic experience. However, as we allow Him, God will use time and circumstances in our lives as part of His ministry to mend and heal our hearts. We can forgive and allow God to eliminate any bitterness or grudges in our hearts. Proverbs 19:11 teaches, "A man's wisdom gives him patience; it is to his glory to overlook an offense."

Only with a forgiving heart can we allow the Holy Spirit to live and work through us. As we do this, our lives will yield and bear the fruit of genuine gentleness, goodness, and kindness to others. God will enable us to love others the way He does. As I was praying for God to do this in my life one morning, He let me feel what He feels. I shared about this with my close friend May, and she encouraged me to write it down. I hope that you will be encouraged as you read my journal excerpt to God:

> *Lord, I woke up in the morning feeling great and feeling your presence by me. I heard Kayli playing in her playroom and went in to greet her. But instead of giving me her usual hugs and kisses greeting, she was pre-occupied with her own things. I think she was reading or listening to her Jump 5 CD again. Even when I asked for my morning hugs and kisses, she turned away. "See the door there?" she said. "Can you go out please?"*
>
> *I was so hurt by her attitude. She is about to turn eight years old this fall, and I can already sense a change in her attitude toward us. Her affection has been teetering up and down. I usually discipline her really strongly by talking about her bad behaviour and attitude, and if required I would give her a time out or take something away from her.*

That morning, instead of getting really angry and forcing her to change, I left her room and went into my room and started to cry! I went to my bed, planted my face into my pillow, and cried and cried!

For some reason, instead of getting angry at her, I felt in my heart the anguish and pain you feel when we turn our love away from you, Lord. You cannot make us love You. I want Kayli to show me her love and affection on her own and not because I am coercing her. I felt deep sadness and anguish as all the pain and broken heartedness seem to come from You. I felt my spirit grieving in Your place. It was the strangest feeling I have ever had!

When I went downstairs to see Bill, he immediately knew I was crying, even though I was trying to contain it. When he asked me what was wrong, I broke down and could barely share how I felt that morning. He thought I was upset at Kayli, but I said, "No, this time I am crying because I feel so sad and bad about how I hurt the Lord."

I felt pain because of the way Kayli had been toward me, but I reject You and hurt You because I do not show how grateful I am to You and how much I really love You. I felt Your pain Lord, and I am so sorry. I am so sorry for sinning against You, and I am so sorry for the pain You feel from others who continue to sin and forget that You are God Almighty, our Lord, our Father who loves us and wants a loving relationship with us. You do not want to coerce or force Your love upon us. Lord, I did not just learn that, I really felt Your sorrow.

That morning I not only offered forgiveness to Kayli, but I also received forgiveness from God again. I thank God for the sadness that I felt so I could feel just a small part of the pain He feels when we forget His love. We have so much to be thankful for. We have a God who is our Heavenly Father; He "is compassionate and gracious, slow to anger, abounding in love. He will not always accuse, nor will he harbor his anger forever; he does not treat us as our sins deserve or repay us according to our iniquities.... As a father has compassion on his children, so the LORD has compassion on those who fear him" (Ps. 103:8–10, 13).

AN INSIGHTFUL CHALLENGE

When we are in a tough situation, it is very hard to remain calm and not become easily excited. Whether we are on the giving or receiving end of words in challenging relationships, it is difficult to be gentle. Are you facing this kind of problem right now? Have you seen or heard something that is not correct, and do you realize that you need to lovingly approach someone about it? Have you turned a blind eye to problems and held them in? Are you harboring negative and bitter thoughts about someone? Has it been difficult for you to forgive someone who has wronged you?

When we allow the Holy Spirit to control us, God's love and forgiveness will fill our hearts and make us more like Him. We will be able to display genuine gentleness to others, and God will be glorified. Allow God to give you a loving and gentle heart.

> Therefore, as God's chosen people, holy and dearly loved, clothe yourselves with compassion, kindness, humility, gentleness and patience. Bear with each other and forgive whatever grievances you may have against one another. Forgive as the Lord forgave you. And over all these virtues put on love, which binds them all together in perfect unity.
> —COLOSSIANS 3:12–14

11

The Mask of Satisfaction
and Happiness

Whoever loves money never has money enough;
whoever loves wealth is never satisfied with
his income. This too is meaningless.
—ECCLESIASTES 5:10

D O YOU LOVE to go on fast rides like the roller coaster or tilt-a-whirl spinners and feel your heart beat a hundred times faster than its normal rate? How about death-defying activities like bungee jumping, parachuting, paragliding, rock-climbing, and snowboarding? All these things have one thing in common—they pump adrenaline into your body and create excitement about meeting your goals. I have a friend who wanted to try bungee jumping, even though she was totally afraid of heights. She said if she could do that, it would help her realize that she can overcome almost anything else in her life.

It is in our nature to seek a higher purpose in life. Many of us pursue active sports, challenging careers, and various relationships and religions to find the one thing that will satisfy our inner longings. If you're like me, you may take up a new hobby until your original passion for it is gone. You may try to revive your interest in the hobby, or you may just move on to something else that will give you a thrill. Perhaps that is why many of us love to travel—to enjoy new experiences in exotic places. In a similar way, a husband and wife may become bored with each other and seek other companions to fill their needs and desires.

Our minds and hearts tend to thirst for new things, and we are never satisfied with the mediocre. We are not content in our circumstances, and we have an insatiable desire for more. Wanting more is not necessarily bad. However, we must be careful about how we fill our desires and needs. Do we fill them with things that only give us temporary satisfaction, or do we fill them with things that give us permanent and eternal satisfaction?

Jesus promised to give us "living water" so that we will never thirst again (John 4:10–14). We just have to reach out and take it! But was Jesus really referring to physical water? No, He knew that our physical needs are only temporary but our spiritual needs are permanent. We have an inner longing, a spiritual thirst to be fulfilled and complete, and it can only be met through a relationship with the living God.

In John 7:37–39, Jesus spoke again about living water and said that those who believe in Him will have "streams of living water [that] will flow from within him." He was referring to the Holy Spirit, whom He promised to give to those who receive Him. The flow of streams of living water is not just a temporary trickle of water, but a continuous supply of water that will satisfy our thirst and will never run dry.

> The water that I shall give him will become in him a fountain of water springing up into everlasting life.
>
> —John 4:14, nkjv

> "If anyone is thirsty, let him come to me and drink. Whoever believes in me, as the Scripture has said, streams of living water will flow from within him." By this he meant the Spirit, whom those who believed in him were later to receive. Up to

that time the Spirit had not been given, since Jesus had not yet been glorified.

—JOHN 7:37–39

LESSONS ON TRUE SATISFACTION AND CONTENTMENT

As I consider Jesus's promise of living water, I am reminded of *Ladder 49*, a movie about firemen and their lives on their own home front. In one scene, a fireman's wife, who was pregnant, told her husband that she was afraid. She said, "It's not just about us anymore, it's more than that." Rubbing her tummy, she continued, "You forgot what we have. We have to think about our new family. You can't just think about what's best for you and what you want in your job."[1]

I have shared something similar with my husband, "It's not just about us, and it's not just me and our daughter Kayli." I said this because I felt that we had forgotten about another important entity in our family—the Holy Spirit. It is so easy to forget that the Holy Spirit, the third person in the triune Godhead, is part of our family and lives in us. God is in our midst, and we must take Him into account.

When we forget that the Holy Spirit should be at work in our lives, we take Him for granted and we thirst for other things that will never satisfy us. Only the Holy Spirit can quench our thirst. We need to tap into Him so that His living water will overflow our lives and there will be no need to look for external things to fill it.

Our family learned a lesson in finding satisfaction and contentment in God on a recent trip to the Oregon coast. Before our family left, Bill booked five reputable hotels to meet our lodging needs along the way. He spent countless hours researching each hotel to ensure that among other things, it had an indoor pool and spa. Therefore, we were greatly disappointed when one of them, part of a well-known hotel chain, provided inferior amenities and services. The clerk was not as friendly as we expected, and the hotel pool and spa were being renovated.

I prayed and asked God to help us enjoy what we had and to also show us that He was in control of everything. Thank God, He answered my prayer. He enabled us to be calm and content with what was given to us—a decent hotel where we were all safe and sound with a roof over our heads. And when Bill voiced our dissatisfactions to the manager, we received 50 percent off our hotel rate because the hotel's mission is to provide a 100 percent satisfaction rate. We learned to trust that God was indeed in control and would make everything right for us.

This incident reminded me how quickly we forget the goodness of God. We always want more. However, God wants to teach us to be content in all our circumstances and grateful for our present blessings. He wants us to be confident that He will always provide, sometimes in unexpected ways.

WE FIND SATISFACTION IN COMMITMENT TO GOD

I attended two beautiful wedding ceremonies this year and they caused me to reflect on my own wedding. One of the things that has stayed with me is the special moment Bill and I repeated our wedding vows. Our vows are the commitment—the promise—we made to each other and to God. Our commitment is not just to each other, but to God. He is our accountability partner.

> At the beginning of creation God "made them male and female." For this reason a man will leave his father and mother and be united to his wife, and the two will become one flesh. So they are no longer two, but one. Therefore *what God has joined together, let man not separate.*
> —MARK 10:6–9, EMPHASIS ADDED

Everyone strives to have a "marriage made in heaven." In front of family and friends a couple may display affection and love, but as soon as they are behind closed doors, the real truth about their problems spills out. Both husband and wife wear masks of happiness that hide their hurt and their grudges against each other. When they are alone, they are cold to each other and they complain and argue and hurt each other deeply. Their feelings of love and respect for each other fade away, and separation and divorce seem to be the only solution. By the time they get to this stage, they ask themselves, "What happened?"

Falling in love involves feelings. Staying in love involves not just feelings, but, more importantly, commitment. If love is based only on feelings, a marriage relationship will never survive. Having gone through my own marriage battles and having listened to stories of countless others, I am convinced that only a commitment to God can save one's marriage. When you are in a quarrel with your mate, your feelings may tell you to do something that is harmful to your marriage. We can love someone one day because they are treating us well. However, if we are not grounded and committed in our vows to each other and to God, it's so easy to give up when trials come our way.

We strive to be satisfied and happy in marriage. When we are not, we search for things to fill the void in our lives. Some people indulge in food to temporarily silence their sadness, and some may drink or take drugs to make themselves forget. Some engage in extramarital affairs, some go on wild shopping sprees (unfortunately this is my weakness), and some sit at home and watch movies or TV sitcoms all day. All these responses fail to give us genuine contentment through the difficulties in marriage.

However, God has provided an answer for us: commitment to God. When we are committed to Him and know that we are accountable for our actions, we will tend to hang in there. If we have committed our vows and our lives to God, we can have no higher and stronger accountability partner in our lives and in marriage.

A HARMFUL SOURCE OF PLEASURE

Most of us seek to find satisfaction and pleasure in coveting. We do not place enough emphasis on the last of the Ten Commandments, which forbids us to covet, and we do not seem to realize how harmful it is to disobey it. However, the fact that the Tenth Commandment is a separate commandment shows that it was very important for God to warn us against coveting:

> You shall not covet your neighbor's house; you shall not covet your neighbor's wife, nor his male servant, nor his female servant, nor his ox, nor his donkey, nor anything that is your neighbor's.
>
> —EXODUS 20:17, NKJV

Perhaps we do not take this seriously because we feel that we don't "covet our neighbor's house, wife, servant, ox, donkey, or anything that they own." But if we look at how Jesus explains who our neighbor is in the New Testament (see Luke 10:29–37), we realize that our neighbor can be anyone, not just the person living next door. We are to love our neighbors as ourselves (Matt. 22:39).

We covet when we yearn to have something that we think will fill our temporary needs. We want it because others have it, not because we need it. We don't want to lack something that others have. Coveting stems from envious eyes and an envious heart. We envy because we want to have the same thing as others, or even worse, because we want to be better than others. We may covet not just material wealth and possessions but also resources, job positions or titles or status, power, prestige, and even people.

Do you remember what Satan wanted? He coveted God's position and authority. He wanted not just to be as powerful as God, he wanted to be God! He wanted to be better. Ecclesiastes reminds us of our vanity and how it is like "chasing after the wind." Picture yourself chasing after the wind, trying to catch something you can't see and obtain.

> And I saw that all labor and all achievement spring from man's envy of his neighbor. This too is meaningless, a chasing after the wind.
>
> —ECCLESIASTES 4:4

Needing and wanting are two different things. God provides for our needs, but it is our sinful nature to want things just for the sake of having them. Marketing advertisements and friends encourage us to buy things, not because we really need them, but because they are the latest trend or fashion. This is one of Satan's plots to spoil our hearts with unhealthy desires. How can we overcome such desires? Like any other sin that invades our lives, we need to come clean, confess, and repent to God and ask for His help to control our urges. If we need personal support, it is important that we enlist the help of a trusted accountability partner.

As I think about the danger of coveting, I am reminded of an educational exhibit I saw at the Pacific Science Center in Seattle, Washington. It showed the differences between habit, compulsive behavior, and addiction and helped me see how the things I do affect me. Habit was defined as something we repeatedly do until it becomes learned. Compulsive behavior was identified as repeating an activity over and over again without realizing why. And addiction was explained as engaging in something even when we know it is harmful to us.

If we do not address our sin of coveting, it will become a habit that may turn into compulsive behavior and eventually an addiction. If the latter stage happens, it will be very painful to correct.

Coveting may lead to stealing if one does not have the means of acquiring something. It creates inner turmoil and battles within us. James accurately writes:

> What causes fights and quarrels among you? Don't they come from your desires that battle within you? You want something but don't get it. You kill and covet, but you cannot have what you want. You quarrel and fight. You do not have, because you do not ask God. When you ask, you do not receive, because you ask with wrong motives, that you may spend what you get on your pleasures.
>
> —James 4:1–3

The Secret of Contentment

Today's society leads us to believe that we can find satisfaction, contentment, and peace in the security of owning things. This false sense of security is measured by how much money we have stored away and the size of our investments in our cars, our home, and any property we may have. However, the truth of the kingdom of God is completely opposite. Christ Jesus said that He, not the world, gives us the peace and contentment we really need. "Peace I leave with you; my peace I give you. I do not give to you as the world gives. Do not let your hearts be troubled and do not be afraid" (John 14:27).

Success in the kingdom of God is found in seeking God and His godly ways. To be first we must be last, to be exalted we must be humbled, to be a leader we must be a servant, to be rich we need to be poor, to enter into God's kingdom we must be like little children, to be satisfied we need to be content with what we already have, to be content we need to surrender all, to be at peace we need to trust.

The apostle Paul wrote humbly and honestly about his secret of contentment:

> I am not saying this because I am in need, for I have learned
> to be content whatever the circumstances. I know what it is to
> be in need, and I know what it is to have plenty. I have learned
> the secret of being content in any and every situation, whether
> well fed or hungry, whether living in plenty or in want. I can
> do everything through him who gives me strength.
>
> —PHILIPPIANS 4:11–13

Paul trusted in Christ Jesus. He realized that he had a living Savior who could provide for him in every circumstance. He also wrote to Timothy about the importance of finding true contentment in pursuing godly ways. What is the point of coveting and hoarding material wealth we cannot take with us when we leave this earth? Rather than trying to find satisfaction in material wealth, we should focus our energy and passion in pursuing the things of God. Listen to Paul's words:

> Now godliness with contentment is great gain. For we
> brought nothing into this world, and it is certain we can
> carry nothing out. And having food and clothing, with these
> we shall be content. But those who desire to be rich fall into
> temptation and a snare, and into many foolish and harmful
> lusts which drown men in destruction and perdition. For the
> love of money is a root of all kinds of evil, for which some
> have strayed from the faith in their greediness, and pierced
> themselves through with many sorrows. But you, O man of
> God, flee these things and pursue righteousness, godliness,
> faith, love, patience, gentleness.
>
> —1 TIMOTHY 6:6–11, NKJV

We must not invest in temporary earthly things that we cannot take with us but invest in eternal things that will count in the kingdom of God. As we do this, we can trust that we have a sovereign God and

Father in heaven and that He will never leave us nor forsake us. We do not need to covet what others have, but we can be content with what we already have, knowing that God will always provide for us.

Hebrews 13:5 says, "Let your conduct be without covetousness; be content with such things as you have. For He Himself has said, 'I will never leave you nor forsake you'" (NKJV). Our heavenly Father loves us so much, and He knows what is best for us. He will supply everything we need "according to His riches in glory by Christ Jesus" (Phil. 4:19, NKJV).

As I write about the secret of contentment, I recognize that my heart is not always centered on the things of God. Too often I find myself wearing the mask of satisfaction and contentment because it is expected that Christians will be content and joyful in all circumstances. It is my personal quest to learn to experience the true joy of living in the presence of God moment by moment.

Not until I released and surrendered the things I had coveted did I truly feel at peace and content with the things God has blessed me. However, this pilgrimage is not as easy as it sounds. I keep returning to the fact that true joy is not focused on me. Rather it is about Jesus and others. I remind myself of this daily by placing the letters J-O-Y—an acronym for placing Jesus first, Others second, and Yourself last—around my home.

AN INSIGHTFUL CHALLENGE

Are you satisfied with what you have? Are you grateful for your job, your home, and the relationships you have? Or are you sometimes green with envy? Are you constantly trying to pursue more material wealth and financial gain because you think it will make you feel better? Is it hard for you to be content without getting more? On a scale of one to ten, with ten being extremely satisfied, how satisfied are you with what you have?

Do you want to experience true contentment and joy? The challenge is to surrender all that you are and all that you have to Jesus. Ask Him to give you a new heart that thirsts after the things of God and seeks to be satisfied in Him. Ask for His peace, joy, strength, and riches so that you will never be in need. Experience true joy in finding contentment in Jesus—He alone will satisfy all your needs.

Agur wrote a compelling Proverb:

> I am the most ignorant of men; I do not have a man's understanding.
> I have not learned wisdom, nor have I knowledge of the Holy One.
>
> —PROVERBS 30:2–3

Yet, as he continued to write, his words showed that he was a very wise man and had a heart for the mighty God:

> Two things I ask of you, O Lord; do not refuse me before I die:
> Keep falsehood and lies far from me; give me neither poverty nor riches, but give me only my daily bread.
> Otherwise, I may have too much and disown you and say, 'Who is the Lord?' Or I may become poor and steal, and so dishonor the name of my God."
>
> —PROVERBS 30:7–9

May we be more like Agur.

> Praise the LORD, O my soul, and forget not all his benefits....who satisfies your desires with good things so that your youth is renewed like the eagle's.
>
> —PSALM 103:2, 5

12

The Mask of Optimism

Do not boast about tomorrow, for you do not
know what a day may bring forth.
—PROVERBS 27:1

SOME PEOPLE SAY that I have a very positive attitude and outlook on life. I have never really thought of myself that way, although I have yearned and prayed to see things God's way. I have always thought that I had a very negative view on many things, but perhaps, over time, God has refined and shaped my thinking to see things in a positive light. However, I continue to fight the tendency to go back to my own way of seeing things from a negative perspective.

It is ironic that I used to train and counsel people to see the light at the end of the tunnel and hope in the midst of darkness. As I taught them to have a positive mental attitude, I shared the following scenario in my sessions with people who needed to tweak their attitudes:

> It's a beautiful day and you're driving down the highway on your way to work. All of a sudden, a car cuts you off and forces you to brake really hard. Do you get really upset and curse, or do you think that the driver who just gave you a mini heart attack did not maliciously set out to ruin your day?
>
> If you choose the former, you are making a decision to have a bad day, a conscious choice to allow it to affect

you. The driver does not even know who you are, and he was probably distracted and rushing off to an event. If you take a negative attitude with you into your work, your day is already ruined just as it is starting! You forget that less than ten seconds ago you were having a wonderful day. It is funny how a little change can affect your whole day.

Although I trained this and believed it, I don't practice it when things don't go my way. I allow silly little interruptions and changes to my schedule to get the best of me. I think it's because I want control too much and I see the negative view too easily. My husband, Bill, reminds me that what we think determines our behavior and how we behave will determine our success. The key for us then is to saturate our thoughts in the ways of God and allow the Holy Spirit to lead us in how we behave. If our way is negative, let's choose God's positive way.

THE PROBLEMS OF GAD AND SAD

Worry is a part of my problem. In fact, I have a nickname that I actually coined for myself—Giant Worry Wart. It's not an attractive name, but sometimes I feel that it really fits me. I have heard dozens of sermons that told me not to worry, and my family and friends have also reminded me that I should not worry. Yet, I worry so much that I worry about worrying too much, and I worry about the guilt of worrying! It is no wonder, as I mentioned in Chapter 3, I was medically assessed as having a mild generalized anxiety disorder (GAD). I need continuous prayers to surrender this weakness in my life to God.

When we worry, we express our lack of trust and faith in our sovereign Lord. Why do we need to worry about something we cannot control? Why do we worry when we know that God knows and intends the best for us? His promises are steadfast and unchanging and He has promised that He will never leave us nor forsake us (Deut. 31:6; Heb. 13:5). He assures us that He has plans not to harm us but plans to allow us to prosper and to have a future (Jer. 29:11).

So why do we worry? I once read that if we worry we should pray, and if we're not going to pray about it, it's not worth worrying about. Jesus told us to first seek His kingdom, and He promised that He will always take care of us. He said that we should not be anxious and worry about tomorrow (Matt. 6:33–34).

What does it mean to seek the kingdom of God? Pastor Tim Tze from my local church once taught what it means to seek the kingship of God. If we seek God and allow Him to reign as King in our lives, we, as royal citizens, should obey Him and let Him be in control of our lives. I recently read Holly Wagner's book *When It Pours, He Reigns.*[1] Isn't the title so true? Sometimes we go through our own little storms and forget that God is our mighty King who reigns in our lives. We should not worry or be afraid.

In addition to having a generalized anxiety disorder, I have attitude and depressive mood swings that seem to occur more strongly during the late autumn and winter months. This is typical of people who have the Seasonal Affective Disorder (SAD) because there is generally less sunlight during the winter season, and lack of light affects behavior. SAD is different than winter blues or cabin fever; it is a form of depressive behavior that is triggered by seasons.

People who suffer with SAD are robbed of a happy outlook and a positive attitude. It is interesting that the acronym itself describes exactly what this disorder causes millions of people to suffer— sadness. I purchased a home blue light therapy to treat my condition. Once a day for forty-five minutes to an hour, I used a special lamp that mimicked the sun's light spectrum. I noticed immediately that I was not as tired or sluggish and I was able to skip my afternoon naps. I had increased energy, which allowed me to have a happier and more positive disposition.

It is no coincidence that not only do I need more sunlight but more of the Son's light in my life. It is Jesus Christ who shines His light into my darkness to reveal the things I needed to surrender to Him. I needed both kinds of light in my life: sunlight for my physical and mental health and the Son's light for my spiritual health. Having enough light in our lives is truly therapeutic.

THE FOREST AND THE TREES

If you have ever been in a business seminar or a training session on goal setting, you may have heard the analogy of the forest and the trees. We need to see the big picture—the entire forest and not just the trees—to plan for the future and set goals. Sometimes we get so caught up in dealing with all the details—the trees—that we lose sight of our original purpose and goal—the forest. Having an optimistic outlook will enable us to see the whole forest, including the way out of the forest. However, having a pessimistic outlook will cause us to get stuck in front of a tree and become lost in the forest.

God took me back to this analogy during my healing retreat. This time, however, I saw it from a different perspective. I had prided myself for years in not just training others to see the forest but in my ability to see the forest. If I can see the forest, I feel like I am in control; when I am in control, I feel powerful. God showed me that this is a false sense of power. It is really not for me to see the whole forest! God created all the trees and the forest. He's up there and He sees everything! I can never see the whole forest, and I was not meant to see it!

I can only see the trees in front of me and perhaps a path to other trees. I must learn to surrender and trust that if I continue to follow His path, He will lead me out of the forest! God continues to plant this Proverbs 16:1 in my heart, which tells us that we can make our plans, but the final outcome is in God's hands. I can dream, plan, and hope all I want, but I have to realize that it is God who is sovereign and controls everything. Similarly Proverbs 20:24 says, "A man's steps are directed by the LORD. How then can anyone understand his own way?"

We are curious and want to know the outcome to everything. In the Old Testament, the prophet Daniel asked God to tell him the outcome of what He had revealed to him. God reminded him that there are certain things that are left to be unknown and "sealed until the time of the end" (Dan. 12:8–9). God has "set eternity in the hearts of men; yet they cannot fathom what God has done from the beginning to the end" (Eccles. 3:11).

In the New Testament, James wrote that we "do not even know what will happen tomorrow." We are like "a mist that appears for a little while and then vanishes." Therefore, we should say, "If it is the Lord's will, we will live and do this or that" (James 4:14–15). James was right; we do not know what tomorrow will hold for us. We can only trust that God's sovereignty will allow us to do the things we have planned, and we must continue to seek and do His revealed will. (See Ephesians 5:8–17.)

God wants us to live and enjoy an optimistic life as King Solomon described in the Book of Ecclesiastes. It is "the gift of God":

> I know that there is nothing better for men than to be happy and do good while they live. That everyone may eat and drink, and find satisfaction in all his toil—this is the gift of God. I know that everything God does will endure forever; nothing can be added to it and nothing taken from it. God does it so that men will revere him.
>
> —ECCLESIASTES 3:12–14

We were not meant to see the whole picture. If we could, we wouldn't need to trust and rely on God, who has written our stories—both in His secret will and in His revealed will. The exciting thing is that we will be with God at the end of our life journey. Until then, each day is an exciting mystery (see Romans 8:28–30), and God intends for us to walk with Him daily and enjoy the journey with Him.

So how do we relate to the forest and the trees? I choose to trust God daily and to see, experience, and learn from each tree I encounter. God will reveal the forest to us in His time. And ultimately we will come out of the forest having experienced the fullness of His grace and a greater appreciation of God's plan for our lives.

GOD GIVES ENCOURAGEMENT AND COURAGE

In Chapter 8 I shared how the trilogy movies based on *Lord of the Rings*, J. R. R. Tolkien's novel saga, spoke to issues related to the mask of devotion. One of my favorite characters in Tolkien's well-beloved stories is Frodo's best friend Sam. Frodo and Sam were ordinary young hobbits who embarked on an extraordinary expedition to save Middle-Earth. Sam's character, especially his commitment and loyalty to Frodo, is one of the most touching and heart-felt elements in the story. He is an example of the encouragement God provides for our struggles we face with the mask of optimism.

Throughout their dangerous and tiring task of taking the ring to the destination where it was to be destroyed, Sam was relentless in encouraging and protecting Frodo. He even sacrificed his own health and gave their last food portions for Frodo to eat. He was a great encourager and committed friend. One of my favorite parts in *Return of the King* was when Sam and Frodo made it to the foot of the volcano where Frodo was to destroy the ring. They were at their final destination, but Frodo faltered because he was too weak to take another step. As he lifted his weary friend up, Sam said these wonderful words, "I can't carry it [the ring] for you...But I can carry you."[2]

What a beautiful depiction of love and sacrifice! What a wonderful reminder of what Jesus Christ has done and continues to do for us. Without Sam, Frodo would have never completed his mission.

Without Christ, we would never complete God's plans for our life. As Jesus gives us His grace and help each day, He also sends people to encourage us when we are discouraged and need a listening ear. He gives us friends like the hobbit named Sam to inspire us with hope, courage, and confidence in our abilities.

How blessed I felt when I realized that God had given me the gift of encouragement! I can see the best in others and recognize their potential; I can see the good in something that may seem bad to others. I am hopeful when things are bleak, and I try to promote peace when there is discord. I try to encourage rather than discourage, and I see the glass as half full rather than half empty. Yet, while I am able to encourage others, I cannot seem to encourage myself. It seems as if I have no reserve of encouragement left for me.

Without encouragement from others, I become pessimistic about myself. I lack the positive energy to believe God's plans for my life and the courage to act on them. To encourage myself, I wear a necklace inscribed with the following: "The only courage you ever need is the courage to live your heart's desire." It is difficult to live out the desires of our hearts if we are afraid to fail. But sometimes it is in failing that we learn and become better.

As we draw nearer to God, our desires will become more aligned with His. God will answer our desires as we simply trust Him and take the first step of faith to fulfill them. Because it will take courage on our part, I cling to God's command to Joshua: "Be strong and courageous. Do not be terrified; do not be discouraged, for the LORD your God will be with you wherever you go" (Josh. 1:9). Our journey here on earth is like a battlefield. We can be strong and courageous because we trust that God will be with us no matter what.

Courage can take many different forms. After I shared about my weaknesses and my depressive-suicidal state with my high school friends, one of my girlfriends commended me for my courage. It takes courage to speak out and express a different point of view than others. It takes courage to be a light amidst the darkness. It takes courage to stay positive and keep trying in the face of adversity. It takes courage to keep hope alive despite what others may say. And it takes courage to do the things of God even when you can't see the final outcome.

Being faithful is part of courage. It means that we are strong through Christ's power and refuse to give up. The courage and faith He gives will enable us to focus on intangible, eternal things and invest in them. As the apostle Paul wrote, "So we fix our eyes not on what is seen, but on what is unseen. For what is seen is temporary, but what is unseen is eternal" (2 Cor. 4:18).

POSSIBILITY THINKING

Have you heard of possibility thinking? It is thinking and acting as if a future outcome is possible. It is being hopeful and positive because of the belief that something can be achieved. Possibility thinking focuses on each person's own self-will and power to control their destiny. Without Christ, it lacks a true source of power. However, when we trust God and know that He is our source of power, we can practice possibility thinking.

Jesus gave us many examples of possibility thinking. When a man brought his mute, epileptic, and demon-possessed son to Jesus, he asked Him if He could do anything about it. Jesus said to him, "If you *can*?...Everything is possible for him who believes." And "immediately the boy's father exclaimed, 'I do believe; help me overcome my unbelief!'" (Mark 9:14–29). After Jesus had driven the evil spirit out of the boy, His disciples asked Him privately why they could not do the same thing. Jesus told them that they had to ask in prayer for that to happen.

I believe that Jesus was teaching His disciples, and also the father and his son, that we need to truly believe and not doubt that God can do all things. James reminded us of this when he wrote that we must "believe and not doubt, because he [or she] who doubts is like a wave of the sea, blown and tossed by the wind" (James 1:6). If we doubt when we ask, how can we even deserve to receive God's answer? We become "double-minded" and "unstable in all [that we do]" (James 1:7–8).

When the disciples were faced with the pessimistic outlook that it may be difficult for anyone to be saved, Jesus delivered one of His greatest assurances: "With man this is impossible, but not with God; all things are possible with God" (Mark 10:27; Matt. 19:26). This profound truth applies to us today. All things are possible for us because we believe and trust in our God who can do all things for us. The possibilities are endless if we truly trust and believe in what God can do.

OUR DIVINE WEAVER'S PLAN

Each summer our family usually goes to Whidbey Island in Washington. Last summer, we stayed at Oak Bay Harbor where there were many quaint stores including a small Christian book and gift shop. I was compelled to buy a hanging cloth canvas with the following poem by an unknown author:

The Weaver

My life is but a weaving
between the Lord and me;
I cannot choose the colors, He worketh steadily.
Ofttimes He weaveth sorrow
and I in foolish pride
forget He sees the upper and I, the underside.
Not 'till the loom is silent and the shuttles cease to fly
Shall God unroll the canvas and explain the reason why.

> The dark threads are as needful in the Weaver's skillful
> hand
> As the threads of gold and silver in the pattern He has
> planned.

"I really need to get this," I told Bill, "because I need it as a reminder." And it does remind me that God has His perfect pattern planned out for me. When I fight against His will for me, I create knots. However, God works in me to untangle those knots so He can finish His canvas in me.

Perhaps you have heard the famous quote by Babatunde Olatunji, "Yesterday is history. Tomorrow is a mystery. And today? Today is a gift. That's why we call it the present."[3] Wow! It is so simple, but true. We are to trust in God and live our lives the way He wants us to. We need to enjoy our daily moments with Him and make the best of each day. Yes, today is a gift from God. We should not allow our past to hinder us and we must not worry about tomorrow because it is a mystery. No one knows the future except God, and we can trust Him to weave the pattern He has planned for the canvas of our lives

An Insightful Challenge

Do you wear the mask of optimism? Do you encourage others to see things positively, but inside you really doubt what you say? Do you have a tendency to view things in a pessimistic way? When you are presented with challenges, are you easily discouraged?

True optimism grows out of faith. Hebrews 11:1 describes faith as "being sure of what we hope for and certain of what we do not see." We are optimistic because we believe that God is in total control. Even though we cannot see what will happen, we can place our faith in His loving promises. If we put our trust and hope in God, all things are possible. Believe that God intends the best for you.

"For I know the plans I have for you," declares the LORD, "plans to prosper you and not to harm you, plans to give you hope and a future."

—JEREMIAH 29:11

13

The Mask of Sociability

A man of many companions may come to ruin, but there is a friend who sticks closer than a brother.
—PROVERBS 18:24

HAVE YOU EVER tried to take a picture of a butterfly? This slender insect, which has broad wings and flutters around, doesn't stay still for very long! You won't see a butterfly perched with other butterflies for any length of time, unless they are mating. They flutter all around with other butterflies, but they seem to be alone most of the time.

The term *social butterfly* has been coined to describe people who resemble the butterfly. Dictionary.com defines social butterfly as "a person who flits aimlessly from one interest or group to another,"[1] This label is generally given to people who have the trait of sociability—being sociable. The adjective *sociable* is defined as "seeking or enjoying the companionship of others"[2] A sociable person is inclined to associate with others and crave their companionship for the sake of feeling better. Sadly, this is a temporary fix.

I have been called a social butterfly many times. I used to take pride in that, but now I realize it's not really something to be proud of. What does it say about me if I flit aimlessly from one group of friends to another? The more sociable I am, the less time I have to build stronger, more meaningful relationships. My heart becomes divided when I am preoccupied with a large group of friends.

THE NEED FOR QUALITY RELATIONSHIPS

There is a difference between having many friends and having quality friends. I have a girlfriend whom I greatly admire, but at one time I thought she was selling herself short by not having very many friends. I used to tease her about being picky and selective in her choice of friends and mates. Now I realize that she was the wise one. She invested her time in building meaningful, quality relationships while I spent all my time flitting around different groups of friends.

I now realize that I have a security issue. I don't know why, but I feel more secure when I have more friends. Maybe it's also because I love variety. At any rate, as long as I can remember, I have had many circles of friends. At secondary school, I had at least five different groups of friends: my "neighborhood friends," the "popular gang," the "quiet group," the "wild party friends," and my brother's friends.

After I gave my heart to Jesus, I gained even more friends from church and Bible classes. When I entered the university, I added more circles of friends: the "hanging out group," the "lunch group," the "study group," and the "International Visa students group." Alongside these groups of friends, I had my work colleagues and staff friends. Every time I moved to a different job environment, I would have a new group of friends. And even though I left the company, I would still maintain one to three close contacts. Building new ministries along the way for God also allowed me to add new groups of friends.

Now, after more than forty years of life, I have accumulated many circles of friends. I have been afraid to let go of them and have tried to reconnect with them even when they have moved on with their lives. However, everything came to a head when I spiraled into my depression. You would think that someone who had so many friends would never feel lonely or depressed, but I was to learn that the number of friends I had would not satisfy my heart. Although I was surrounded by friends, I was isolated in my room.

How can one have so many friends and have no one to turn to? As I have already mentioned, part of the problem was my pride, which hindered me from sharing the "real me" with others. Also, I had not invested the time required to maintain close quality relationships. I could not turn to anyone because I did not trust anyone at a level that would allow me to share my feelings, fears, and pains. I was a social butterfly whose wings were clipped, and I retreated into my cocoon to hide as if I was a silkworm.

Through this experience, I felt loneliness—a longing for companionship—and lonesomeness—a feeling of sadness and isolation. I felt more of the latter because I suffered feelings of isolation even though I did not lack for company. I lacked close, quality relationships with my friends and also with God. I was preoccupied with my problems, and I was trying to resolve them on my own.

We were not meant to be alone. God designed us to have a close intimate relationship with Him and with others. In the beginning of time when God created Eve for Adam, He created her as a companion and helper for man. "The LORD God said, 'It is not good for the man to be alone. I will make a helper suitable for him'" (Gen. 2:18).

In their innocence, both Adam and Eve enjoyed living in the presence of God. However, when the crafty serpent lured Eve into disobeying God, they were alienated from Him and loneliness was birthed into the world. The whole human race inherited their disobedience and its consequences. Today the enemy continues to lure us from giving our time, our resources, and our hearts to developing intimacy with God. This lack is the root cause of our loneliness.

THE COMPANY WE KEEP

The Bible has a lot to say about the company we keep. Throughout the Old Testament we learn how the Israelites strayed from God when they befriended those who worshiped other gods. The New Testament warns against this very thing when it commands us to "not be yoked together with unbelievers" (2 Cor. 6:14). Many interpret this verse as a warning for Christians to stay away from unbelievers. However, if this were the case, how would it be possible for the unsaved to hear of God's salvation plan?

The warning not to be yoked means that we are not to walk with or hold the same attitudes as the ungodly. A yoke is the wooden beam placed over two animals that work together. A donkey cannot work with an ox because they walk differently and such is the case for an unbeliever and a believer. We are to take the yoke of Christ and walk with Him. (See Matthew 11:28–29.) My brother Chi suggested the following paraphrase for 2 Corinthians 6:14–18: "Do not walk with the unbelievers in their ungodly attitudes and ways. Are you not children of God? Did He not say that in the Scriptures? Therefore, let's walk like children of God."

We can keep company with unbelievers, but we must guard our hearts to follow in the ways of Christ. Proverbs 12:26 says, "A righteous man is cautious in friendship, but the way of the wicked leads them astray." As we seek God's will about the company we keep, we must always use Jesus as our role model. Jesus ate with those who were rejected, sat with the sinners, and shared God's love with them. He taught us that we should associate with sinners but not with their attitudes, aspirations, and worldly ways that would lead us astray. We must not forget that we are sinners who have been saved by God's grace.

As we share the love of Christ with unbelievers through friendship, God will also direct us into "best-friend" relationships with those who can help us grow closer to Christ. A close friend will be one who is fun to be with, has a strong listening ear, and is committed to always be there for you. Other characteristics will include loyalty, honesty and strong integrity, wisdom, and a positive, encouraging, and loving attitude.

I personally require that a best friend be a person who is accountable to me, encourages me to be better for God, and loves me without my masks, despite my imperfections. It is equally important for me to have permission to be encouraging and accountable to a best friend.

However, when it comes to having good close friends, it should be as simple as something my daughter told me. One time I saw Kayli dub a girl her best friend within a few hours of meeting her. When I asked Kayli what made her new friend a best friend, she replied, "She is nice to me and plays well with me!" Good friendship warms a heart.

The Gift of Unconditional Love

Over the years I have realized that God surrounds us with close friends who have different personalities and gifts and come to our aid when we need them. As I think of close friends, my heart automatically identifies my sister Ellie as my best female friend—my best male friend is my husband, Bill, of course. I have been really blessed because God gave her to me as my sister by birth, but as we always tell each other we are best friends by choice.

At my surprise fortieth birthday party, my sister read a speech that took me back to our childhood and adolescent years and reminded me again how special our relationship has been. "You support me in everything I do, whether it's good or bad," she said. "You just give and give and never expect anything in return…that unconditional love is the most amazing gift you can ever give me, Sis."

Of course her speech left me crying, because everything she said about me is also what I feel about her. When she commented on sacrifices I made for her, I think of the sacrifices she made for me. She visited me almost every day when I was in the hospital, and she was right there helping me when I became a first-time mom. When I desperately needed my healing retreat, she offered her home to me. The list is endless.

My other best friend, Winnie, is a non-family member. We have a special relationship because even though I do not see her often, we have a kindred spirit. She would give her heart to me if she could; she prays for me and encourages me and is always genuine; she shares her fears and imperfections with me and allows me to do the same with her. We stay connected through e-mail, cards, and phone calls since we cannot see each other face-to-face as often as we like. Staying connected is the key, especially when it is a spiritual connection. You know you are close to someone when you haven't seen them for a very long time, but it's as if you were never apart when you do get together.

I have three other close loyal friends—May, Wendy, and Betty. They are great listeners and provide sound wise advice. Most of all, they have the gift of encouragement that speaks to my heart. They are there not only for me, but for my entire family. In fact, I consider them as my own family.

Why am I writing about these special friends? Hopefully it will encourage you to think about the close friends you have. Friends who are the closest give you encouragement and active support, and I hope that you have at least one you can count on. It's easy to take close friends for granted. When you have too many friends, your time is divided among them and you tend to forget those who are the closest to you. Because you know they will always be there, you tend to let your relationships with them slide a bit. This can also happen in our relationship with our spouses, our children, and God.

It is so important that we do not take God for granted. He is the one who always loves and always forgives. He is slow to anger and filled with compassion and mercy. Not only is Jesus Christ our Lord, our God, our Savior, and our counselor, but He is also our friend. Indeed He is our true *best* friend. We connect with Jesus through prayer, reading the Word of God, music, worship, fellowship, and just being still and enjoying His presence.

We tend to consider someone a close friend if that person expresses friendship with tangible actions. If you say you care but you're not there when someone needs you, that person will not consider you a good friend. This is true in the way some people treat their relationship with God. If God does not respond to their prayer needs as they expect, they think He does not care. This, of course, is untrue, but we live in a fallen world and we find it difficult to love someone if we do not see and feel something tangible.

When I think about my sister saying that I extend unconditional love to her, I have to admit that it is not entirely true. I do have conditions. I tend to reciprocate because of her positive actions towards me. We stay connected with others because we expect that they will connect with us. We extend a listening ear because we expect the same in return. When we extend love, there are conditions attached.

None of us can truly give unconditional love the way Jesus has shown it toward us; for Christ died for us while we were still sinners and were rejecting Him (Rom. 5:8). He continues to connect with us even when we feel disconnected from Him. The closest we can come to loving and giving unconditionally is when we extend love to others who cannot return anything to us. Jesus talked about this when He commanded us to "love your enemies and pray for those who persecute you" (Matt. 5:44). "If you love those who love you, what reward will you get?" Similarly, "If you greet only your brothers, what are you doing more than others?" (Matt. 5:46–47).

It is not easy to love someone who fails to love us as we expect or return any favors to us. We must learn from the selfless, unconditional love of Jesus for us. As we walk more closely with Christ and become more like Him, we will learn to extend His love to others in a genuine way. The more connected we are with Christ, the more we can connect with others unconditionally.

TOWARD A GREATER DEGREE OF INTIMACY

When I counsel people, I tell them, "If you want a friend, you have to be a friend first." If we want solid, meaningful relationships, we have to open up and be honest and transparent. However, we tend to blame someone else when this does not happen. That is what our first parents did when God questioned them about their disobedience in the Garden of Eden. Eve blamed it on the serpent, and Adam blamed it on Eve, "The woman that you put here with me" (Gen. 3:12). In essence, Adam was really blaming God!

I remember lonely, painful times when I have cried out to God. *Lord, where are You and who can I turn to? Why do I feel so alone? Where are my friends now? You have promised me, Lord, that You will not forsake me!* It's so easy to live in a self-pity mode and blame God and others for our personal troubles. Sadly, the more we do this, the more isolated we become.

To have a greater degree of intimacy in our relationships, we have to make a conscious effort to reach out to others. If we need help, we need to ask for help. If we are not willing to admit our need of forgiveness to God, we cannot receive it. However, if we draw closer to God by investing in the discipline of spending time with God, we will establish a more intimate relationship with Him.

Similarly, as we invest our time in communicating with our loved ones, our relationships will grow stronger. Building strong intimate relationships always involves both parties. As we ask for help from others, we must remember to also return help to them. God designed us to give and receive intimacy, and we therefore have a void in our lives if we do not have healthy intimate relationships. Only God, through the spiritual ministry of His love and the physical expressions of love from others, can fill our void. He will always be there for us.

RESTING IN GOD'S PRESENCE

Have you ever tried to sit still and not do anything at all? What is the first thing you think of? Let's try this exercise together now. Read this entire list first and then follow the instructions:

- Mark this page before you put the book down.

- Close your eyes.

- Breathe deeply ten times.

- Come back to this section when you are done.

If you followed the instructions, you were probably preoccupied with counting to ten. In following the instructions and breathing ten times, you had to mentally count to ten in your head. If the requirement of breathing ten times were removed, I can almost guarantee that your mind would wander. You may start thinking about your list of things to do or you may actually fall asleep. It is difficult for us to sit still. We have to be doing something.

How then, do we rest in God's presence? It is simpler than you think. Repeat the above exercise, but this time don't count your number of breaths. Instead, add the following three steps:

- Ask God to speak to your heart as you close your eyes to meditate.

- Reflect on a favorite passage; meditate on it, and let your heart and mind drift to be a part of it.

- As you are meditating, you will feel God's presence surround you and He will speak to your heart. Be sure to thank Him for whatever you learn.

This simple exercise is only one way of resting in God's presence and allowing yourself to consciously be still before Him, reflect on Him, and enjoy Him. As you practice this, you will learn how it feels to be more aware of God and His presence in everything you do.

I am smiling as I write because I can feel and enjoy God's presence. When you fold your laundry, do the dishes, clean the house, tend to your garden, work on your computer, you can reflect on God and know that He is right there. Rest in His presence and allow Him to speak to you through everything that you do. You will be surprised by what you can learn from Him when you are still. You will realize that you are never alone because God will always be with you.

AN INSIGHTFUL CHALLENGE

How do you feel about your social status? Are you blessed beyond measure because you have so many friends that you are never lonely? Can you think of at least two or three persons who you can call right now if something happens to you? If not, why not? When you are in a large group, are you the type who mingles with everyone? How do you feel after everyone has gone home? Do you feel alone in a large group? Do you ever feel out of place?

Can you feel God's presence in the midst of large crowds? Do you feel God's presence when you are alone? Our Savior, the Lord Jesus Christ, promises that even though He is God, He is also our friend.

He gives us eternal security and friendship with Him. Make Him your best friend today.

> Oh, for the days when I was in my prime, when God's intimate friendship blessed my house.
>
> —JOB 29:4

14

The Mask of Sincerity and Righteousness

Let us not love with words or tongue
but with actions and in truth.
—1 JOHN 3:18

WHY DO WE go to church? Do we go because we truly desire to give our praises to the Lord? Or do we go because others expect us to go, because it is the Christian thing to do? What are our motives? Do we wear a mask of piousness?

One time when I was a substitute teacher for a group of teenagers, I asked them some leading questions about why we go to church. Each time I asked a question they excitedly shouted, "Jesus!" When I probed them for a more specific reason, they still said "Jesus!" and explained, "The answer always goes back to Jesus somehow." I finally got a list of the true reason the teens were going to church and it included: meeting people, learning about Jesus, singing songs. Ultimately an honest discussion led to "because our parents expect us to."

This stuck with me for the longest time. The teens did not know that the real reason for going to church is our desire to worship Jesus, to give thanks and reverence to the Lord who came down from heaven to die as a sacrifice for our sins. Christ came so that we could be reconciled to God and be worthy to worship Him.

What does it mean to live a victorious Christian life? Is it just about going to church, serving where needed, teaching others, reading the Bible, and praying with others? Sometimes it is difficult to know our real motives and we can end up with rituals and a compromised relationship with God. We deceive ourselves and end up living a life of hypocrisy.

When I discovered that I was wearing a mask of sincerity, I realized that I was turning my relationship with God into a religion. I judged others and compared them to myself. I thought I had a sincere passion for the Lord's work, but they did not. I was so wrong—we are all imperfect, and it is not up to us to judge each other. My pride broke to pieces as God revealed the sinful motives of my heart. God was refining me to be more Christ-like—more of Him and less of me.

GOD UNMASKS OUR MOTIVES

It is difficult to separate the mask of perfection, the mask of devotion, and the mask of sincerity and righteousness from each other. Although they are distinctly different, they go hand in hand. Our pride makes us feel like we have to do our best to show our devotion and be righteous before others so we can feel worthy. In the end, even though we may be sincere and devoted, what really matters is the motive of our hearts. As the apostle Paul taught, "it is by grace you have been saved, through faith—and it is not from yourselves, it is the gift of God—not by works, so that no one can boast" (Ephesians 2:8–9).

Barbara Johnson, whose witty writing style shares God's truth with humor and simplicity in her book *Fresh Elastic for Stretched-Out Moms,* has addressed the importance of our motives. She has stated, "God only called you to be faithful; He did not call you to be successful!"[1] In other words, God is not interested in what we do for

Him. He is interested in our faithfulness to Him, and He works in our lives to reveal motives that dishonor Him.

So often we are judgmental of others whose lives reflect obvious sinful motives. Bill and I have always been fascinated with mystery shows in which the good guys catch the bad guys. As we have watched the popular TV series of the *CSI: Crime Scene Investigation*, we have seen lies unearthed as suspects are tracked down and questioned. Each person who is investigated seems to have hidden motives, and the shows are filled with deceit, greed, sex, power, and corruption— everything that God abhors.

Our tendency is to judge the suspects on *CSI* as worse than us. However, when we see things through God's eyes, He opens our hearts to recognize that we are no better off than they are. We need to be mindful of our own motives and ensure that we are following God's will and not our own.

THE DANGER OF AFFIRMATION

Have you ever struggled to prove yourself to others? You want to show that you are a true servant of God by volunteering and helping in many different ministries. As people start affirming how good you are, their affirmations become your sole motivation for serving. It is no longer to help others in the name of the Lord, but to receive affirmation and praise from others.

We are easily swayed by the affirmation of others. After I confessed the ugly motives of my heart to my fellowship group, Pastor Tim Tze shared with me, "Affirmation is like a two-edged sword, on one side it helps to encourage us, on the other side it will tempt us to think of ourselves over God." Serving with the wrong motives will make us forget the real reason we were serving in the first place. Pride creeps in and we don't even know it.

This is why Jesus warned us many times not to become hypocrites.

Two examples from Matthew 6 stand out—one related to giving to others and the other to praying:

> Beware of practicing your righteousness before men to be noticed by them; otherwise you have no reward with your Father who is in heaven. So when you give to the poor, do not sound a trumpet before you, as the hypocrites do in the synagogues and in the streets, so that they may be honored by men. Truly I say to you, they have their reward in full. But when you give to the poor, do not let your left hand know what your right hand is doing, so that your giving will be in secret; and your Father who sees what is done in secret will reward you.
>
> MATTHEW 6:1–4, NASB

> When you pray, you are not to be like the hypocrites; for they love to stand and pray in the synagogues and on the street corners so that they may be seen by men. Truly I say to you, they have their reward in full. But you, when you pray, go into your inner room, close your door and pray to your Father who is in secret, and your Father who sees what is done in secret will reward you. And when you are praying, do not use meaningless repetition as the Gentiles do, for they suppose that they will be heard for their many words. So do not be like them; for your Father knows what you need before you ask Him.
>
> —MATTHEW 6:5–8, NASB

These examples teach us to protect ourselves from the temptation to receive credit and affirmation for ourselves. When we give and help anonymously, the credit will not be ours but God's. Similarly, when we pray secretly and sincerely, God will hear and honor our prayers. This is not to say that we cannot honor God when we give and pray publicly; the important thing is that we give the credit to God.

When we know that we may be tempted with pride and hypocrisy, we must guard against it by giving and praying in secret. This will ensure that we stay true to our motive to honor God, who sees everything and will reward us. We should not expect or need affirmation from this world. We are called to be different; we are called to shine for Jesus. Our motives must be pure so that all glory and honor will go to the Lord.

WHAT PLANK?

I love the analogy Jesus used when He warned us about judging others.

> Why do you look at the speck of sawdust in your brother's eye and pay no attention to the plank in your own eye? How can you say to your brother, "Brother, let me take the speck out of your eye," when you yourself fail to see the plank in your own eye? You hypocrite, first take the plank out of your eye, and then you will see clearly to remove the speck from your brother's eye.
>
> —LUKE 6:41–42; MATTHEW 7:3–5

You know that you're heading for danger if you can read the above passage and not see yourself in the analogy. When I used to read or hear about that passage, I would say to myself "Yeah, Jesus, you are so right, so many people are hypocritical. They judge me and others and they don't even know it and they are ruining your reputation." Then God revealed to me that I was the hypocrite who should remove the plank from my own eye first! I never would have admitted before that I was the type who would judge others. I tried to stay true, unbiased, and pious. However, when you think you are trying to stay out of trouble and believe you're always right, you become self-righteous.

We all have our own stories of how God speaks His truth to us.

Mine was the struggle I had with my siblings about our responsibilities to the family. I had always felt that I had the blessing of supporting my parents, and I took on the responsibility of helping them not only financially but also by giving of my time. I painted such a rosy picture of myself doing these honorable things for them, and I reminded myself that it was such an achievement for the youngest of the siblings to do so.

However, I did not know that I had put on a mask of sincerity. Deep down, I felt bitter and resentful, especially with the lack of support from a particular sibling. My judgemental heart prevented me from learning how to love and serve my family unconditionally. As God showed me this, He revealed that if I can't love and serve with my own relatives, how can I ever learn to love and serve those within and without my church family?

> If you love those who love you, what credit is that to you? Even "sinners" love those who love them. And if you do good to those who are good to you, what credit is that to you? Even "sinners" do that. And if you lend to those from whom you expect repayment, what credit is that to you? Even "sinners" lend to "sinners," expecting to be repaid in full. But love your enemies, do good to them, and lend to them without expecting to get anything back. Then your reward will be great, and you will be sons of the Most High, because he is kind to the ungrateful and wicked. Be merciful, just as your Father is merciful."
>
> —LUKE 6:32–36

THE COURAGE TO COME CLEAN AND BE HONEST

As I think about unveiling the mask of sincerity, I am reminded of how God stopped me from running to hide in another church. God reached my heart when a sister in the Lord told me the reason she and her family had left their home church to go to a much larger church. They were afraid they would be asked to serve at their home church, and they were not ready to do so for personal reasons. Therefore, they went to a larger church to hide.

I understood this because I wanted to leave my home church for the same reason. I thought I would not feel guilty for not serving at a bigger church because they would have enough servants. At my home church, however, I did not want to disappoint others. I did not want to feel guilty, and I was afraid to say no to my brothers and sisters in the Lord. It would have been easier to run away than reveal my sinful motive to others, but God intervened. Listen to what He said to me:

> *"Helen, this is wrong. You need to repent of this sin and turn away from this thought. You cannot run. The problem will still be there. You need to face it head on, as you already shared with your fellowship group and some of your friends. As hard as it is, Helen, I will give you the courage and the strength from the Holy Spirit to openly share and tell others what you are going through. You need to come clean and be honest; tell them the reason why you cannot serve.*
>
> *You need to sit at My feet. I will raise others. Never, Helen, never feel obligated to serve, never be "guilted" into serving others. Always serve with the right motives, out of love for others not out of guilt. I don't want you to put a mask on, Helen. I have not created my children to live in fear and guilt. I want you to live in love and joy and not in pretense. Come out of your hiding place. Know that I am God. Do not be afraid of what others say. Bear My name, and you will shine so that I may be glorified.*
>
> *I will give you the strength. Yes, you feel weak and defeated now, but the enemy is lying to you. You know how*

*much I love you. I have affirmed you; look around at what
I have given you. You must hear my voice: I will give you
the courage to not run, and I will enable you to come out of
your shell and deal with the things that have been troubling
you all these years—the things that you have hidden deep
down in your heart. I will shine My light in your heart and
consume all your darkness. I have already revealed all the
ugliness that I abhor, and you have heeded and repented.
Welcome back into my presence, Helen."*

Try as we might, we cannot hide from God or from others. Our
problems will not go away unless we first admit them and deal with
them. Let God help you do this.

Knowledge Can Be Dangerous

The classroom wall of my high school English class displayed a poster
with the following message:

The more you study, the more you know,
The more you know, the more you forget.
So why study?

This quote made complete sense to me at the time, but I now realize
that studying to gain more knowledge is a coveted thing. And yet
gaining too much knowledge can also be a dangerous thing. Think of
what happened to Adam and Eve when they disobeyed God and ate
the fruit from the tree of the knowledge of good and evil. They realized that they were naked and sewed fig leaves to cover themselves,
and when they heard the sound of God walking in the garden, they
hid themselves.

God asked them about the sin they had committed, and they tried
to justify their disobedient behavior by making excuses and blaming

others. Eve had wanted to attain wisdom after listening to the promise of the crafty serpent, and now she blamed the serpent. (See Genesis 3.) She learned that when we feel we are wise enough and know what is best for us, we forget that God's grace gives us wisdom to discern. We look to ourselves for knowledge and leave God out.

It is very dangerous to study and gain wisdom and knowledge and think that we are better than others. We justify our own actions to suit ourselves. In fact, it is the very hypocrisy Jesus exposed in the Pharisees:

> You diligently study the Scriptures because you think that by them you possess eternal life. These are the Scriptures that testify about me, yet you refuse to come to me to have life. I do not accept praise from men, but I know you. I know that you do not have the love of God in your hearts. I have come in my Father's name, and you do not accept me; but if someone else comes in his own name, you will accept him. How can you believe if you accept praise from one another, yet make no effort to obtain the praise that comes from the only God?
>
> —JOHN 5:39–44

When we snub others for not acting or thinking like us, we become like the Pharisees who thought they were more righteous and holy than the rest of the people because they followed all the rules and laws so strictly. Although we know we are saved by grace, we can become hypocrites who only do things to look good if we don't guard our hearts and do things with sincerity.

I confess that I have snubbed others. When I hear someone teach a lesson, I sometimes criticize how it was presented. I may keep my snide remark in my heart, or I critique it to my husband and make him feel just as negative as me. Whether I keep it inside or say it out loud; God knows how I feel. It is not for me to judge and think that I am better than others. I know that when I snub others it's because I want to feel better about my own insecurities. Envy distorts my view and causes me to think or say hurtful things. I have learned that it is so important to surrender these things to God and allow Him to be in control of my life.

THE CONSEQUENCES OF HIDING OUR REAL MOTIVES

Sometimes we may not know what our real motives are. Sometimes we do know what they are, but we try to hide them. The consequences are deadlier when we try to hide our motives, as the story of Ananias and his wife, Sapphira, shows in Acts 5:1–11.

Like many other believers in the church at Jerusalem, Ananias and Sapphira sold a piece of their property to share their profits with the apostles for distribution to the needs of others. However, Ananias's greed got the best of him and he kept back part of the money for himself, with the full knowledge of Sapphira. The problem wasn't that Ananias kept part of the money for himself, rather, it was that he tried to lead others to believe he was giving everything. He tried to look sincere and righteous in front of others.

God used Peter to expose Ananias's mask and confront him with the truth that "you have not lied to men but to God" (Acts 5:4). God took his life, and three hours later, Sapphira came and agreed with her husband's lie. She also died, and great fear went throughout the whole church and all who heard about it. I believe that everyone was afraid not only because of the death of Ananias and Sapphira, but mainly because they knew that they also had wrong motives in their hearts at one time or another. It was a huge wakeup call for the church then, and it continues to stand as a warning against hiding our real motives in our hearts.

GOD WILL REWARD OUR FAITHFULNESS

Sometimes I feel envious of other people's gifts, talents, and faith. I feel inadequate and wish that I could be more like them. However, in Romans 12 I am reminded that God gives us faith, and He also decides who gets what gifts by His grace. We are to exercise our gifts by the faith God gives us.

> For by the grace given me I say to every one of you: Do not think of yourself more highly than you ought, but rather think of yourself with sober judgment, in accordance with the measure of faith *God has given you.* Just as each of us has one body with many members, and these members do not all have the same function, so in Christ we who are many form one body, and each member belongs to all the others. We have different gifts, according to the grace given us. If a man's gift is prophesying, let him use it in proportion to his faith. If it is serving, let him serve; if it is teaching, let him teach; if it is encouraging, let him encourage; if it is contributing to the needs of others, let him give generously; if it is leadership, let him govern diligently; if it is showing mercy, let him do it cheerfully.
>
> —ROMANS 12:3–8, emphasis added

In the parable of the talents, the people who were resourceful with the talents entrusted to them received more talents when their master returned. However, the person who didn't do anything with the talent entrusted to him had his talent taken away. (See Matthew 25:14–28.) God wants us to live a life of freedom. He does not want us to worry about our inadequacies because He is the one who enables us to do things for Him. This is the sovereignty of God, which we will never understand because He chooses and knows what is good for all His creation. How can we receive more from God when we don't do much with what He has already given us?

God is more interested in our faithfulness to Him than in how much we do for Him. God will reward us for our faithfulness even in performing a small task for Him as long as we are obedient to Him and use what He has given us wisely.

> Well done, good and faithful servant! You have been faithful with a few things; I will put you in charge of many things. Come and share your master's happiness!
> —MATTHEW 25:21

LESSONS FROM A STAR

One autumn season, when my daughter, Kayli, was six years old, I bought a nice star necklace pendant for her. It had the acronym of STAR on the front, and the phrase Seek Truth And Righteousness was inscribed on the back. The pendant reminded me of Kayli because I call her my "little Star." But how could I explain the inscription to her?

As I thought of *truth*, God reminded me of Jesus's words in John 14:6: "I am the way and the truth and the life. No one comes to the Father except through me." I told Kayli that the STAR meant for her to follow Jesus. He would teach her how to be good, and she could become a star shining for Him. She was happy to learn this and wore the necklace joyfully.

That year God inspired me to make this message the theme for the annual Christmas party I host for the FAB Ladies Group. When Jesus came into the world to live among us, He chose a star, a bright light that shined into the darkness of the night so that the magi from the East would have a guide to lead them to Him (Matt. 2:1–3). The star led them until it stopped right above where the child Jesus was staying. Immediately when they found Jesus, they bowed down and worshiped Him because they knew that they had found their King (Matt. 2:7–12).

Today a lot of people try to seek God and find Him, but Jesus is the only one who is the way, the truth, and the life. No one can come to the Father except through Him (John 14:6). He is the Truth, so if we want to seek the truth, we need to seek Jesus. When we seek to know who Jesus is, He will answer and we will find Him. We will bow down and worship Him like the wise men did because His truth will be revealed to us.

What is this truth? It is that Jesus came to this earth with the sole purpose of becoming a substitutionary sacrifice. He came to die on the cross for our sins so that we, who are not righteous at all, may be forgiven and made righteous; He came to restore us to a relationship with God. A star is a reminder for us to Seek Truth And Righteousness—Seek the Truth and seek Jesus while He may be found.

As I spoke about these things with the Ladies Group that night, I confessed all my hidden lies. I told them about my pain and struggles with deep sadness and despair and my thoughts of taking my own life again. And I shared that I was serving God and the women's ministry with the wrong motives. When I prepared the lessons and organized the material to be used, it was a chore and not a ministry that I desired to serve.

The only positive motivation I felt for the FAB Ladies' group was that they, the attendees, were expecting to receive something from the day's activities. My source of affirmation was their "*oohs* and *aahs*" and their positive comments on my designs. I had lost focus of what the ministry was about—a vehicle to attract women to hear the message of God and to learn to enjoy God's gifts in the creative things we can make, and the friendships we can forge.

For me personally the star reminded me that I must Speak Truthfully And Repent! I must speak truthfully and repent of my ways so that I can walk in Jesus' ways. I need to ensure that my heart has the right motives and the right intentions, not to seek approval from people, but to do what God has called me to do.

That was the night I shared the news that I was going to take a sabbatical rest in my ministries and in my career so I could start my healing process. I needed affirmation from God and not from others. My heart required time to heal. It was important that my heart's motives were pure. Whatever I did, I needed to do it out of love and not out of obligation in anyway.

A Lesson from Kayli

My daughter is one of God's great blessings in my life, and I learn so much from her. God used Kayli to teach me the following after my healing retreat:

> I had a nice time listening to Kayli's week and all that she has gone through. Kayli wrote me a beautiful letter that she gave me to read at the beach; it was affixed with her one and only dragonfly sticker that she gave me because she knew it was my favorite. She wrote, "You're the best mommy, I love you, Mommy, I miss you so muce [I know she meant much], Love Kayli." It melted my heart and made me cry.
>
> We went home to nap, and as I cuddled with Kayli in my bed, she read the My Mom's the Best Mom[2] book to me, until I feel asleep. She later awoke me, and asked me to follow her heart sticky notes that she had pasted everywhere. I was so tired that I still wanted to nap, but Kayli started crying because her plans were changed. I knew how she felt. She wanted to please me, and had all her plans laid out, so I forced myself to get up to follow her notes. She was so cute, the first note said: follow the trail of notes. Then, go to the door, go down the steps, go to the table. (She stuck the last note on the Hamataro pasta can.)

Mommy, please cook this for me to eat, please. (She is way too cute!)

I made Kayli's can of Hamatoro pasta and she ate the whole can with two cups of milk. She also repeated her Sparky scriptures to me again and she kept asking me if I was proud of her as she had learned five verses for this week.

She reminded me of myself trying to please my mom in everything I did, and she was seeking approval, which I gladly gave her. I remember that my own mother would hardly have any positive affirmation for me; nothing was good enough—it was either too little, too late, or not enough of something. That always stuck with me, and that is why I still try to seek approval and try to please everyone today.

No matter how old or young we are, we want to please others. Our challenge is to be more like Paul when he wrote to the church of the Thessalonians: "*We are not trying to please men but God, who tests our hearts. You know we never used flattery, nor did we put on a mask to cover up greed—God is our witness. We were not looking for praise from men, not from you or anyone else*" (1 Thess. 2:4–6, emphasis added).

Serving with No Hidden Agenda

I have always wanted to please everyone. I would do my best to be at the top, even if it meant sacrificing my sleep, time, and energy. I counted it a blessing to help others and enjoyed making people happy. I soaked up people's hurts like a sponge and made them mine, even to the point of neglecting my own pain. There was no time to share my feelings, and worse yet, as I finally just discovered, I was too afraid to tell others my own hurts.

Others leaned on me for strength. How could I even bear to tell them that I am not as strong as they think I am? How could I admit that I am weak and vulnerable, especially to my non-Christian friends who were wondering about knowing God in an intimate way? How could they understand that I am just a forgiven sinner and not perfect?

I was embarrassed to show how wishy-washy my faith was; I struggled with my flesh and spirit daily, and I was filled with such sadness. The worse I felt, the more I took upon myself—keeping myself busy by counseling others and volunteering to serve in more areas. I thought that the more I became involved with others, the more I could be affirmed by others and by God. Of course the more involved I was, the more I was caught up in doing things for the wrong reasons.

God broke me and showed me what I really needed. I didn't need to do anything to be worthy before God. I had forgotten that my righteousness is not the result of anything I can do to attain it, it is because Christ died for me and I received Him into my life by faith. Although we know that we are saved by God's grace and not by our works, we always try to do more to account for it. If we could put a magnifying glass to our hearts and see our motives, it would be a scary thing. Some of us may be sincere in our ministries, but others of us may be serving out of guilt or obligation.

We may not know it, but we may be serving in certain ministries because we desire popularity and a higher profile. We may want to serve in areas where we can be recognized by those we are serving. Others may choose to serve because everyone else is, and they feel they have to serve to fit in.

What is your heart's motive in serving? Have you ever felt obligated to do something? Do you feel resentment and bitterness in serving because you did not really want to be involved in that capacity to begin with? We have to be careful about the way we serve; we are not serving ourselves. We should not have any hidden agendas when we serve. When we serve, we should serve in the Holy Spirit and not from our selfish desires. The apostle Paul exhorted the Galatian Christians:

> If anyone thinks he is something when he is nothing, he deceives himself. Each one should test his own actions. Then he can take pride in himself, without comparing himself to somebody else, for each one should carry his own load.
>
> —GALATIANS 6:3–5

> Do not be deceived: God cannot be mocked. A man reaps what he sows. The one who sows to please his sinful nature, from that nature will reap destruction; the one who sows to please the Spirit, from the Spirit will reap eternal life. Let us not become weary in doing good, for at the proper time we will reap a harvest if we do not give up. Therefore, as we have opportunity, let us do good to all people, especially to those who belong to the family of believers.
>
> —GALATIANS 6:7–10

How do we overcome the temptation to accept praise from others even when we serve with sincerity? I had trouble doing that when I realized my weakness in pleasing others and the danger of accepting credit for my service. When I prayed to the Lord, He answered by reminding me that it is "by the grace of God I am what I am" (1 Cor. 15:10). Jesus Christ alone deserves all honor and praise. It is only through Christ that we can be made righteous and counted worthy to be called servants of God. Let's serve in humility through Christ's righteousness, not our own.

AN INSIGHTFUL CHALLENGE

God calls us to do a personal "heart check" to see if our motives are aligned with what He wants us to do. God is not interested in how much we do for Him but where our hearts are. No matter how much we do, we will never do enough to attain righteousness. We can be righteous only by God's grace, because Christ died for us and imputed His righteousness to us.

Surrender your pride to God, and refuse to listen to the enemy's lies. Christ will humble your heart and restore your joy in Him as you allow His righteousness to work through you:

> …not having a righteousness of my own that comes from the law, but that which is through faith in Christ—the righteousness that comes from God and is by faith.
>
> —PHILIPPIANS 3:9

SECTION III

AFTER WE UNVEIL OUR MASKS

15

We Find Ourselves at War

But each one is tempted when, by his own evil
desire, he is dragged away and enticed. Then, after
desire has conceived, it gives birth to sin; and sin,
when it is full-grown, gives birth to death.
—JAMES 1:14–15

As WE UNVEIL our masks, we make ourselves vulnerable to spiritual warfare. Satan, the enemy of our souls, attacks us because he does not want us to expose his lies. He knows that he cannot fight against the Holy Spirit and His ministry through a pure and holy heart, so he tries to manipulate our hearts. He does not want us to be effective servants for Christ, and he will do anything to disrupt God's work. However, if we set our minds and hearts on the things of God and surrender to the Holy Spirit's leading, God will lead us into victory. To this end, we must receive and practice the counsel of Proverbs 4:23, "Above all else, guard your heart."

As we fight against Satan, he tempts us by using our old nature—our inherent evil desire to sin—against us. In Chapter 8, "The Mask of Devotion," I mentioned my struggle with the enemy's lies and my desire to satisfy my inner selfish desires instead of doing the will of God. We wear masks because we listen to the enemy's lies and are lured away from seeking and following the heart of God. Satan's number one goal is to take us away from loving and serving God wholeheartedly, and he will use masks to do that.

THE REALITY OF SPIRITUAL WARFARE

We are at war, not only with our own self-will, but also with the enemy of our souls. We must be spiritually alert to recognize the spiritual warfare in which we are engaged, and we must also be prepared for it. This war is the battle for each person's heart and soul. The apostle Paul wrote that we fight "not against flesh and blood," but "against the powers of this dark world" and "spiritual forces of evil" (Eph. 6:12). We are fighting a spiritual battle that can only be won by using the proper weapons—spiritual weapons—effectively.

> For though we live in the world, we do not wage war as the world does. The weapons we fight with are not the weapons of the world. On the contrary, they have divine power to demolish strongholds. We demolish arguments and every pretension that sets itself up against the knowledge of God, and we take captive every thought to make it obedient to Christ.
> —2 CORINTHIANS 10:3–5

When the motives of our hearts are right with God, we will desire to serve Him faithfully. The enemy and his evil cohorts will begin their tactical maneuvers on us and perhaps interrupt us with unexpected setbacks as we serve God in an exciting ministry He has entrusted to us. We may experience problems related to an accident, the loss of a job, disputes with others, or even the loss of a loved one. Such things, which distract or discourage us from continuing our service for Christ, are not coincidences. In reality, they are forms of demonic attack the enemy has sent to disrupt God's work. (See 1 Thessalonians 2:18.)

In his book *Waking the Dead*, John Eldredge wrote that "things are not what they seem"¹ in this world. I can personally attest that *nothing is as it seems* in our world. We cannot think that we are so grounded in our faith that the enemy will not attack. I used to believe the enemy's lie that if you are a strong Christian, you cannot be penetrated by the devil and his evil demons. I was really wrong.

True Christians cannot be possessed by demons, but we can still be distracted and deceived if we're not on guard. I fell into the deception of Satan when I became too self-reliant. My motives for serving in ministry came from my own strength and not from God's strength. Satan uses our pride to make us become self-righteous instead of dependent on Jesus Christ's righteousness in us. (See Chapter 14, "The Mask of Sincerity and Righteousness.") We all need to be equipped for the battle if we are going to be victorious.

Once again, the key is that we guard our hearts. If we do not, the enemy will see an open window of opportunity to break in and take over the entire fortress. We need to recognize the power of Satan (Acts 26:18) and the fact that it is impossible to conquer him in our own strength. Satan will try to get us "alone" through disbelief in God's promises or through isolation from other believers. However, God wants us to have victory over Satan, and the Spirit in us is stronger than the enemy. (See 1 John 4:4.) We can defeat the enemy in the power of the Holy Spirit who dwells in us. It is the Lord who fights for us, as we ask Him for guidance and help.

A PRACTICAL WARFARE STRATEGY

As we recognize the reality of spiritual warfare, we must receive and practice God's strong warning for us to understand the strategies and tactics of the enemy. The Bible reminds us to be "alert" and know that "the devil prowls around like the roaring lion looking for someone to devour"; we need to "resist the devil" and "he will flee" (James 4:7).

Be self-controlled and alert. *Your enemy the devil prowls around like a roaring lion looking for someone to devour. Resist him, standing firm in the faith,* because you know that your brothers throughout the world are undergoing the same kind of sufferings.

—1 PETER 5:8–9, emphasis added

How can we stay alert and resist the devil? Here are three key suggestions:

1. Follow Jesus's Example

We can learn from what Jesus did when Satan tempted Him.

Then Jesus was led by the Spirit into the desert to be tempted by the devil. After fasting forty days and forty nights, he was hungry. The tempter came to him and said, "If you are the Son of God, tell these stones to become bread." Jesus answered, *"It is written: 'Man does not live on bread alone, but on every word that comes from the mouth of God.'"*

Then the devil took him to the holy city and had him stand on the highest point of the temple. "If you are the Son of God," he said, "throw yourself down. For it is written: 'He will command his angels concerning you, and they will lift you up in their hands, so that you will not strike your foot against a stone.'" Jesus answered him, *"It is also written: 'Do not put the Lord your God to the test.'"*

Again, the devil took him to a very high mountain and showed him all the kingdoms of the world and their splendor. "All this I will give you," he said, "if you will bow down and worship me." Jesus said to him, *"Away from me, Satan! For it is written: 'Worship the Lord your God, and serve him only.'"* Then the devil left him, and angels came and attended him.

—MATTHEW 4:1–11, emphasis added

Each time the devil tempted Jesus, He resisted the devil by using the Word of God: "It is written...it is written...it is written." Even though He was the Son of God, He used no supernatural powers, but simply proclaimed God's truth. He showed us that we too can overcome temptation by the power of the Word of God. We must commit ourselves to know God's Word and His truth in our hearts and our daily lives so we can use it, too, when temptation comes.

2. Stay out of compromising situations

When we face difficult choices in our lives, we need to ask ourselves, "Is it constructive?" "Is it good?" We need to be focused on what is good and pure (Phil. 4:8). I agree with what Steve Russo wrote in his book *Halloween*:

> Not everything is constructive. God has given each one of us a free will and the freedom to choose. Knowing how far to exercise this liberty can sometimes be difficult to discern, especially in the things that the Bible is silent upon as to being right or wrong. The apostle Paul addressed this issue with the Corinthian church: "Everything is permissible, but not everything is beneficial (1 Corinthians 10:23). As Christians, we must exercise our freedom in such a way to build up our spiritual life and to encourage others. We must be careful when it comes to questionable things, the gray areas of life that are not specifically forbidden in the Bible."[2]

We must be careful that we do not set ourselves up for failure by putting ourselves in a compromising situation where we will be tempted in an area of weakness. Even if we think we are strong, the devil is swift and cunning and can attack us at any given moment. For example, a recovering alcoholic knows that he or she should not hang out in a bar or near a liquor store.

Because the first two days of my menstruation affects my mood swings and makes me more emotionally vulnerable, I purposely avoid attending any engagement that may give the enemy an advantage against me. This helps to protect me from saying and doing things that may hurt others. I have learned this the hard way, and I am thankful that I have been restored to those I have offended as I confessed my wrongs against them and asked their forgiveness.

> You, my brothers, were called to be free. But do not use your freedom to indulge the sinful nature; rather, serve one another in love.
> —GALATIANS 5:13

3. Daily put on the "whole armor of God" and pray!

After my much needed healing retreat, God showed me that I must *always* be mindful that we are in "The Battle Zone" and I must continually be equipped to fight in the battle. Satan knows our weaknesses, and he uses them against us to make us ineffective in our service for the Lord. Extra caution is required for any masks that are unveiled because this is where he will keep attacking. To avoid injury in the spiritual warfare in which we are involved, we must daily put on the "whole armor of God" (Eph. 6:11, NKJV). This includes fervent prayers. Each time you pray, the enemy shudders because he knows the power of prayers. Read more on this in Chapter 16, "We Put On the Armor of God" and the section on "Continuous Prayers."

GOD HEALS OUR WOUNDS

No one is invincible. The stronger we think we are, the more vulnerable we are to an attack by the enemy. Our pride, arrogance, and self-reliance take God out the picture and leave us without the strength He gives us by the Holy Spirit. Into this void, the devil comes to play with our minds and penetrate and divide our hearts. He casts his lies telling us that God has abandoned us and we don't need God. If we listen to the enemy's lies, we will lose hope. We will lose our faith in God and His promises, and that's exactly what Satan wants us to believe.

Fortunately for us, God will never abandon us. His promises will never fail. He has given us a security deposit—His Holy Spirit—and we need to live and be led by the Holy Spirit.

> So then, brothers [and sisters], we are debtors, not to the flesh, to live according to the flesh. For if you live according to the flesh you will die, but if by the Spirit you put to death the deeds of the body, you will live.
> —ROMANS 8:12–13, ESV

When we listen to the enemy's lies and are wounded by them, the Holy Spirit, who lives in our hearts, is grieved. He groans within us, and we may experience an uneasy feeling that something is wrong. When this happens and God convicts us of sin, we must retreat to a place where we can repent and renounce any lies that are against God's will for our lives. This will enable healing to begin.

Jesus Christ bore our pains and our wounds when He was crucified on the cross. He died for all our sins—past, present, and future. He knows that we are not perfect—if we were, we would not need a Savior. Praise God that He forgives all who are willing to come to Him for healing. We need to receive healing for our hearts because our hearts matter to God. "For I will restore health to you, and your wounds I will heal, declares the LORD" (Jer. 30:17, ESV).

We are saved through God's love, mercy, and grace. Nothing we can do will change that because God has already done it all. God has special plans for each of us. He created each of us to do good works, and He is preparing us for the spiritual battles we face. We just need to rest and receive healing from God who will strengthen us with

His power to face the evil lies and works of the enemy. The following verses remind us of God's gracious provision to heal us:

> But because of his great love for us, God, who is rich in mercy, made us alive with Christ even when we were dead in transgressions—*it is by grace you have been saved.*
> —Ephesians 2:4–5, emphasis added

> *For it is by grace you have been saved, through faith—and this not from yourselves, it is the gift of God*—not by works, so that no one can boast. For we are God's workmanship, created in Christ Jesus to do good works, which God prepared in advance for us to do.
> —Ephesians 2:8–10, emphasis added

> We were under great pressure, far beyond our ability to endure, so that we despaired even of life.... This happened that we might *not rely on ourselves but on God, who raises the dead.*
> —2 Corinthians 1:8–9, emphasis added

God healed my heart when it was broken, shattered to pieces by the enemy. I briefly tell about this in the following excerpt from the daily journal I kept when I went on my healing retreat:

> *Day 4: Healing*
> *...I know that the battle is already won for Christ, but my flesh is being tempted by Satan to go away from Jesus. I need to equip and arm myself with the full armor of God daily, or I'll be wounded. I know that this morning if I had spent time in meditation with You, Lord, and put on my armor first, the enemy would not have been able to penetrate my heart. My heart was not protected and hence the enemy saw and went for my weak spot. But You were there,*

Lord, when I prayed for help and strength, and You healed me. Thank You, Lord, for this. This is when I know that You are so real—when I am vulnerable and in my weakest state, when I've fallen and I can't get up, You pick me up and give me the will and strength to live.

Heal me, O LORD, and I shall be healed; save me, and I shall be saved, for you are my praise.

—JEREMIAH 17:14, ESV

GOD PRESCRIBES "GOOD MEDICINE"

When we are wounded on the battlefield, we need medicine to help in the healing process. Proverbs 17:22 speaks about this when it says, "A cheerful heart is good medicine, but a crushed spirit dries up the bones." Since this is true, we must learn how to make our hearts cheerful. The Bible has given us the following prescription:

Spiritual Food

God instructs us to feed in His Word daily to receive spiritual nourishment. Just as we must eat the proper natural food to be physically healthy and strong, we must also receive the right balance of biblical truth to be spiritually healthy. We may be tempted to rush into our daily devotions and quickly read God's Word only because it is *expected* of us. However, God desires that we come to Him with the right motives in our hearts, to read His Word because we want to hear, learn, and be refined and refreshed by Him. We will receive healing and strength as we ask God to guide us and speak to us through His Holy Spirit before we read His Word. As you consider these things, you may find it helpful to review the section "Making God Our Focus" in Chapter 7.

Living Water

We need to drink "spiritual liquid" and lots of it. This spiritual liquid is the water that Jesus promises to give us, the life He wants us to live so that we will never thirst. It is the *living water*—the Holy Spirit—that will strengthen us and guide us. Just as we must drink natural water to be physically refreshed, we must drink the living water to be spiritually refreshed. We can drink more of this *living water* when we are filled with the Holy Spirit.

To be filled with the Holy Spirit, we must yield our lives to His control and allow Him to lead us. We can surrender to our old natural self or we can surrender to the control of the Holy Spirit. If we are not continually filled with the Holy Spirit, we will do things out of our old self and our own strength. We will grieve and quench the Holy Spirit. We may also quench the Spirit when we neglect to pray, witness, read the Word of God, or ignore the Holy Spirit's promptings in our life.

Because the Holy Spirit lives in our hearts, we need to protect and guard our hearts. We can only be filled with the Holy Spirit if we confess and repent of any sin that is blocking Him from working inside of us. When we try to do things out of our strength, we will become tired, burned out, and even spiritually depressed. However, when we are filled with the Holy Spirit, we have the power of God in us and we are able to win any battles. We are able to live more effectively for God and give glory to Him.

> Do not get drunk on wine, which leads to debauchery. Instead, be filled with the Spirit.
>
> —Ephesians 5:18

Prayer

God calls us to pray. We are to confess and repent of anything that blocks the Holy Spirit from working in our lives. We are to pray for help and strength from God and for protection against the enemy. And we are to give thanks for all circumstances so that our hearts will be equipped to trust in the sovereignty of God. You can read more about the importance of this in the section "Continuous Prayers" in Chapter 16.

God's promises

When we feel depressed or defeated, we need to remember His precious promises. Here are a few:

> Never will I leave you; never will I forsake you.
> —HEBREWS 13:5

> Come to me, all you who are weary and burdened, and I will give you rest. Take my yoke upon you and learn from me, for I am gentle and humble in heart, and you will find rest for your souls. For my yoke is easy and my burden is light.
> —MATTHEW 11:28–30

> Peace I leave with you; my peace I give you. I do not give to you as the world gives. Do not let your hearts be troubled and do not be afraid.
> —JOHN 14:27

> But thanks be to God! He gives us the victory through our Lord Jesus Christ. Therefore, my dear brothers, stand firm. Let nothing move you. Always give yourselves fully to the work of the Lord, because you know that your labor in the Lord is not in vain.
> —1 CORINTHIANS 15:57–58

> But we are not of those who shrink back and are destroyed, but of those who believe and are saved.
> —HEBREWS 10:39

Now it is God who makes both us and you stand firm in Christ. He anointed us, set his seal of ownership on us, and put his Spirit in our hearts as a deposit, guaranteeing what is to come.

—2 CORINTHIANS 1:21–22

Rejoice in the Lord always. I will say it again: Rejoice! Let your gentleness be evident to all. The Lord is near. Do not be anxious about anything, but in everything, by prayer and petition, with thanksgiving, present your requests to God. And the peace of God, which transcends all understanding, will guard your hearts and your minds in Christ Jesus

—PHILIPPIANS 4:4–7

For God did not give us a spirit of timidity, but a spirit of power, of love and of self-discipline.

—2 TIMOTHY 1:7

AN INSIGHTFUL CHALLENGE

Do you frequently find yourself battling with everyday things? Do circumstances around you affect the way you behave? Have you ever asked God to help you with the struggles in your heart and your battles with the enemy? Do you feel vulnerable and the enemy seems to be always one step ahead of you? Has your heart been wounded too many times, and you feel that it will never heal? Do you feel more like a "casualty of war" rather than a "wounded soldier"? Do you realize that you have the power to resist the devil through Christ? God will never abandon you. Even if you falter, He gives you time to rest and prepares you to become a better warrior for Him. Submit yourself to God. Allow God to equip you with His power and wisdom to overcome your own inner battles and the enemy's scheming tactics.

> Submit yourselves, then, to God. Resist the devil, and he will flee from you.
>
> —JAMES 4:7

16

We Put On the Armor of God

Finally, be strong in the Lord and in the strength of his might. Put on the whole armor of God, that you may be able to stand against the schemes of the devil.
—EPHESIANS 6:10-11, ESV

THE APOSTLE PAUL, writing in Ephesians 6:12-18, exhorted us to prepare for spiritual warfare by putting on protective gear that will keep us from being wounded in the battle. Paul had lots of opportunity to analyze the armor of the Roman soldiers who guarded him in his prison cell, and he depicted "the whole armor of God" as that which a Roman soldier would wear into battle. In this chapter, we will examine each of the following pieces of the armor God has provided to equip us for battle:

- The belt of truth
- The breastplate of righteousness
- The shoes of peace
- The shield of faith
- The helmet of salvation
- The sword of the Spirit
- Continuous prayers

THE "BELT OF TRUTH"

Stand therefore, having fastened on the belt of truth.
—EPHESIANS 6:14, ESV

The belt was worn around the waist of a Roman soldier to support and hold his clothing gear together. It was usually worn loose on non-battle days. When the Roman soldier was preparing for battle, he tied his belt tightly around him. His belt was very important because it held his sheath, which stored his sword when it was not in use.

We need to equip ourselves with the belt of truth so that we can be victorious over Satan's lies and deception. The belt of truth houses our spiritual weapons—prayers, praise, and the Word of God, which is the sword of the Spirit. We need to gird ourselves with God's belt of truth to be prepared for our spiritual battles. In other words, we need to live in God's truth with honesty and integrity so we can defeat Satan.

First Peter 1:13 tells us to "prepar[e] your minds for action" (ESV). New King James translates it: "gird up the loins of your mind." In the English Standard Version, the same word translated *minds* in 1 Peter 1:13 is translated *belt* in Ephesians 6:14. In both verses, the context is the same. We are to walk in truth and righteousness, preparing to go when Christ returns. Our minds must be saturated in God's truth.

My brother Chi, a history buff on wars and battle gear, has told me that belts were not issued at random to the Roman soldiers. Each soldier carefully chose his own belt according to his own taste, budget, and wealth. Since we are wealthy in Christ, we can go forth to battle with a richly truthful lifestyle and display our riches in Christ to the world.

In Chapter 4, "The Mask of Honesty," I shared a journal excerpt that included my confession that I have told some little white lies. If we overlook the small lies in our lives, they will compound into a bigger lie and the enemy will take advantage of us. Our lives must be built according to God's standard of truth. We cannot make things up and justify our actions to make them seem right. White is white, and black is black. There is no grey. A lie is a lie. Truth is God's truth, and it is pure. The truth may hurt, but it protects and brings fairness to everyone.

I fell into spiritual depression because of the lies I had believed about myself. These lies, which were the masks I wore for many years, started as something small, like saying I was happy about someone else's success when I was deeply jealous inside. However, each time I lied, I abandoned God's belt of truth. My lies blocked God's truth and the Holy Spirit from working in my life, and Satan attacked and used my masks against me.

The belt of truth equips us to be truthful with God, others, and ourselves so that we can be sanctified—set apart from the world to fulfill God's purpose. (See John 17:15–19.) We cannot be sanctified if we are dishonest and hypocritical. However, if we stay focused on God's truth, we will not be lured into the sins that would entangle us.

As we gird ourselves with the belt of truth, we allow the Holy Spirit to give us wisdom and discernment to recognize Satan's evil tactics against us. (See Hebrews 4:12.) The Holy Spirit is the Spirit of truth, who provides strong leadership and guidance for us. As Jesus said, "But when he, the Spirit of truth, comes, he will guide you into all truth. He will not speak on his own; he will speak only what he hears, and he will tell you what is yet to come" (John 16:13).

It is so important that we ask God to reveal all our hidden lies so that we can renounce them. To truly live in freedom, we must be honest and true. Jesus said, "You will know the truth, and the truth will set you free" (John 8:32).

> For your love is ever before me, and I walk continually in your truth.
>
> —PSALM 26:3

The "Breastplate of Righteousness"

...and having put on the breastplate of righteousness.
—Ephesians 6:14, esv

The breastplate was the piece of armor that the Roman soldier wore to protect his heart and his back, if the enemy attacked from behind. *The Nelson Study Bible: New King James Version* describes it this way: "The breastplate of Roman times went completely around the body, so that the back of a warrior was also protected. The breastplate was made of metal."[1]

We need the breastplate of righteousness because none of us is righteous in the sight of God. "There is no one righteous, not even one" (Rom. 3:10). The good news is that God, through His loving grace, sent His son Jesus Christ to die for our sins and our unrighteousness. When we accept by faith that Jesus redeems us, His righteousness is imputed to us.

> This righteousness from God comes through faith in Jesus Christ to all who believe. There is no difference, for all have sinned and fall short of the glory of God, and are justified freely by his grace through the redemption that came by Christ Jesus.
>
> —Romans 3:22–24

As I considered the complete protective covering provided by the breastplate of righteousness, I recalled something I learned when I worked for a chocolate manufacturer. In one of the production processes, nuts are entirely enrobed in chocolate to make them sweet. To put on the breastplate of righteousness is similar, for our lives are *enrobed* in the righteousness of Jesus Christ. We who were not righteous are made righteous—sweet because of Christ!

In addition to imputing Christ's righteousness to us when we believe, God calls each of us to obey the gospel and live in submission to Christ. It is not good enough for us to just hear and know of God's saving grace. We must also act in obedience by faith. "For it is not those who hear the law who are righteous in God's sight, but it is those who obey the law who will be declared righteous" (Romans 2:13). (See also Romans 3:20.) We are not saved by works but our actions show that we are saved. (See James 2:21–23.)

When we don the breastplate of righteousness, we believe by faith that we can live righteously in Christ because of what He has done for us. We know that we can walk in integrity and goodness because of what Jesus has accomplished. We need to be mindful of the intentions of our hearts and take care that we serve God in humility through Christ's righteousness. We need to remember that we do not do things in our righteousness, but in the righteousness and powerful name of Jesus who is the King of kings!

> Righteousness from God comes through faith in Jesus Christ to all who believe.
>
> —ROMANS 3:22

THE "SHOES OF PEACE"

> ...and, as shoes for your feet, having put on the readiness given by the gospel of peace.
>
> —EPHESIANS 6:15, ESV

In her book *The Heartache No One Sees*, Sheila's Walsh encourages her readers to be ready for battle. She writes the following about the shoes of peace:

Once the breastplate was fitted into position, a soldier would put on his strong army boots. When they were off duty, the soldiers wore sandals, but for battle, especially in winter, they

wore strong, thick boots that ensured a solid footing. Histo-
rians have attributed the military successes of Alexander the
Great and of Julius Caesar to the fact that their armies were
equipped with such heavy boots; therefore, they could march
day after day over rough territory.[2]

Just as the proper footwear protected the Roman soldier, the peace
of God through Jesus Christ is footwear that protects us as we trod
through the enemy's ground. It keeps us from stumbling or allowing
the enemy to gain a foothold in our lives. What is "the gospel of
peace"? Some say that it is being ready always to share the gospel,
the message of salvation by grace through faith in Christ. From the
context, however, it more likely refers to our standing as those who
have peace with God because of the gospel. This peace is achieved
because the gospel unites us to God and also with one another. (See
Ephesians 2:11–19.)

We have sure footing because we stand on the gospel of peace, a
strong foundation that is sure and secure. But we do much more than
stand. The shoes of peace make us ready to push forward and take the
offensive in battle. We can advance with sure footing in our spiritual
strides because we have peace—not war—with God. He is on our side!
"If God is for us, who can be against us?" (Rom. 8:31). We were once
enemies of God, but now we are reconciled to Him (Rom. 5:10; Eph.
2:16). God gives the shoes of peace so we can do battle for Him as an
ambassador for Christ.

Because of my disability, it is very important for me to have good,
stable footwear that provides comfort when I walk. I recall when
God broke my pride, and I went to have my feet fitted for custom
orthotics. This special raised insole is placed inside a shoe to provide
stability and comfort in walking. Initially my foot ached when I used
my new orthotics, but I gradually noticed a significant difference in

my walk. I was even able to walk longer distances without my ankles and legs tiring out.

My disability also requires that I guard against slipping and falling when I walk on a spill or a wet spot. To help me do this, I have a shoe repairman adhere a skid-proof material to the bottom of my shoes. If I must do this to have the proper physical shoes, how much more important it is for me to have the proper "spiritual shoes" that will keep me from slipping when I walk on dangerous battle grounds!

The best part of the shoes of peace is that we do not have to change them for different occasions. We all have shoes of peace that we can wear daily, and we can be confident and walk solidly in them! However, just as it was with my custom orthotics, we can walk more effectively the more we wear them. In Chapter 12, "The Mask of Optimism," I warned against being worried or afraid. If we let the enemy deceive us this way, we will lose our footing. We will be so consumed with our problems that we are not effective in our spiritual combat for God.

When I think of our battle gear that will help us in our spiritual battles, it makes total sense that we are to have our feet fitted with the shoes of peace. Jesus promised, "Peace I leave with you; my peace I give you. I do not give to you as the world gives. Do not let your hearts be troubled and do not be afraid" (John 14:27). When we believe the gospel and trust God daily, we have the personal, inner peace that will enable us to keep our footing in our daily spiritual battles.

And the peace of God, which transcends all understanding, will guard your hearts and your minds in Christ Jesus.

—PHILIPPIANS 4:7

The "Shield of Faith"

In all circumstances take up the shield of faith, with which
you can extinguish all the flaming darts of the evil one.
—Ephesians 6:16, esv

The shield, one of the most important pieces of the Roman soldier's armor, protected the bearer from all sorts of attacks. Soldiers sometimes protected themselves from volleys of their enemy's arrows by crouching behind a large shield. According to Max Anders in his *New Christian's Handbook*, "The surface of these large shields was either metal or leather over wood soaked in water, which could repel or withstand flaming arrows from the enemies."[3]

Paul wrote that our shield of faith will not only deflect and protect us from anything the enemy throws our way, but it also "can extinguish *all* the flaming darts of the evil one" (Eph. 6:16, esv, emphasis added). That's a lot of protection from one shield! It is so important that we have a strong shield of faith to hold up against anything the enemy throws at us. We *do* have such a shield as we walk close to God by hiding His Word in our hearts and worshiping Him and praying continually.

Bill and I recently bought a new deck of cards for our daughter Kayli. These cards are unique because their facings have the coats of arms and the flags of all the Canadian Provinces, as well as geography and heritage facts. Each coat of arms displays the different symbols that were used on shields and flags when soldiers engaged in battles in the olden days. Most of the heraldry has lion or crown designs that speak of strength just as the lion symbolizes the king of beasts. The emblems would remind the soldiers who they were fighting for, and they carried them into battle with great honor.

I was so excited to learn about the heraldic arms and mottoes of the Provinces because they depict what each Province believed in. God, in His sovereignty, inspired past leaders to choose our country and provincial mottoes to give Him honor and glory. For example, the card deck identified the motto for Newfoundland and Labrador as "Seek Ye First the Kingdom of God,"[4] a phrase from Matthew 6:33, KJV. And when I did research on the history behind Canada's motto, I was happy to learn that my country's motto, *A Mari usque ad Mare*—Latin for "from sea to sea," was based on Psalm 72:8, (KJV), "He shall have dominion also from sea to sea, and from the river unto the ends of the earth."[5]

When I think of the shield of faith, I choose Psalm 28:7 as my motto: "The LORD is my strength and my shield; my heart trusts in Him, and I am helped." This reminds me that no matter how difficult the conditions of the battle may be, the almighty God, my Lord and also my Father in heaven, will always protect me. I will trust that He is sovereign and that He intends His best for me. I will be strong, knowing that He is right beside me to shelter me. I am reminded of God's faithful promise to Joshua, "Be strong and courageous. Do not be terrified; do not be discouraged, for the LORD your God will be with you wherever you go" (Joshua 1:9).

Can you visualize a soldier under heavy attack? The only way he can protect himself is to lift up his shield to block the enemy's bombardment. I remember dark times when I was under heavy attack. I felt that I had lost my sense of purpose, and it seemed that God was so far away. I was afraid I would lose everything. The enemy would not let up—he knew how weak I was and kept shooting his "fiery darts" (Eph. 6:16, NKJV) and piercing my heart. I was weak, and yet something stronger—God Himself—was helping me. I can't explain it, but I remember experiencing it.

God is the shield for our lives. Without Him as our shield, we would be crushed completely. God does not want us to be hurt and He gives us the weapons we need. However, we must pick them up and keep them with us. It would be foolish for a Roman soldier to go into battle without carrying his shield. He would only do that if he was overconfident in his own abilities or lost his shield during combat. Similarly, when we trust in our own abilities and not in the power of God, we will be without protection. Only our faith in the one and only powerful God will save us.

We must always be on guard and "take up the shield of faith" in "all circumstances" (Eph. 6:16, ESV) because the devil shoots his fiery darts at us at all times. It is important to remember that God is our shield (Gen. 15:1; Ps. 18:2). Our shield of faith is simply trusting in who God is. We must believe God's promises and trust in His truth. Our weak faith may change with our feelings, but God is always faithful. He will never change, and He is able to keep us safe. He is mighty and powerful, and He is able to deliver us. Let us keep our faith in God not in ourselves!

> Every word of God is flawless; he is a shield to those who take refuge in him.
>
> —Proverbs 30:5

The "Helmet of Salvation"

...and take the helmet of salvation.

—Ephesians 6:17, ESV

The Roman soldier wore a helmet to protect his head from injury as he fought in the battle. As we fight in the spiritual battles we face, we must wear the helmet of salvation to receive protection from thoughts the enemy may use against us. When I think of the helmet of salvation, I am reminded that God has promised salvation to us because of what Christ completed on the cross. He covers and protects our heads—our minds and our thoughts—by His strength and His deliverance for us. We can agree with the psalmist David, "O God the Lord, the strength of my salvation, You have covered my head in the day of battle" (Psalm 140:7, NKJV).

In addition to providing protection, the helmet of the Roman soldier was designed to make him look tall and noble. As soldiers in God's army, the helmet of salvation is a source of identity that we are victors through Christ. Because we wear the helmet of salvation, we can stand firm and believe the truth of God's love for us, even if the enemy tries to use our minds and thoughts against us. We are "more than conquerors" through Christ. As we do battle, we can claim God's truth and His promise that absolutely nothing will separate us from His love.

> In all these things *we are more than conquerors through him who loved us.* For I am convinced that neither death nor life, neither angels nor demons, neither the present nor the future, nor any powers, neither height nor depth, nor anything else in all creation, will be able to separate us from the love of God that is in Christ Jesus our Lord.
>
> —ROMANS 8:37–39, emphasis added

I wear many different hats—and I am referring to *real* hats. Kayli's classmates call me the "Hat Lady" because I always wear a hat when I pick her up from school. I have acquired a variety of hats for two reasons. First, wearing hats helps protect my head from the different weather elements, such as heat, rain, snow, and cold weather. Just as I wear a different hat to protect my head from different weather elements, I don my helmet of salvation to protect my mind from different attacks and lies of the enemy and even from my own self-condemnation.

And second, I feel more complete if I wear a hat. It feels strange if I go outdoors without a hat. In a similar way, when we put on our helmet of salvation, we place our trust in God for our salvation and protection. We do not have confidence in our emotions or abilities, but in the hope of salvation through Christ Jesus.

Let us be self-controlled, putting on faith and love as a breastplate, and the hope of salvation as a helmet. For God did not
appoint us to suffer wrath but to receive salvation through
our Lord Jesus Christ. He died for us so that, whether we are
awake or asleep, we may live together with him. Therefore
encourage one another and build each other up.
—1 Thessalonians 5:8–11

The Lord is my light and my salvation—whom shall I fear?
—Psalm 27:1

The "Sword of the Spirit"

...and the sword of the Spirit, which is the word of God.
—Ephesians 6:17, esv

My brother Chi, who was fascinated with swords when we were
growing up, has told me that the swords used by the Roman soldiers
were really heavy. Because of this, a soldier would require good
training to be able to wield his sword with one hand. While today's
collectors may acquire swords for decorative purposes or for display,
the sword of the Roman soldier was made for use in battle. When
used properly, it was a lethal weapon.

The sword of the Spirit—the Word of God—is an offensive weapon.
We go into spiritual battle and fight the enemy with the power of the
Word of God. Actually it is God who fights for us; without the Spirit
wielding the sword for us, we would lose. As we look to God's Word
and respond to Satan's lies with Scripture, the Spirit gives us victory.
Satan and his evil cohorts will leave us alone because they cannot
fight against the power of God.

When Jesus was tempted by Satan in the wilderness, He resisted
Satan by declaring God's Word. (See Matthew 4:3–11.) He showed by
His example that we must wield the sword of Spirit when the enemy

attacks us. We too must fight back by audibly declaring the Word of God. When we are spiritually attacked, we can speak aloud our promise in Hebrews 13:5, NKJV, "It is written that God has promised me He will never leave me nor forsake me, in the power and in the name of Jesus Christ—leave me alone Satan and stop making me feel this way!"

The sword of the Spirit, our standard for truth and integrity, is housed in its sheath in the belt of truth. We claim and declare God's Word—His truth—to protect us and to attack the enemy. Just as the soldier needs to be trained to wield his sword properly; we must be intimate with God, grounded in His Word, so we can use Scripture appropriately and effectively. We can be victorious in battle as we speak and use God's Word at the right time in the right way.

> For the word of God is living and active. Sharper than any double-edged sword.
>
> —HEBREWS 4:12

"CONTINUOUS PRAYERS"

> And pray in the Spirit on all occasions with all kinds of prayers and requests. With this in mind, be alert and always keep on praying for all the saints.
>
> —EPHESIANS 6:18

Continuous prayer is vital part of putting on the armor of God and being victorious in the spiritual warfare we face. This truth is often illustrated in the history of Israel, and we find one example of this in 1 Chronicles 5:18–22. These verses tell how chosen men of the Reubenites, the Gadites, and the half-tribe of Manasseh were led to battle against their enemies and submitted themselves to God in prayer. They showed reverence to God and put their reliance on Him, not their own abilities. Because they trusted in God, He answered their prayers and gave them victory.

> They were helped in fighting them, and God handed the Hagrites and all their allies over to them, because they cried out to him during the battle. *He answered their prayers, because they trusted in him.*
> —1 Chronicles 5:20, emphasis added

Second Chronicles 20 presents King Jehoshaphat as one who was humble in prayer and showed reliance on God to fight the enemy. He gathered the entire nation together for a huge prayer meeting before God (see 2 Chronicles 20:1–30) and then displayed an attitude of trust in God even as the army went into battle. Scripture says that he "appointed men to sing to the Lord and to praise him" with the refrain, "Give thanks to the Lord, for his love endures forever" (2 Chron. 20:21).

What a beautiful sight to envision—a group of people singing and praising God as they led an army into battle. God blessed King Jehoshaphat for his humility and faith; He caused Judah's enemies to turn against each other, and by the time the army of Judah got to the battlefield, its enemies had already destroyed each other. What an amazing triumph and victory Judah had that day!

God's power to intervene on our behalf when we pray is exactly the same for us in the battles we face. If we are in right relationship with God, our prayers and our trust in God's power will defeat Satan and his demons that battle against our minds and hearts. God will thwart Satan and his evil schemes. Regardless of our circumstances, we can pray to our mighty God and praise Him. Indeed let us "Give thanks to the Lord, for his love endures forever" (2 Chron. 20:21).

When bad things happen to us, we sometimes forget to turn to God in prayer. Instead, we rely on ourselves or ask others to help us first. However, we should first turn to God because He is our source of strength. If we become confident in our own abilities and fail to pray to God, we will suffer defeat, even if we are wearing our full armor gear. Prayer is not a magical formula to help us win, it is an inward and outward sign that we are placing our faith and reliance on God to give us victory. When we pray, we humble ourselves and show our total reliance in our living God.

In the New Testament, Jesus taught the great importance of using prayer to fight the enemy when He warned his disciples in the Garden of Gethsemane to keep praying. Too often we are like the disciples who fell asleep. Many times our inner and external battles are so great that we give up and are exhausted from our despair. We forget to "get up and pray so that [we] will not fall into temptation" (Luke 22:46).

The night before He was crucified, Jesus prayed for his disciples and for us. "My prayer is not that you take them out of the world," He said, "but that you protect them from the evil one" (John 17:15). We can learn from Christ's example to pray for others so that God will protect them from the evil one. Our prayers must be continuous not only for ourselves but for all the saints.

If you believe, you will receive whatever you ask for in prayer.
—MATTHEW 21:22

BE DRESSED AND READY

As we consider the armor God has provided for us, we must be vigilant to equip ourselves for the spiritual battles we face. One way we can do this is to put on the full armor of God as we prepare ourselves for the day ahead. To help you do this, I offer the following confessions and prayers for you to speak audibly or pray in your heart as you get dressed each morning:

Belting or buttoning your trousers or skirt: *I am putting on God's belt of truth.*

Buttoning or zipping up a top or a jacket: *I am enrobed in Jesus Christ's righteousness and will walk in His way.*

Brushing your hair, adding a hair accessory, or putting on a hat or cap: *I am wearing my helmet of salvation as Christ's protection for my mind and my thoughts.*

Putting on your slippers or shoes: *I am grounded in the gospel of peace.*

Picking up your purse, briefcase, or bag or putting on your watch or glasses: *I am taking my shield of faith with me.*

Putting on a necklace, or picking up the keys to your house and your car: *I have the sword of the Spirit and am ready to apply God's promises and truth.*

As you begin your day's activities or leave the house, pray: *Lord, I am wearing your whole armor. Protect me from the enemy. I trust in You.*

When we consciously don the whole armor of God on, we are saying that we are confident to fight our daily spiritual battles—not in our flesh, but in the power and strength of God. It is the Lord who fights for us!

> Finally, be strong in the Lord and in the strength of his might. Put on the whole armor of God, that you may be able to stand against the schemes of the devil.
> —EPHESIANS 6:10–11, ESV

A PRAYER FOR STRENGTH IN THE BATTLE

We all have times when we feel especially weak in the battles we are facing. Perhaps the following prayer will strengthen your faith to release the ministry of God's victorious presence and power in your life:

Lord, forgive me when I feel inadequate to serve You, forgive me when I listen to Satan's lies instead of Your Spirit. Lord, help me not to get trapped in my enemy's snares. Satan sends his troops and surrounds me and I feel defeated. My heart needs healing. Lord, I even fight within myself, battling my old selfish ways. Lord, I know that I am not defeated because You have promised in Your word that nothing can separate me from Your love. You have sent your angels to guard me, and I have the power of Your Holy Spirit.

Help me, Lord, to put on my full armor each day, so that I can fight the enemy's attacks and my old nature, which tries to creep in. Lord, help me gird myself with Your belt of truth, and put on the breastplate of righteousness You have provided to protect my heart from the enemy. I stand firm on Your gospel of peace, and lift up the shield of faith in You. Lord, help me to defeat the enemy with the sword of the Spirit, which is Your Word.

Lord, I am reminded that my struggle is not against flesh and blood, but against the rulers, against the powers, against the world forces of this darkness, and against the spiritual forces of wickedness in the heavenly places.

Thank you, Lord, for sending Your angels to help me and for Your precious Word and the empowerment of Your Holy Spirit. I know, O Lord, that Jesus is on my side, I shall not be afraid, because Jesus Christ has already defeated the enemy and triumphed over evil. Help me, O Lord, to come boldly before You and do the task You have set before me. I will not be afraid to do anything, for You have chosen me to serve in Your mission. Lord, thank you for choosing me to be Your child. I pray for all these things, in the name and power of my Lord Jesus Christ, Amen.

Remember the Lord, who is great and awesome, and fight.

—Nehemiah 4:14

An Insightful Challenge

Do you know the role you play in spiritual warfare? How equipped are you daily? What must you do now to stand firm at the end? Are you ready to fight by faith? Intend to allow God to use you. God has equipped you to fight, and He promises to give you victory. Yield to Him today! Let God fight your Battles!

This is what the Lord says to you: 'Do not be afraid or discouraged...For the battle is not yours, but God's.'

—2 Chronicles 20:15

Conclusion

And we, who with unveiled faces all reflect the Lord's glory,
are being transformed into his likeness with ever-increasing
glory, which comes from the Lord, who is the Spirit.
—2 CORINTHIANS 3:18

WHAT IS THE fruit of unveiling our masks? What benefits does God graciously give us? The enemy wants us to feel naked and ashamed, as Adam and Eve did when they disobeyed God. He has deceived all of us, like our first parents, to wear masks and cover our true selves because we do not want God or other people to see the real us. However, God does not intend for us to live in shame. He wants us to be what I call "naked in the truth" so we can enjoy the freedom of living in Christ.

> But whenever anyone turns to the Lord, the veil is taken away. Now the Lord is the Spirit, and where the Spirit of the Lord is, there is freedom.
> —2 CORINTHIANS 3:16–17

God gave His Son Jesus Christ to ransom us from sin and its penalty and restore us to Himself. God wants us to remove our masks, to be naked before Him, and to enjoy the freedom of living in Christ and reflecting His glory. When we take off our masks, we allow God's Spirit to work in us and through us. We can truly with "unveiled faces" reflect God's glory as we are transformed into His likeness (2 Cor. 3:18).

Let us not be like the Israelites who kept their hearts veiled even when they read God's truth. (See 2 Corinthians 3:14–15.) God does not want us to hide behind our veils and be what others expect us to be. As we uncover our veils through Christ's power, He releases us to grow into all He has for us. In these concluding pages of this book, I identify seven ways this happens.

WE RECOGNIZE THE TRUTH

My daughter, Kayli, and I have enjoyed reading the Hans Christian Andersen classic, "The Emperor's New Clothes."[1] In this story, a proud, vain emperor with a passion for dressing up and flaunting himself was deceived by two impostor weavers to invest in their most beautiful cloth imaginable. They claimed that their cloth was not only uncommonly beautiful but it also had a special property that made it invisible to anyone who was not fit for his job, or who was unpardonably stupid.

Each royal servant was asked to inspect how the weavers were progressing on the emperor's garment; and each one, although they could not see anything, did not want to admit that they were not fit for office, or, worse yet, that they were stupid. So everyone pretended that the garments being woven were unimaginably beautiful, as the weavers continued their charade of weaving and cutting their invisible cloth.

When the garment was completed, the emperor's worst nightmare came true as he discovered that he could see nothing. However, he did not want to admit to anyone that he was not fit to be emperor or that he was unpardonably stupid. As the emperor lied and even boasted about how splendid his garment was, he was actually standing naked—OK, maybe in his royal undergarments—before his court.

The absurdity of it all was obvious when all the courts men and townsfolk exclaimed how gorgeous the emperor was as he showed off his new special garment in a procession! Even the chamberlains who held the emperor's train pretended to lift and hold the garment in the air! No one wanted to disclose that they could not see anything, for fear they would be unfit for their position and risk being known as stupid.

Finally, however, a little boy's voice rang over the noise of the foolish crowd, "But the emperor has nothing on!"

"Just listen to that innocent child," the father said.

Now, however, the people started to whisper to one another, until they all burst out, "But he has nothing on!" The moment of truth had been revealed for everyone. Although, the emperor realized that they were right and that indeed he had been fooled, he still walked back with his chamberlains in the procession with his head held up even more uprightly. Everyone knew that they had all been fooled.

We may laugh at the absurdity and foolishness of the emperor and his subjects, but we tend to behave the same way in similar circumstances. No one wants to admit that anything is wrong. The truth does not mean as much as what others may think of us. We tend to keep the truth to ourselves because we don't want to appear foolish and outside of the norm. We want to fit in.

However, when we try to hide the truth, we are actually fooling ourselves. We are fools when we don't embrace the real truth of what is happening. We may keep God's truth to ourselves because we do not want others to think negatively of us. The little boy who spoke up in *The Emperor's New Clothes* reminds me of the Holy Spirit, who speaks God's truth in our hearts. We must choose whether we will believe and act upon it. Will we finally admit that we are wrong like the townspeople, or will we continue to keep our pride and be like the emperor who continued with his façade?

It is difficult for us to admit that we follow the ways of men. Although the emperor was naked, he made himself believe that he was wearing the finest clothes. I wonder if demons are like the impostor weavers who con us into believing and acting like something we are not. We wear masks to cover the real us. We try to fool others, but we cannot fool God. We can hide but we cannot hide from God. As the writer of Hebrews reminds us, "Nothing in all creation is hidden from God's sight. Everything is uncovered and laid bare before the eyes of him to whom we must give account" (Heb. 4:13).

If we will recognize the truth, it is worth the risk to take our masks off and be made a fool so that we can be humbled and refined by God. Only by letting go of our masks are we able to let God work in us to reflect His glory to others.

WE REFLECT GOD'S GLORY

In his book *Waking the Dead*, John Eldredge addressed the importance of taking our masks off and reflecting God's glory:

> We are in the process of being unveiled. We were created to reflect God's glory, born to bear his image, and he ransomed us to reflect that glory again. Every heart was a given a mythic glory, and that glory is being restored. Remember the mission of Christ: "I have come to give you back your heart and set you free." For as Saint Irenaeus said, "The glory of God is man fully alive."[2]

We cannot reflect God's glory with masks on. Yet, as Eldredge said, "Most of us spend our energy trying to hide that fact, through all the veils we put on and the false selves we create."[3] "Far better to spend our energy trying to recover the image of God and unveil it for His glory."[4] When we unveil our masks, we feel that we are vulnerable and unprotected. That, however, is the enemy's lie. When we unveil our masks, we may stand naked before God and others, but we also allow God to come in to restore us and allow His mighty power to protect us. We must open our hearts and let God reveal what we need to be restored to Him. We are meant to reflect God's glory—to let God in.

Some of us are afraid of being different and standing up for the truth. Eldredge's response to this fact was: "It is an awkward thing to shimmer when everyone else around you is not, to walk in glory with an unveiled face when everyone else is veiling his."[5] However, if we keep our masks on, we cannot love the way God intends for us to love. When our hearts are hiding, how can we express our love and live out Christ's two greatest commandments to "love the Lord your God with all your heart and with all your soul and with all your mind" and to "love your neighbor as yourself" (Matthew 22:37–39)?

We do well to consider Eldredge's comment about expressing love without masks:

> You cannot love another person from a false self. You cannot love another while you are hiding. How can you help them to freedom while you remain captive? You cannot love another unless you offer her your heart. It takes courage to live from your heart."[6]

Yes, it takes courage to walk a different path than others. Following Christ requires us to walk through a small gate and on a narrow road, and many will not find it (Matt. 7:13–14). We need to stick to the narrow road and not stray from it. When we unveil our masks and allow God to restore our hearts to Him, something wonderful happens—we are renewed, and we feel alive again. Let us reclaim our joy and love in the One who came to redeem us to Himself. May we all pray as David did: "restore to me the joy of your salvation and grant me a willing spirit, to sustain me" (Ps. 51:12).

WE SURRENDER OURSELVES
TO THE HOLY SPIRIT

I recently watched *Herbie: Fully Loaded*,[7] the re-make of the movie *The Love Bug*.[8] In the movie, Herbie, a Volkswagen car with life and personality, directed and controlled the driving instead of the driver, Maggie Peyton. The more Maggie tried to fight against Herbie's driving direction, the harder it was for her to drive at all. During an impromptu street race led by Herbie, Maggie was able to race and win against the top driver when she finally allowed Herbie to take over the driving. Maggie realized that when she surrendered control to Herbie, she was able to partner together with him to drive well.

This reminded me of the Holy Spirit living in me. I need to allow the Holy Spirit to be in the driver's seat to lead and direct me because He knows what is best for me. Unfortunately, I am a really bad back-seat driver. I am too impatient to wait for the outcome, and I want to control the situation. I tend to question His every move in my life when it's a different course than where I want to go. I am just like Maggie Peyton who tried to fight against what was best for her. Yet, the more I surrender to the Holy Spirit, the more He can work through me. I have learned the truth of Paul's teaching:

> For if you live according to the sinful nature, you will die; but if by the Spirit you put to death the misdeeds of the body, you will live.
>
> —ROMANS 8:13

During the final NASCAR race when Maggie was stuck and cornered by other race cars, she wanted to give up. However, her father came to her and encouraged her to believe that she could complete the race and win it. With renewed confidence from her dad's words, she, together with Herbie, continued and raced to victory.

I have a Heavenly Father who knows my heart's desires. When I am weak, He comes and reminds me that He is right there with me. He gives me confidence to continue the race when I feel that I am *jammed in* by my struggles and cannot go on in this journey. He gives me the extra boost I need to *accelerate* forward in my journey with Him. You and I can trust God to help us complete our course and be victorious for Him. "For it is God who works in you to will and to act according to his good purpose" (Phil. 2:13).

WE ARE VICTORIOUS IN BATTLE

We will not have smooth sailing when we unveil our masks and repent before God. It is a daily struggle to keep our masks off; it is a process we go through. In spite of the difficulties we face in this process, we can walk in freedom and victory. The more we understand this, the more we will want to take our masks off.

Recently my family and I were going out to meet a close friend for a date. As we were getting ready to leave, Bill and I found ourselves fighting over an unresolved issue. Normally we would have gone anyway and pretended that nothing was wrong until we returned home. This time, however, being aware of the enemy's schemes, I asked my husband to call our friend and ask her to pray for us and keep us accountable. Because we revealed the truth and asked for help from God and our friend, we were able to resolve our issue and moved forward immediately.

It is still a struggle for me to keep motivated to listen and do God's will in my life. I am easily led back to the ways of the world and enticed to give in to my old natural desires. My mind and heart struggle with the issue of my significance. As Billy Graham has recognized, we will face such struggles. In his book *The Holy Spirit*, he wrote "Sin will always be a continuing problem—our lives will always be marked with defeat and discouragement—as long as we try to keep "self" at the center of our lives."[9]

Even though we have inner battles, God is faithful. He calls us to face our battles by contending with Satan and his evil cohorts and our own selfish nature. Our battles may seem endless, and we may feel defeated even before we start. However, God promises that victory rests with Him.

> The horse is made ready for the day of battle, *but victory rests with the* LORD.
> —PROVERBS 21:31, emphasis added

Satan will not attack those who have already fallen away from God because they do not care about God and will be ineffective in serving Him. Satan *will* attack those who are seeking to know God more and desire to serve God faithfully. Satan knows that he will not win the war, but he keeps fighting in an effort to pull down those God will use in effective service. I like the analogy from Pastor Jon Couson, written in a book by Bickel and Jantz:[10]

> Imagine a dinner party in the backyard of someone's home. All of the guests are dressed nicely and milling around. A group of pranksters at the party notice that one of their friends is standing close to the swimming pool. They grab him and carry him to the edge to throw him into the water. Now, the guy knows he is going to get dunked. But under the "misery loves company" impulse, he grabs, fights, and claws to bring as many others as possible into the water with him. He may be going down, but he's not going alone if he can help it. And so it is with Satan.

God has equipped us with the power of His Holy Spirit—our secret weapon for winning our spiritual battles. When we try to fight the enemy and our old nature with the strength of our flesh, we will definitely falter and lose. The secret is that we need to yield ourselves to the Holy Spirit so that He can empower us to put off the old and put on the new.[11] When we surrender ourselves to be led by the power of the Holy Spirit, He enables us to be victorious. We must constantly be on guard against anything that distracts from following the leading of the Holy Spirit.

Jesus Christ calls us to step off the thrones of our lives and let Him rule over us completely. Dying daily in Christ will have new significance in our lives as we allow Him to be our King. Jesus taught, "If anyone would come after me, he must deny himself and take up his cross daily and follow me" (Luke 9:23). Our battles are continuous, but victory is ours through Christ.

WE BECOME MORE LIKE CHRIST

It seems impossible to not wear some sort of mask in the journey of life. The enemy constantly entices us to do this, and we need to continuously surrender to God and ask Him to show us how to take our masks off. We must spend time in the Lord's presence so we can have an intimate relationship with Him, and we must allow ourselves to be led by the Holy Spirit. We need to recognize God's voice, and not yield to our own nor the enemy's.

In some tribes, people wear masks into battle to scare their opponents and to protect themselves. However, because we are in a spiritual battle, only the full armor of God will give us the protection we need. Masks only cover up our faces, while the full armor of God protects our bodies and our hearts entirely, as we learned in Chapter 16, "We Put on the Armor of God."

As we unveil each mask, we give God permission to transform us.

To become more like Christ is a daily, life-long process. Billy Graham has described it this way:

> Each day we should seek to understand more from God's Word. We should pray that God will help us see our sin each day. Each day we should confess and repent. And each day we should submit our wills to His will. We should so walk in faith that He is continually filling us as we submit to Him. Each day we should walk in obedience to His Word.[12]

We cannot become truly naked before God until we meet Him face to face in heaven. That is when we will fully reflect His glory, when He will transform our earthly bodies into glorious bodies like Christ (Phil. 3:21; 1 Cor. 15:40–54). I am longing for that day.

WE ARE SET FREE TO LIVE TRUTHFULLY

I don't want to live a life of restrictions. I don't want to be rule-bound, I want to live freely. These words echo in our hearts when we strive to do things our own way. However, we don't realize that God does want us to live freely. God has given us His written Word, the Bible, as well the Holy Spirit, to guide us into His truth and provide direction for our lives. His rules—His truth—do not take away our freedom, but actually give us freedom and increase our enjoyment in life.

Imagine two teams playing hockey without any rules or regulations. No one would know what the boundaries were, and no one would know who actually won the game. And the players would probably end up slashing each other to death. When people are confused, they make up their own rules, and then they fight or hurt others who don't agree. People prefer to know what the boundaries are so they can be free to enjoy the game.

Life is like that. God has given us His truth, which tells us what we can do and what we must not do. He has established what is "in bounds" and what is "out of bounds." If we play within His rules, we will have freedom and enjoyment in life. However, if we break the rules or try to camouflage the truth, we will hurt ourselves and others. As God reveals His truth and His will to us, we can obey Him and enjoy our relationship with Him. We can also love others sincerely without hypocrisy. As the Apostle Peter wrote, "Having purified your souls by your obedience to the truth for a sincere brotherly love, love one another earnestly from a pure heart" (1 Pet. 1:22, ESV).

Jesus promises us a life of freedom in Him. The apostle Paul taught, "It is for freedom that Christ has set us free" (Gal. 5:1). He died in our place to ransom us from the bondage of sin and bring us back to Himself so we can live in His truth. We do not need to engage in the activities of our old sinful nature or try to do things "our way" to be free. We are freed from slavery to our past ways and to the enemy so that we can serve a new Master. Jesus, our new Master, has provided the only way for us to live in freedom. The apostle John declared this when he wrote, "So if the Son sets you free, you will be free indeed" (John 8:36).

By abiding in Christ and His truth, we have freedom to love, freedom to live truthfully, freedom to enjoy life without guilt or shame, freedom to serve God wholeheartedly. We are set free to live the way God intended for us to live, not hindered by falsehoods but having genuine love for each other. Paul explained, "[We] were called to be free," but we should "not use [our] freedom to indulge the sinful nature; rather, serve one another in love" (Gal. 5:13).

We no longer need to hide behind our masks of pretense to be someone we're not. As we live in the light of God's truth, we will attract others into our lives. People will discover that we are genuine and they will desire to remove their masks. When our relationships are open and transparent, genuine relationships will bud and grow. We have the freedom to truly serve others out of love.

WE "REPENT AND LIVE!"

Of the seven things that Proverbs 6:16–19 identifies as detestable to the Lord, more than half of them relate to falseness and lies. They include: "haughty eyes, a lying tongue,...a heart that devises wicked schemes,...a false witness who pours out lies and a man who stirs up dissension among brothers." God hates falseness. When we keep our masks on, we don't just hurt ourselves, we hurt God.

The masks I have discussed in this book do not constitute a comprehensive list; they do, however, reveal some of the real dangers we face. In response to these masks, I have repented before God first and I have also asked forgiveness from others, both family and friends, for my deception. I was too ashamed to tell others that I was going through a period of depression and not leading the victorious Christian life I felt I should. Instead I was living a self-reliant life, a life to please the world and not God, a life focused on the work of God rather than God Himself.

God is not interested in what we do for Him—our successes; instead, He is interested in our obedience to Him. (See 1 Samuel 15:22; John 14:15; 15:10.) I have sinned before God, and He has shown me grace. He has forgiven me because Jesus died for my past, present, and future sins. He desires to continue His work of grace as Billy Graham has explained: "We Christians are to be "progressively sanctified" or "made righteous" in holiness as we daily abide in Christ—and obey His Word."[13]

I confessed in Chapter 12 that I was always a giant worry wart, and I am trying hard not to morph back into one. As I have written this book and shared God's truth about the masks we wear, I have experienced deep guilt and also worry about how others may perceive me and how they may be affected. God has comforted me with 2 Corinthians 7:10, "Godly sorrow brings repentance that leads to salvation and leaves no regret, but worldly sorrow brings death." I want to be more like Paul—he did not regret sharing with others, even if it meant hurting them for a little while, because it led them to repentance. "For you became sorrowful as God intended and so were not harmed in any way" (2 Cor. 7:9).

God has allowed me to go through the struggles I have shared in this book so that I can warn others about the dangers we face when we do not guard our hearts. We need to continually abide in the Holy Spirit so we can hear and obey God's directions. I desire that my personal testimony and God's truth will help you come to God in repentance and be reconciled to Him. As you unveil your masks to one another, offer forgiveness, not judgment in your relationships with each other:

> The reason I wrote you was to see if you would stand the test and be obedient in everything. If you forgive anyone, I also forgive him. And what I have forgiven—if there was anything to forgive—I have forgiven in the sight of Christ for your sake, in order that Satan might not outwit us. For we are not unaware of his schemes.
> —2 CORINTHIANS 2:9–11

My prayer is that you will have a sincere and joyfully intimate relationship with God and others. Allow Him to create right motives in your heart. I mimic what Paul wrote in 2 Corinthians 2:4, "For I wrote you out of great distress and anguish of heart and with many tears, not to grieve you but to let you know the depth of my love for you." God has shown me that I must "come out of hiding" to reveal what He has shown me. I want to share with others what I have both heard from God and also experienced, not to grieve your Spirit nor to stumble your faith, but to show you my love and my weaknesses.

We were meant to live an abundant life in Jesus Christ. Godly sorrow leads to repentance. It's going to hurt for a bit, but the end results will be amazing. Unveil your heart. "Repent and live!" (Ezekiel 18:32).

> In my anguish I cried to the LORD, and he answered by setting me free.
>
> —PSALM 118:5

Appendix 1

A Summary of Truth About Unveiling Masks

Masks/Lies	What was really under the mask? (the truth)	God's deliverance
1. Mask of Healthiness	deteriorating health, physical and spiritual	God the Healer
2. Mask of Honesty	lies, deception, cover ups	truth/freedom in Christ
3. Mask of Perfection	pride	humility, grace through Christ
4. Mask of Strength	weakness, fear	the power of the Holy Spirit
5. Mask of Busyness/ Productivity	laziness, unproductivity	effectiveness, growth from God
6. Mask of Devotion	idolatry	God's faithfulness
7. Mask of Patience	impatience, lack of self-control	Holy Spirit-led living

Masks/Lies	What was really under the mask? (the truth)	God's deliverance
8. Mask of Gentleness/ Sweetness	anger/rage, unforgiveness	mercy, forgiveness from God
9. Mask of Satisfaction/ Happiness	sadness, insatiable desires, covetousness	contentment, peace, joy in Christ
10. Mask of Optimism	pessimism, negativity, despair	hope in God's promises
11. Mask of Being Sociable	loneliness, lonesomeness	resting in God's presence
12. Mask of Sincerity/ Righteousness	intentionally wrong motives, hypocrisy	the righteousness of Christ

Appendix 2

A Guide for Unveiling Masks

THIS FIFTEEN-SECTION STUDY guide is geared for the individual who desires to reflect more deeply on the content in this book and also for the small group that wishes to build closer relationships. I recommend that you do Study 1 first, Studies 2–13 in any order you feel led, and Studies 14–15 near the end. Reading the selections for each study section will help you reflect and answer the questions appropriately.

Each study section has three parts: *reflection*, *study*, and *challenge*. The *reflection* questions are aimed to help you reflect on what was written and how it applies to you. The *study* section reinforces the topic of the reading section with biblical passages you can read and review for deeper insights. The *challenge* section is intended to motivate you to act on what you have learned. Whether you use this study guide as an individual or in a group study, it will challenge your mind and heart to evaluate where you stand in your relationship with God and with others.

I recommend that you use this study guide in a group setting. By opening your heart to others and sharing hidden things with them, you will build trust and confidence in your relationships. God wants us to share love and support and to build each other up. (Eph. 4:15–16). He intends for us to enjoy a full abundant life of intimate relationship with Him and with others in the body of Christ. Prayerfully commit yourself to God's truth in this study guide and unveil your heart before Him. Discover how the truth will indeed set you free. He will restore you, transform you, and give you a new heart.

STUDY 1
Read the Preface, the Introduction, and Section I, "The Unveiling of My Masks"

Reflection

1. Reflect on the moment when you asked Jesus to come into your life. How was your life before you received Christ? What led you to trust in Him? How did Christ change your life? How is your current relationship with God? How do you relate to others?

2. Have you ever felt drawn away from God? Have you ever doubted or wanted to give up your faith? If so, what circumstances made you feel that way?

3. Have you ever questioned your identity and asked "Who am I?" or "What is my purpose in life?" Take a moment to reflect on what your purpose is. Do other people see the "real" inside of who you are? Can you identify with what the author is sharing?

4. Have you ever felt bitter or drained after serving in ministry? Do you ever feel like giving up? Do you experience rage, anger, bitterness, or deep sadness? Do you keep it inside or do you seek help? Who do you usually turn to for help?

5. You can fully experience true relief from every sin that hinders you from being healthy and whole through

Christ. How can the acronym *RELIEF* remind you of this?

Study

1. Read 1 John 3:9 and 1 John 5:18. What do these passages tell us? What do they teach you?

2. Read Galatians 5:22–23 and John 15:5–8. Do you feel you are bearing fruit for God? Does fruit come naturally or are you trying hard to emulate it? Why do you think it is so difficult to bear fruit?

3. What can you learn from Bible characters who tried to hide the truth or control things in their lives?

   - Rebekah—Genesis 25:19–28; 27–28:1–5

   - Jonah—Read Jonah chapter 1

   - King David—2 Samuel 11–12:1–14

4. Read John 8:31–32. What is Jesus trying to teach us in this passage?

Challenge

1. What does "wearing a mask" mean to you? Have you ever worn a mask? Pray and ask the Holy Spirit to reveal any masks that you may not even know you are wearing.

2. Do you have a secret that is holding you down? Do you desperately want to share it with others but don't for fear of what others may think of you? Share your secret

with another person or with your group today. How does it feel after you do this?

3. What have you learned from this study and how can you act on it?

STUDY 2
Read Chapter 3: The Mask of Wellness

Reflection

1. Do you or a loved one struggle with physical or emotional pain? Do you or your loved one run to God when you are suffering, or do you run away from Him?

2. What is your reaction when God does not seem to answer your questions on healing?

3. Had you ever heard of "spiritual depression" before you read this book? What does it mean for you personally?

4. What leads to spiritual depression? What will cure it? How can you ensure that your "spiritual diet" will nourish you?

5. What do you think this statement means: "Our internal pain aggravates our external pain"?

Study

1. Read 1 Samuel 16:7. What does this passage tell you?

2. What can you learn from Bible characters who dealt with illnesses?

- The centurion who came to Jesus on behalf of his servant—Matthew 8:5–13

- The blind beggar—John chapter 9

- Paul—2 Corinthians 12:7–10

3. Read Psalm 119:71. What is the psalmist sharing? How does it apply to you?

4. Read Luke 5:31–32. What do you think Jesus is trying to imply in this passage? How does this apply to you personally?

Challenge

1. Have you struggled with any physical, emotional, mental, or spiritual health issues that you have been keeping to yourself? Have you put on the mask of wellness?

2. Share your health needs with another person or with your group today. How does it feel after you do this?

3. What have you learned from this study, and how can you act on it?

STUDY 3
Read Chapter 4: The Mask of Honesty

Reflection

1. Has God revealed something ugly about you?

2. What did you learn from the lessons I shared from *Spiderman 2*? How do they apply to you personally?

3. What does the phrase "be honest with yourself first before you can be honest with others" mean to you?

4. Have you ever told a "white lie"? On a scale of 1–10 (with 10 being honest 100 percent of the time), how consistently do you tell the truth to others?

5. Are you aware of the lies you tell? If so, what do you do about it after you have lied? If not, how can you become aware that you are lying?

Study

1. What can you learn from the following passages?

   - Luke 12:1–3

   - John 3:20–21

   - 1 John 1:5–10

2. What did Christ mean when He said, "I am the way, the truth and the life. No one comes to the Father except through me" (John 14:6)?

Challenge

1. Do you struggle with being truthful? Have you been completely honest with those around you?

2. Share your need for honesty with another person or with your group today. How does it feel after you do this?

3. What have you learned from this study, and how can you act on it?

STUDY 4
Read Chapter 5: The Mask of Perfection

Reflection

1. Are you a perfectionist? If not, do you know someone who is one? What traits do you think a perfectionist typically exhibits? Why do you think someone becomes a perfectionist?

2. How does pride affect the way we do things?

3. What do we mean when we say that "we have to admit imperfection before we can receive help to be better"?

4. Have you ever boasted? Have you ever exaggerated your achievements, accomplishments, and even shopping purchases to others? Why do you think we do this?

Study

1. What is the difference between earthly boasting and heavenly boasting? Read 2 Corinthians 10:17–18.

2. What can you learn from Paul's example of honoring God and giving Him all the glory in all that he did? Read 1 Corinthians 15:10.

3. What do the following scriptures teach about biblical characters who honored God?

- The prayer of the tax collector—Luke 18:9–14

- Mary giving perfume—Matthew 26:6–13; Mark 14:3–9

- Jesus–Philippians 2:3–11

4. What can you learn from the object lesson of Christ washing His disciples' feet? Read John 13:15–16 and Luke 22:26–27.

Challenge

1. Have you ever put on a mask of perfection? Have you kept your imperfections to yourself because you were concerned about what people might think about you or how they might treat you?

2. Share an imperfection with another person or with your group today. How does it feel after you do this?

3. What have you learned from this study, and how can you act on it?

STUDY 5
Read Chapter 6: The Mask of Strength

Reflection

1. What is the difference between a superior complex and an inferior complex? Do you think you have either of them? Why?

2. Can you recall a time when you wanted to put up a strong front in front of others? Why?

3. What is the difference between the "mask of strength" and the "mask of weakness"? Are you wearing one of them? Why?

Study

1. Read Romans 12:3 and John 15:5. What do these scriptures tell you? What is your source of strength?

2. What can you learn about strength and weakness from the following biblical characters?

   - Elijah—1 Kings 18–19

   - Job—Job 1:21; 42:1–6

   - Paul—2 Cor. 10:1; 11:21–31; 12:9–11

3. Read James 4:10 and Isaiah 40:31. What do these passages teach about being humble? What do they identify as the source of our strength?

4. What do Ephesians 5:18 and Zechariah 4:6 say about the power of the Holy Spirit?

Challenge

1. Do you tend to rely on your own strength instead of going to God first? What does completely surrendering your will to the Holy Spirit mean to you?

2. Share an area of weakness with another person or with your group today. How does it feel after you do this?

3. What have you learned from this study, and how can you act on it?

STUDY 6
Read Chapter 7:
The Mask of Busyness and Productivity

Reflection

1. How would you describe your daily routine? It is slow and steady, a normal routine, balanced and productive, or crazy and hectic?

2. What does it mean for you to stop, look, and listen to God?

3. Do you identify more with Mary or Martha in Luke 10:38–42? Why?

4. What did you think of Joan Fong's statement that "most of us are afraid of the stillness because we do not appear to be productive"? Are you afraid of being still? Do you know how to be still? Do you take time to do it?

5. Do you usually schedule your priorities around God, or do you fit Him into your schedule?

Study

1. What do the following biblical characters teach you about taking time to listen to God and obey Him?

   • Samuel—1 Samuel 3:1–10

- Mary—Luke 10:38–42

- Jesus—Mark 14:32–36

2. What did Jesus mean when He said, "Seek first his kingdom and his righteousness, and all these things will be given to you as well" (Matt. 6:33)?

3. Read Psalm 46:10. How does this scripture apply to your daily life? How does God want you to grow in Him?

Challenge

1. Do you struggle with always being too busy? Do you wear the mask of busyness so you can feel and look productive? Are you using your time effectively for God?

2. Are you taking time to read God's Word and pray? Do you spend quality time with God by sitting and listening to what He wants to tell you? What do you do after you hear what God wants you to do?

3. Share the truth about your priorities with another person or with your group today. How does it feel after you do this?

4. What have you learned from this study, and how can you act on it?

STUDY 7
Read Chapter 8: The Mask of Devotion

Reflection

1. What are some of the idols in your life? Who or what do you turn to when you are in trouble? Anything—money, shopping, food, alcohol, drugs, family or friends—can become a substitute for God. Pray and ask God to reveal anything that is blocking your relationship with Him. Ask Him to show you what you should do about it.

2. Are you serving in Christian ministry? Have you ever considered that you can be "married to your ministry"? What do you think will help you know if your ministry becomes an idol?

3. Can you relate to the analogy of Gollum/Sméagol's internal struggle in *The Lord of the Rings—The Two Towers*? Do you struggle with surrendering your will to God? Who is your real master?

4. How can you be sure that God will be faithful to you even though you may be faithless or sway in your loyalty? Read 2 Timothy 2:11–13 and Jeremiah 32:39–42.

Study

1. Proverbs 4:23 warns us to guard our hearts above all else. Why do you think you should heed this warning?

2. What can you learn from biblical characters who struggled to follow God's will and make God their only "Master"?

- King David—Psalm 51

- Rich man—Luke 18:18-29

- Paul—Romans 7:15-25

3. Read Exodus 20:3-4, Mark 12:29-30, and James 4:5. What do these scriptures tell you about God? How should we respond to this?

Challenge

1. Read and memorize Psalm 86:11. Do you struggle with an "undivided heart" in your relationship with God?

2. Do you sincerely want to devote your heart 100 percent to God? Do you want to remove any idols that are blocking your relationship with Him? Is it time to remove your "mask of devotion" and become truly free to love Christ completely?

3. Repent of your devotion to any idol in your life, and confess your sin to God today. Share and pray about this with another person or with your group today. How does it feel after you do this?

4. What have you learned from this study, and how can you act on it?

STUDY 8
Read Chapter 9: The Mask of Patience

Reflection

1. What is your patience level? Where would you rank yourself on a scale of 1–10, with 1 being automatically irritable when you don't see immediate results and 10 being very patient and willing to wait as long as it takes? Why?

2. Can you relate to what the author is trying to convey in her confession that she is "slow to listen, quick to speak, and quick to become angry"? How well do you listen? Why do you think so?

3. What is the meaning of the statement that "faith and patience go hand in hand"?

4. Have you ever gone to bed angry? How did you feel afterward? Did you do anything about the cause of your anger later?

5. Why do you think some people seem to be so patient? What can you do to control your impatience level? What will help you develop patience? How can the Holy Spirit help you?

Study

1. Where does Romans 8:5 direct your focus?

2. Read James 3:9–10 and Ephesians 4:29. What do these passages remind you what your speech is meant for?

3. What can you learn from the patience of biblical characters who waited for God's promises and timing in their lives?

   - Sarah—Genesis 16:1–6; 17:15–16; 18:10–15; 21:1–7

   - Joseph—Genesis 37:1–5, 18–28; 45:1–8

   - Martha and Mary—John 11:1–45

Challenge

1. Do you yearn to be less frustrated and more patient? Is it hard for you to admit that you are wearing the mask of patience? Are you willing to surrender control of your life to God and allow the Holy Spirit to lead you?

2. Confess your impatience to God today, and share your confession with another person or with your group today. How does it feel after you do this?

3. What have you learned from this study, and how can you act on it?

STUDY 9
Read Chapter 10: The Mask of Gentleness and Sweetness

Reflection

1. Can you identify with being a "sweet and sour dish"? Do you sometimes feel like you are playing a sweet and gentle role even when you are really feeling bitter, hurt, or unhappy? Why do you think we play different roles in our lives?

2. "Schmoozing" is flattering or complimenting someone to attain positive affirmation or results. How is it the same as "sugar-coating" a statement? Have you ever "schmoozed" someone or "sugar-coated" your words? When? Why? How did it make you feel?

3. What is the role of a referee in a game? What is the role of a referee in life? When you find yourself in the role of a referee, do you speak gently to conciliate the parties involved? List some things you can learn from Jesus, our "ultimate referee."

4. What is the difference between meekness and weakness? What trait do you portray to others? Why?

5. To have a sincere heart you need a pure heart that produces gentleness and love for others. You must release any bitterness and grudges in an act of forgiveness. How can you learn to forgive from the exhortation of Colossians 3:12–14?

Study

1. The book of James gives a key teaching on the importance of our speech and our attitudes. Read James 3:6–18, and consider how you can apply these verses in your life.

2. Read James 5:19–20 and Galatians 6:1–5. Have you seen or heard of things that need to be corrected? Have you turned a blind eye to problems that need to be addressed? Why do you think it is important to be

accountable and to gently, lovingly correct others if they sin?

3. What can you learn about the following biblical characters as you consider the importance of extending gentleness, mercy, and forgiveness appropriately?

   - The parable of the king and the unmerciful servant—Matthew 18:23–35

   - Paul—2 Corinthians 10:1–6

   - Jesus—Luke 23:34

Challenge

1. What is the condition of your heart? Do you have any bitterness or hold any grudges? Have you put on a mask of gentleness to hide the real truth about yourself? Are you ready to completely surrender any unforgiveness to God?

2. Resolve to extend forgiveness to those who have wronged you. If you have the ability to contact them, share your forgiving heart with each of them today—whether it is in person or in writing. How does it feel after you do this?

3. What have you learned from this study, and how can you act on it?

STUDY 10
Read Chapter 11: The Mask of Satisfaction and Happiness

Reflection

1. List ten things that make you feel happy. Circle the ones that are only temporary, and underline the ones that are lasting. Did you underline very many of them? What does this tell you?

2. How content is your heart? Where would you rank yourself on a scale of 1–10, with 10 being completely content? Are you grateful for your job, your home, and the relationships you have? Are you envious of others? Are you constantly trying to pursue more material wealth and recognition because you think it will make you feel better? Why do you think you feel the way you do?

3. Are you married? How is your marriage relationship going? Do you and your spouse display the same feelings toward each other both in public and in private? Why not? What is the difference between feelings and commitment? If you realize that your marriage is at stake, focus on your commitment to God and each other. Seek help from a trusted friend, pastor, or professional Christian counsellor. If you are not married, share these questions with a family member or close friend who is.

4. What did you learn about the differences among habit, compulsiveness, and addiction? Are you aware of any

unhealthy habits in your life? Do others know about it? Enlist the help of a loved one for support or seek professional help for treatment.

5. Society's definition of success is completely opposite of the definition that is taught in the kingdom of God. What does God say about success and contentment in the kingdom of God?

Study

1. What lesson can we learn from the teaching Jesus gave to the Samaritan woman at the well? Read John 4:5–15 and John 7:37–39.

2. How can the following passages help you become more content?

   • Proverbs 30:7–9

   • Philippians 4:11–13

   • 1 Timothy 6:6–11

   • Hebrews 13:5

3. What does God tell you about coveting your neighbor's job, house, and other material things? Read Exodus 20:17 and Ecclesiastes 4:4.

Challenge

1. Do you want to experience true joy and contentment? Do you wear a mask of happiness and satisfaction before others, but struggle with discontentment deep inside?

2. Share the truth about your discontentment with another person or with your group today. Discuss what they are feeling as well. If necessary, find an accountability partner to help you with your struggles. How does it feel after you do this?

3. What have you learned from this study, and how can you act on it?

STUDY 11
Read Chapter 12: The Mask of Optimism

Reflection

1. Do you tend to see events and circumstances in your life as a glass that is "half empty" or "half full"? When trouble comes your way, are you able to see the positive side of your situation? Do your words to others reflect worry, discouragement, or hope? Why?

2. Do you worry a lot? Rank yourself on a scale of 1–10, with 1 meaning that you do not worry at all, and 10 meaning that you worry about everything. What did you learn about worrying? Why do you think you worry? Name one thing you can do today to make you less worried.

3. It's very common to feel "blue" during the winter because most of us do not get enough sunlight. What did this chapter teach you about getting enough sunlight and the "Son's light" in your life? How do

both "light sources" help change your attitude and
your outlook in life? Do you have enough of both?

4. What did you learn from the analogy of the forest and
the trees? Do you tend to see the forest or the trees?
Why?

5. Do you tend to be encouraged or easily discouraged?
What triggers both types of feelings and attitudes?
How does focusing our hope in God's promises enable
us to be more optimistic in life?

Study

1. What can you learn from the story of the man who
brought his mute, epileptic, and demon-possessed son
to Jesus? Read Mark 9:14–29. Does this remind you of
your own faith? How?

2. What do the following passages teach you about faith
and God's promises?

   - Jeremiah 29:11

   - Matthew 6:33–34

   - Deuteronomy 31:6

   - Mark 10:27

   - Luke 17:5–6

   - Hebrews 11:1; 12:2–3

3. What does James 1:2–8 say about our trials and the
way we should pray?

Challenge

1. Do you wear the mask of optimism? Do you encourage others to see things positively, but inwardly doubt what you say? Do you have a tendency to view things in a pessimistic way? Are you easily discouraged when you are presented with challenges?

2. Share your need for encouragement with another person or with your group today. When you encourage someone, do not doubt what you are saying but trust and believe it for yourself. Ask others how they view things. How does it feel after you do this?

3. What have you learned from this study, and how can you act on it?

STUDY 12
Read Chapter 13: The Mask of Sociability

Reflection

1. Do you consider yourself a "social butterfly" or a "silk worm in a cocoon"? When you are in a party atmosphere, is it easy for you to mingle and meet new friends? Or do you tend to retreat into a corner and talk only to those who are familiar?

2. Reflect and think about the friends you have. Would you say you have a lot of friends or a few friends? Would you consider them quality close friends? If close friends are those who will drop everything and be

there for you in the time of need, how many of them do you have?

3. Do you tend to host or attend parties? If you tend to host parties, how do you feel after everyone leaves? If you are more likely to attend parties, how do you feel after you leave the party?

4. Loneliness is a longing for companionship, while lonesomeness is a feeling of sadness and isolation. Have you experienced either one? When and why?

5. Do you have a best friend? List ten qualities that you love about them. Circle the three that are most important to you, and reflect on them. Do you have them? The qualities that are important to you are usually the ones you want to have. Is this true for you? How can you extend desirable qualities to others?

6. What makes you feel connected to others? What makes you feel connected to God?

7. How can you learn to rest in God's presence and not feel lonely?

Study

1. The Bible teaches that the company we keep affects who we are. Read Proverbs 12:26. It also commands us to not be unequally yoked with unbelievers. Read 2 Corinthians 6:14–18. Have you learned what this really means? Read also Matthew 11:28–29. Using Jesus

as your example, how can you apply these scriptures to your social life?

2. Read Matthew 5:43–47. What do these words of Jesus teach us about loving and serving others?

Challenge

1. Are you wearing the "mask of sociability"? Do you tend to mix well with others and appear to have lots of friends, but feel lonely and disconnected when you're left alone? Isn't it time to take off your mask and become the person God designed you to be?

2. Share your feelings of loneliness with another person or with your group today. How does it feel after you do this?

3. What have you learned from this study, and how can you act on it?

STUDY 13
Read Chapter 14: The Mask of
Sincerity and Righteousness

Reflection

1. What did this section teach you about the reasons we may have for going to church? Why do you go to church?

2. Are you currently serving in your church or in any other ministry? What is your heart's motive for serving?

Would you continue to serve if you did not receive any affirmation for your ministry? How would you respond? Pastor Tim Tze has said that affirmation is like a two-edged sword. What did he mean by that? When would it be healthy to have positive affirmation from others?

3. Barbara Johnson says that God called you to be faithful; He did not call you to be successful. What does this statement mean to you?

4. Do you watch reality TV shows? Why do they interest you? What do you learn from watching these types of shows?

5. Why is it important to serve in humility through Christ's righteousness? What have you learned about your heart's motives?

Study

1. In what two areas does Jesus warn us not to become hypocrites? What can you do when you find yourself tempted with the wrong motives? Read Matthew 6:1–8.

2. What do the following scriptures teach you about sincerity and righteousness?

    - Luke 6:41–42

    - Acts 5:1–11

    - Romans 12:3–8

    - 1 Thessalonians 2:3–6

    - Galatians 6:12–15

3. How do you overcome the temptation to accept praise from others even when your heart's motive may be sincere? Read 1 Corinthians 15:10 and Philippians 1:9–11; 3:7–9.

Challenge

1. Have you considered the possibility that you may be doing the right things for wrong reasons? Sometimes our best intentions may be wrong. Do you sometimes don the "mask of sincerity and righteousness"? Isn't it time to come clean and be authentic with others?

2. Confess any wrong motives in your heart to another person or to your group today. How does it feel after you do this?

3. What have you learned from this study, and how can you act on it?

STUDY 14
Read Section III: After We Unveil Our Masks

Reflection

1. What happens when you do not guard your heart? How does your "old nature" become your enemy? Have you ever suffered a spiritual attack? What were the circumstances? How is your heart now? What are some remedies you can use to help with the healing process?

2. When you continually yield to the Holy Spirit, you can be filled with His power and strength. Have you ever

felt "drained" rather than "full"? Why do you think that happens? What can you do to stay filled with the Holy Spirit?

3. What is the difference between spiritual warfare with your own self-will and spiritual warfare with the enemy?

4. List the three key suggestions that can protect you from future spiritual attacks. Reflect on them.

Study

1. To be equipped for spiritual battle, you need to wear the "full armor of God."

   Read Ephesians 6:10–17 and write down why each piece of armor is equally important to wear:

   - The belt of truth—(also read 1 Peter 1:13; John 16:13; John 17:15–19)

   - The breastplate of righteousness—(also read Romans 3:20–24)

   - The shoes of peace—(also read Ephesians 2:1–5, 11–19; Romans 8:31)

   - The shield of faith—(also read Psalm 18:2; 28:7; Joshua 1:9)

   - The helmet of salvation—(also read Psalm 140:7; Romans 8:37–39; 1 Thessalonians 5:8–11)

   - The sword of the Spirit-(also read Matthew 4:3–11; Hebrews 4:12)

2. Why is it equally important to continually pray for yourself and others? Read Ephesians 6:18; Luke 22:46; Matthew 21:22.

3. Read James 4:7. What does it mean to "submit ourselves to God" and to "resist the devil"?

Challenge

1. Are you dressed and ready for spiritual battle?

2. Come to God in prayer and put on each piece of God's armor. Pray the "Prayer for Strength in the Battle," which is at the end of Section III. Tell another person or your group about a time you were spiritually attacked. What did you do to overcome it? What would you do now if it happened again?

3. What have you learned from this study, and how can you act on it?

STUDY 15
Read the Conclusion

Reflection

1. How do you think it feels to be totally free of wearing any masks? Is it possible? Why? What does it mean to be "naked in the truth"?

2. What do you remember about the story of "The Emperor's New Clothes"? What was the "moment of truth"? What did you personally learn from this story?

3. How can you "reflect God's glory"? What will hinder the process?

4. What did the story of *Herbie: Fully Loaded* teach you about your relationship with the Holy Spirit?

5. God promises you a life of freedom and an abundant life with Him. How should you guard against abusing your life of freedom?

6. What happens when you are open and transparent with others?

Study

1. How do the following scriptures teach you about enjoying a joyful and intimate relationship with God and with others?

   - Galatians 5:13–18

   - Psalm 51:10, 12

   - John 8:36

   - Ezekiel 18:32; Psalm 118:5

   - Mark 12:30–3; 1 Peter 1:22

2. After considering God's Word in this study, how should you be like the "wise man who built his house on the rock"? Read Matthew 7:24–27.

Challenge

1. Do you truly desire and yearn for a more intimate and joyful relationship with God and with others? If you

haven't yet done so, surrender to Christ and ask Him to reveal any hidden areas you need to confess and renounce.

2. Using the "Suggested Prayers" in Appendix 3, pray on your own and also with another person or your group. How does it feel after you do this?

3. Which part of this book has spoken to you the most? Why? Have you worn any masks that were not discussed? Have you removed them? If not, why not?

4. If this book has been helpful to you, share it with another person who is walking with you in the journey of life.

چ

To contact Helen's ministry and/or access a free downloadable study guide for easier printable group studies, please visit *www.hosannahouse.ca.*

Appendix 3

Suggested Prayers for Seeking God

G OD KNOWS YOUR heart, and He is not as concerned with your words as much as your heart's attitude and your desire to have a relationship with Him.

> Ask, and it will be given to you; seek, and you will find; knock, and it will be opened to you. For everyone who asks receives, and the one who seeks finds, and to the one who knocks it will be opened.
>
> —LUKE 11:9–10, ESV

A prayer of conscious decision to receive Jesus's free gift of salvation

> *Lord Jesus, I want to know You. Even though I don't know everything about You, I ask You by faith to come into my life and let me trust You. I surrender to You and invite You into my heart to become my Lord and Savior. I ask for Your forgiveness for any wrongdoings in my life. I believe by faith that You died for my sins, You rose again, and You are alive. I believe that You have special plans for me. Thank You for the gift of Your Holy Spirit, which You have promised for those who believe in You. Help me to walk in my new life with You. Thank You, Lord Jesus, Amen.*

A prayer to re-commit your life to Jesus

Lord Jesus, thank You that You are watching every step in my life. I thank You for dying for my sins. I ask that You forgive me when I don't remember that You have control in my life. I want You to be Lord in my life. You know my desires and plans. I pray that You renew my passion to walk more closely with You. Empower me with Your Holy Spirit so that I can be equipped to do my best for You. Help me to fulfill Your purpose in my life. Thank You, Lord Jesus. I pray all these things in Your name. Amen.

A prayer for restoration of intimate relationship with God

Heavenly Father, I come before You with thanksgiving and a humble and grateful heart. Lord, You are the One who created me. You are the One who loved me so much that You sent Your one and only Son, Jesus Christ, to die for my sin. Lord, help me to trust in Your unfailing love and to do Your will. Father, thank You for the gift of the Holy Spirit, which is given to those who place their trust in Jesus Christ. Lord, convict my heart and show me anything that is grieving Your Holy Spirit from effectively working in my life. Reveal anything that is blocking me from having a closer and more intimate relationship with You.

Lord, if I am wearing any masks, I ask that You reveal them to me. Help me to remove my masks. Help me to stand firm and true to You and to others. Remove my pride, and help me to change. Renew my heart, restore the joy of my salvation in You, and grant me a willing spirit to sustain me. Lord, thank you for the hope I have in You. Use my life to give You all the glory and honor. I pray all these things in the power and in the name of the Lord Jesus Christ. Amen.

A prayer for God to reveal any hidden mask of sin

Heavenly Father, I come before You in all nakedness. You know everything that is in my heart even before I mention anything. Lord, I pray in Jesus's name that You will help me through the Holy Spirit and reveal any masks I may be wearing. Help me to unveil them. Convict my heart to renounce and repent of anything that is stopping me from a closer walk with You. Teach me Your truth. Help me to walk in Your truth. Lord, let me live in Your truth. Change my heart to thirst after Your will and not mine. Lord, help me to hear Your voice and obey. I pray all these things in the name of my Savior, Jesus Christ. Amen.

A prayer of repentance and confession of unveiled mask

Heavenly Father, thank You that You are a compassionate God, full of mercy and grace. Lord, thank You for showing me that I have donned the mask of _____. Lord, I repent of my sin against You and ask that You, through Your Holy Spirit, will change my heart so that I will not keep this mask on. Lord, forgive me for being so prideful, so foolish, and even so afraid that I have to hide behind my mask. Lord, my trust and hope are in You. What can man do to me? Grant me the courage to confess and share with others about the mask I have on. Lord, I desire to walk in faithful obedience to You and not to please others. Lord, I surrender to You and ask that Your Holy Spirit will lead me to live in Your truth and obey Your will in my life. Thank You, Father. In Jesus' precious name I pray. Amen.

A prayer of praise and thanksgiving for a renewed heart and relationship

> *Abba Father, I praise You because You have answered my prayers to hear You in my life! Lord, I stand in awe of how mighty You are, yet You love someone like me. I was broken, and You healed me. I was sinful, and You forgave me. I was full of pride, yet You humbled me. I needed You, and You are always here for me. Abba Father God, thank You for my new heart. Help me to love and serve others genuinely through Your set of eyes. Grant me a joyful spirit to serve joyfully and lovingly.*
>
> *Thank You for the relationship I have with You because of Christ Jesus. Thank You for giving me the confidence that Your grace is indeed sufficient for me. I praise Your name. May all that I do and all that I say declare Your goodness and give You all the glory. Lord God Almighty, You alone deserve all honor and praise. Use me, Lord, to shine so that Your glory may be revealed in me. In Jesus' powerful name I pray. Amen.*

A prayer of faith to be filled with the Holy Spirit

Remember that the Holy Spirit already dwells inside you if you have invited Jesus to be Lord in your life. "In him you also, when you heard the word of truth, the gospel of your salvation, and believed in him, were sealed with the promised Holy Spirit" (Eph. 1:13, esv).

The Holy Spirit is waiting for you to allow Him to fill you. Submit and yield to God's Lordship. "According to your faith will it be done to you," (Matt. 9:29). "He rewards those who earnestly seek Him" (Heb. 11:6). Ask and you will receive. (See John 4:10.)

Just as I learned from Bill Bright, I suggest that you pray and surrender to God's will. Then claim the fullness of the Holy Spirit as an expression of your faith in God's command and promise.

Heavenly Father, You are so full of love and grace towards me. I desire to have a more intimate relationship with You. I realize that I have so much hidden sin before You. I admit that I have not allowed You to be in full control of my life. I confess that I have been controlling my own life and not allowing the Holy Spirit to have full reign. I thank You that I can come before You and receive forgiveness because of the sacrifice Jesus Christ made for me on Calvary's cross. I now confess and turn away from any sins that are blocking me from You.

I yield and surrender full control of my life to Jesus Christ. I want Him to be the master and the Lord of my life. By faith, I ask You to fill me with the Holy Spirit. You have commanded me to be filled, and I claim Your promise that You will fill me if I ask according to Your will and in the name of Jesus Christ.

Father God, to show my faith, I want to thank You for filling me with Your Holy Spirit and leading my life. I ask that You help me to continually yield my will to the Holy Spirit every moment of my life. Guide me to continuously abide in You and obey Your Spirit's leading in my life. I claim and ask all these things in the power and saving grace of my Lord Jesus Christ. Amen.

Appendix 4

A Glossary of Medical Terminology

ACUPUNCTURE—Today in most western cultures it is considered a "new alternative" medicine. In reality acupuncture medical treatment has been practiced for over 5,000 years. Basically, acupuncture is the insertion of very fine needles (sometimes in conjunction with electrical stimulus) on the body's surface, in order to influence physiological functioning of the body.

Source: Jeffrey A. Singer, www.acupuncture.com/education/theory/acuintro.htm.

ANXIETY DISORDER—Anxiety is a normal reaction to stress. It helps one deal with a tense situation in the office, study harder for an exam, and keep focused on an important speech. In general, it helps one cope. But when anxiety becomes an excessive, irrational dread of everyday situations, it becomes a disabling disorder. Anxiety disorders affect about 40 million Americans age 18 years and older (about 18 percent) in a given year, causing them to be filled with fearfulness and uncertainty. Unlike the relatively mild, brief anxiety caused by a stressful event (such as speaking in public or a first date), anxiety disorders last at least 6 months and can get worse if they are not treated. Anxiety disorders commonly occur along with other mental or physical illnesses, including alcohol or substance abuse, which may mask anxiety symptoms or make them worse. In some cases, these other illnesses need to be treated before a person will respond to treatment for the anxiety disorder.

Five major types of anxiety disorders are:

- Generalized Anxiety Disorder (GAD) (refer to Generalized Anxiety Disorder for more info)

- Obsessive-Compulsive Disorder (OCD)

- Panic Disorder

- Post-Traumatic Stress Disorder (PTSD)

- Social Phobia (or Social Anxiety Disorder)

Source: http://www.nimh.nih.gov/publicat/anxiety.cfm#anx1.

ARTHROSCOPIC SURGERY—Arthroscopy is a way for a surgeon to look into your joint with a camera. The most common type of arthroscopy is arthroscopic knee surgery. Other common arthroscopic surgeries include shoulder, elbow, wrist, ankle, and hip arthroscopy.

Source: www.orthopedics.about.com/od/arthroscopy/.

DEPRESSIVE DISORDER—Depressive disorders come in different forms, just as is the case with other illnesses such as heart disease. Depression affects women, men, and the elderly, and even children.

Major depression is manifested by a combination of symptoms (see symptom list) that interfere with the ability to work, study, sleep, eat, and enjoy once pleasurable activities. Such a disabling episode of depression may occur only once but more commonly occurs several times in a lifetime. A less severe type of depression, **dysthymia**, involves long-term, chronic symptoms that do not disable, but keep one from functioning well or from feeling good.

Another type of depression is **bipolar disorder**, also called manic-depressive illness. Not nearly as prevalent as other forms of depressive disorders, bipolar disorder is characterized by cycling mood changes: severe highs (mania) and lows (depression). Sometimes the mood switches are dramatic and rapid, but most often they are gradual. When in the depressed cycle, an individual can have any or all of the symptoms of a depressive disorder. When in the manic cycle, the individual may be overactive, over talkative, and have a great deal of energy.

Symptoms of Depression and Mania

Not everyone who is depressed or manic experiences every symptom. Some people experience a few symptoms, some many. Severity of symptoms varies with individuals and also varies over time.

Depression

- Persistent sad, anxious, or "empty" mood

- Feelings of hopelessness, pessimism

- Feelings of guilt, worthlessness, helplessness

- Loss of interest or pleasure in hobbies/activities that were once enjoyed, including sex

- Decreased energy, fatigue, being "slowed down"

- Difficulty concentrating, remembering, making decisions

- Insomnia, early-morning awakening, or oversleeping

- Appetite and/or weight loss or overeating and weight gain

- Thoughts of death or suicide, suicide attempts

- Restlessness, irritability

- Persistent physical symptoms that do not respond to treatment, such as headaches, digestive disorders, and chronic pain

Mania

- Abnormal or excessive elation

- Unusual irritability

- Decreased need for sleep

- Grandiose notions

- Increased talking

- Racing thoughts

- Increased sexual desire

- Markedly increased energy

- Poor judgment

- Inappropriate social behavior

Causes of Depression

Some types of depression run in families, suggesting that a biological vulnerability can be inherited. However, it can also occur in people who have no family history of depression. Whether inherited or not, major depressive disorder is often associated with changes in brain structures or brain function. People who have low self-esteem, who consistently view themselves and the world with pessimism or who are readily overwhelmed by stress, are prone to depression.

In recent years, researchers have shown that physical changes in the body can be accompanied by mental changes as well. Medical illnesses such as stroke, heart attack, cancer, Parkinson's disease, and hormonal disorders can cause depressive illness, making the sick person apathetic and unwilling to care for his or her physical needs, thus prolonging the recovery period. Also, a serious loss, difficult relationship, financial problem, or any stressful change in life patterns can trigger a depressive episode.

Diagnostic evaluation and treatment

The first step to getting appropriate treatment for depression is a physical examination by a physician. Certain medications as well as some medical conditions such as a viral infection can cause the same symptoms as depression, and the physician should rule out these possibilities through examination, interview, and lab tests. If a physical cause for the depression is ruled out, a psychological evaluation should be done, by the physician or by referral to a psychiatrist or psychologist.

Source: http://www.nimh.nih.gov/publicat/depression.cfm#ptdepl, The National Institute of Mental Health, (NIH Publication No. 00-3561, 2000) Info is new version of the 1994 edition of *Plain Talk About Depression* and was written by Margaret Strock, Public Information and Communications Branch, National Institute of Mental Health (NIMH).

How to help yourself if you are depressed

Depressive disorders make one feel exhausted, worthless, helpless, and hopeless. Such negative thoughts and feelings make some people feel like giving up. It is important to realize that these negative views are part of the depression and typically do not accurately reflect the actual circumstances. Negative thinking fades as treatment begins to take effect. In the meantime:

- Set realistic goals in light of the depression and assume a reasonable amount of responsibility.

- Break large tasks into small ones, set priorities, and do what you can as you are able.

- Try to be with other people and confide in someone; it is usually better than being alone and secretive.

- Participate in activities that make you feel better.

- Mild exercise, going to a movie, a ballgame, or participating in religious, social, or other activities may help.

- Expect your mood to improve gradually, not immediately. Feeling better takes time.

- It is advisable to postpone important decisions until your depression has lifted. Before deciding to make a significant transition such as changing jobs or getting married or divorced discuss it with others who know you well and have a more objective view of your situation.

- People rarely "snap out of" depression. But they can feel a little better day-by-day.

- Remember, positive thinking will replace the negative thinking that is part of the depression and will disappear as your depression responds to treatment.

- Let your family and friends help you.

How family and friends can help the depressed person

The most important thing anyone can do for a depressed person is to help him or her get an appropriate diagnosis and treatment. This may involve encouraging the individual to stay with treatment until symptoms begin to abate (several weeks), or to seek different treatment if no improvement occurs. The second most important thing is to offer emotional support. This involves understanding, patience, affection, and encouragement.

Engage the depressed person in conversation and listen carefully. Do not disparage feelings expressed, but point out realities and offer hope. Do not ignore remarks about suicide. Report them to the depressed person's therapist. Invite the depressed person for walks, outings, to the movies, and other activities. Be gently insistent if your invitation is refused. Encourage participation in some activities that once gave pleasure, such as hobbies, sports, religious or cultural activities, but do not push the depressed person to undertake too much too soon. The depressed person needs diversion and company, but too many demands can increase feelings of failure.

Do not accuse the depressed person of faking illness or of laziness, or expect him or her to "snap out of it." Eventually, with treatment, most people do get better. Keep that in mind, and keep reassuring the depressed person that, with time and help, he or she will feel better.

Where to get help

Here are some types of people and places that will make a referral to or provide diagnostic and treatment services: family doctors, mental health specialists, such as psychiatrists, social workers, family service, clergy, employee assistance programs, and/or local psychiatric societies.

Source: http://www.nimh.nih.gov/publicat/depression.cfm#ptdep1, The National Institute of Mental Health, (NIH Publication No. 00-3561, 2000) Info is new version of 1994 edition of Plain Talk About Depression written by Margaret Strock, Public Information and Communications Branch, National Institute of Mental Health (NIMH).

GENERALIZED ANXIETY DISORDER—People with generalized anxiety disorder (GAD) go through the day filled with exaggerated worry and tension, even though there is little or nothing to provoke it. They anticipate disaster and are overly concerned about health issues, money, family problems, or difficulties at work. Sometimes just the thought of getting through the day produces anxiety.

GAD is diagnosed when a person worries excessively about a variety of everyday problems for at least six months. People with GAD can't seem to get rid of their concerns, even though they usually realize that their anxiety is more intense than the situation warrants. They can't relax, startle easily, and have difficulty concentrating. Often they have trouble falling asleep or staying asleep. Physical symptoms that often accompany the anxiety include fatigue, headaches, muscle tension, muscle aches, difficulty swallowing, trembling, twitching, irritability, sweating, nausea, lightheadedness, having to go to the bathroom frequently, feeling out of breath, and hot flashes.

Source: http://www.nimh.nih.gov/publicat/anxiety.cfm#anx1.

MENOPAUSE—Menopause is the period of time when a woman stops having her monthly period and experiences symptoms related to the lack of estrogen production. By definition, a woman is in menopause after her periods have stopped for one year. It is a normal part of aging and marks the end of a woman's reproductive years. Menopause typically occurs in a woman's late 40s to early 50s. However, women who have their ovaries surgically removed undergo "sudden" menopause.

The drop in estrogen levels during perimenopause and menopause triggers physical as well as emotional changes—such as depression or anxiety and changes in memory. Some physical changes include irregular or skipped periods, heavier or lighter periods, and hot flashes.

Coping with the symptoms of menopause

There are many other ways you can ease menopause symptoms and maintain your health. In general, these tips include ways to cope with mood swings, fears, and depression:

- Find a self-calming skill to practice such as yoga, meditation, or slow, deep breathing.

- Avoid tranquilizers.

- Engage in a creative outlet or hobby that fosters a sense of achievement.

- Stay connected with your family and community; nurture your friendships.

- Seek emotional support from friends, family members, or a professional counselor when needed.

- Take steps to stay cool during hot flashes, such as wearing loose clothing.

- Keep your bedroom cool to prevent night sweats and disturbed sleep.

- Take medicines, vitamins, and minerals as prescribed by your doctor.

- Eat healthfully and exercise regularly.

What are my options for treating depression during this phase of my life?

Your doctor will try to exclude any medical causes for your depression, such as thyroid problems.

Depression during perimenopause and menopause is treated in much the same way as depression that strikes at any other time; however, there is a growing body of evidence to suggest that estrogen replacement can provide relief of minor phys-ical and emotional symptoms, as well as prevent osteoporosis. However, hormone replacement therapy alone is not effective in treating more severe depression. Antidepressant drug therapy and/or psychotherapy may be necessary.

If you are experiencing symptoms of depression, be sure to talk to your doctor about finding a treatment that will work for you.

Source: www. medlineplus.gov, document under Perimenopause, Menopause, and Depression, (The Cleveland Clinic Foundation, 1995–2005). For additional written health information, please contact the Health Information Center at the Cleveland Clinic (216) 444-3771 or toll-free (800) 223-2273 extension 43771 or visit www .clevelandclinic.org/health/.

MULTIPLE SCLEROSIS—Multiple Sclerosis (MS) is an inflammatory disease of the Central Nervous System (CNS). That's the brain and spinal cord. Predominantly, it is a disease of the "white matter" tissue. The white matter is made up of nerve fibers which are responsible for transmitting communication signals both inter-nally within the CNS and between the CNS and the nerves supplying rest of the body. In general, people with MS can expe-rience partial or complete loss of any function that is controlled by, or passes through, the brain or spinal cord.

Source: www.mult-sclerosis.org/, Paul Jones.

PERIMENOPAUSE—Perimenopause is the stage of a woman's repro-ductive life that begins 8 to 10 years before menopause, when the ovaries gradually begin to produce less estrogen. Perimenopause lasts up until menopause, the point when the ovaries stop releasing eggs. In the last one to two years of perimenopause, the decrease in estrogen accelerates. At this stage, many women experience menopausal symptoms. (See *menopause* for more information)

Source: www. medlineplus.gov, document under Perimenopause, Menopause, and Depression.

POSTPARTUM DEPRESSION—Postpartum depression is an illness, like diabetes or heart disease. It can be treated with therapy, support networks and medicines such as antidepressants. Although many women get depressed right after childbirth, some women don't feel "down" until several weeks or months later. Depression that occurs within 6 months of childbirth may be postpartum depression.

Here are some symptoms of postpartum depression:

- Loss of interest or pleasure in life

- Loss of appetite

- Less energy and motivation to do things

- A hard time falling asleep or staying asleep

- Sleeping more than usual

- Increased crying or tearfulness

- Feeling worthless, hopeless, or overly guilty

- Feeling restless, irritable, or anxious

- Unexplained weight loss or gain

- Feeling like life isn't worth living

- Having thoughts about hurting yourself

- Worrying about hurting your baby

Are mood changes common after childbirth?

Many women have mood swings after they have a baby. One minute they feel happy, the next minute they start to cry. They may feel a little depressed, have a hard time concentrating, lose their appetite, or find that they cannot sleep well even when the baby is asleep. These symptoms usually start about 3 to 4 days after delivery and may last several days.

If you're a new mother and have any of these symptoms, you have what are called the "baby blues." The "blues" are considered a normal part of early motherhood and usually go away within 10 days after delivery. However, some women have worse symptoms, or symptoms last longer. That is called "postpartum depression."

Who gets postpartum depression?

- Postpartum depression is more likely if you have had any of the following:
- Previous postpartum depression
- Depression not related to pregnancy
- Severe premenstrual syndrome (PMS)
- A difficult marriage
- Few family members or friends to talk to or depend on
- Stressful life events during the pregnancy or after childbirth

Why do women get postpartum depression?

The exact cause isn't known. Hormone levels change during pregnancy and right after childbirth. Those hormone changes may produce chemical changes in the brain that play a part in causing depression.

Feeling depressed doesn't mean that you're a bad person, that you did something wrong, or that you brought it on yourself.

How long does postpartum depression last?

It's hard to say. Some women feel better within a few weeks, but others feel depressed or "not themselves" for many months. Women who have more severe symptoms of depression or who have had depression in the past may take longer to get well.

Source: Written by familydoctor.org editorial staff; source: American Academy of Family Physicians, www.familydoctor.org/index.xml.

RESTLESS LEG SYNDROME—Restless leg syndrome (RLS) is a disorder of sensation and movements that affect both men and women. It can occur at any age, including during childhood, but often worsens with age and becomes a problem for older adults. RLS affects the quality of sleep, which in turn can interfere with daytime activities. Some cases of RLS are related to other conditions, such as pregnancy, iron-deficiency anemia or kidney failure.

What does it feel like to have RLS?

People who have RLS sometimes say it's difficult to describe their symptoms. If you have RLS, you may have a "creepy-crawly" feeling in your legs that makes you want to move around. Because this feeling tends to start when you're lying still, you may have trouble sleeping at night. Or, you may find that you have the sensation any time you sit still, such as when you're working at a desk, watching a movie, or reading. Moving your legs makes the feeling go away for a few minutes, but it comes back after you sit or lie still again.

Source: Written by familydoctor.org editorial staff; source: American Academy of Family Physicians, www.familydoctor.org/index.xml.

SEASONAL AFFECTIVE DISORDER—SAD is a form of depressive behavior that is triggered by seasons. Symptoms typically associated with SAD are the following:

- Depression with a fall or winter onset
- Lack of energy
- Decreased interest in work or significant activities
- Increased appetite with weight gain
- Carbohydrate cravings
- Increased sleep, excessive daytime sleepiness
- Social withdrawal
- Afternoon slumps with decreased energy and concentration
- Slow, sluggish, lethargic movement

Source: www.healthline.com.

SPIRITUAL DEPRESSION—There is another kind of depression—spiritual depression. It is a malaise that seems to be upon many people from time to time when they feel "cut off" or "far away" from God. While in it they have no enthusiasm for God's Word. They seem "weary in well doing." They seem ready to collapse under persecution.

Source: David L. Antion, Ph.D., www.Biblestudy.org/basicart/depress .html.

To request the message on Depression write to: GUARDIAN MINISTRIES, P.O. Box 50734, Pasadena, CA. 91115

(Author's note: For help with spiritual depression, I strongly advise you to pray with your pastor, fellowship group, or close friends who are firmly grounded in God's truth.)

TRANSVERSE MYELITIS VIRAL DISEASE—TM is a clinical syndrome in which an immune-mediated process causes neural injury to the spinal cord, resulting in varying degrees of weakness, sensory alterations and autonomic dysfunctions.

Source: www.myelitis.org/abouttm.htm. Written by: Dr. Douglas A. Kerr, Director of the Johns Hopkins Transverse Myelitis Center. Source: "Transverse Myelitis: Pathogenesis, Diagnosis and Treatment," Frontiers in Bioscience 9, 1483–1499, May 1, 2004.

Transverse myelitis (TM) is a neurological syndrome caused by inflammation of the spinal cord. TM is uncommon but not rare. The term *myelitis* is a nonspecific term for inflammation of the spinal cord; transverse refers to involvement across one level of the spinal cord. The spinal cord carries motor nerve fibers to the limbs and trunk and sensory fibers from the body back to the brain. Inflammation within the spinal cord interrupts these pathways and causes the common presenting symptoms of TM which include limb weakness, sensory disturbance, bowel and bladder dysfunction, back pain and radicular pain (pain in the distribution of a single spinal nerve).

Almost all patients will develop leg weakness of varying degrees of severity. Sensation is diminished below the level of spinal cord involvement in the majority of patients. Some experience tingling or numbness in the legs. Pain (ascertained as appreciation of pinprick by the neurologist) and temperature sensation are diminished in the majority of patients. Appreciation of vibration (as caused by a tuning fork) and joint position sense may also be decreased or spared. Bladder and bowel sphincter control are disturbed in the majority of patients. Many patients with TM report a tight banding or girdle-like sensation around the trunk. The trunk may be very sensitive to touch.

Recovery may be absent, partial, or complete and generally begins within 1 to 3 months. Significant recovery is unlikely, if no improvement occurs by 3 months (Feldman, et. al., 1981). Most patients with TM show good to fair recovery. TM is generally a monophasic illness (one-time occurrence); however, a small percentage of patients may suffer a recurrence, especially if there is a predisposing underlying illness.

Source: Dr. Joanne Lynn, www.myelitis.org/tm.htm (The Transverse Myelitis Association, 2004). Dr. Joanne Lynn is an Assistant Professor of Neurology at Ohio State University. Document dated 1997.

Bibliography

Anderson, Hans Christian, "The Emperor's New Clothes," in *Great Illustrated Classics*, Bardfield Center, Essex: Miles Kelly Publishing Ltd., 2004.

Atteberry, Mark, *Walking with God on the Road You Never Wanted to Travel*, Nashville: Thomas Nelson Inc., 2005.

Biebel, David B., and Harold G. Koenig, *New Light on Depression*, Grand Rapids, MI: Zondervan, 2004.

Bright, Bill, *Moving Beyond Discouragement and Defeat*, Orlando, FL: New Life Publications, 1994.

Buchanan, Sue, *A Party Begins in the Heart*, Nashville: Word Publishing, 2001.

Cothern, Clark, *Spirit Controlled Living*, Oregon: Multnomah Publishers Inc., 2000.

Crockett, Kent, *I Once Was Blind But Now I Squint*, Chattanooga, TN: AMG Publishers, 2004.

DeMoss, Nancy Leigh, *Lies Women Believe and the Truth That Sets Them Free*, Chicago: Moody Press, 2001.

Eldredge, John, *Waking the Dead*, Nashville: Thomas Nelson Inc., 2003.

Eldredge, John, and Stasi Eldredge, *Captivating*, Nashville: Thomas Nelson Inc., 2005.

Graham, Billy, *The Holy Spirit*, Dallas, TX: Word Publishing, 1988.

Graham, Ruth, *In Every Pew Sits a Broken Heart*, Grand Rapids, MI: Zondervan, 2004.

Hart, Archibald, and Catherine Hart Weber, *Unveiling Depression in Women*, Grand Rapids, MI: Baker House Publishing, 2002.

Johnson, Barbara, *Boomerang Joy*, Grand Rapids, MI: Zondervan, 2000.

————, *Fresh Elastic for Stretched Out Moms*, Grand Rapids MI: Fleming H. Revell, division of Baker Book House, 2003.

————, *Leaking Laffs between Pampers and Depends*, Nashville: W Publishing Group, 2000.

————, *Mama, Get the Hammer! There's a Fly on Papa's Head!*, Nashville: W Publishing Group, 1994.

————, *Stick a Geranium in Your Hat and Be Happy!*, Nashville: W Publishing Group, 2004.

Lucado, Max, *It's Not About Me*, Brentwood, TN: Integrity Publishers, 2004.

————, *Traveling Light*, Nashville: W Publishing Group, 2001.

Omartian, Stormie, *Just Enough Light for the Step I'm On*, Eugene, OR: Harvest House Publishers, 1999.

Ortberg, John, *If You Want to Walk on Water, You've Got to Get out of the Boat*, Grand Rapids, MI: Zondervan, 2001.

Patterson, Ben, *Deepening Your Conversation with God*, Bloomington, MN: Bethany House Publishers, 2001.

Schaeffer, Dan, *Faking Church*, Uhrichsville, OH: Barbour Publishing Inc., 2004.

Tada, Joni Eareckson, *Holiness in Hidden Places*, Nashville: Thomas Nelson, 1999.

Tan, Siang-Yang, and John Ortberg, *Coping with Depression*, Grand Rapids, MI: Baker Publishing Group, 2004.

Wallace, Peter, *Out of the Quiet*, Colorado Springs: NavPress, 2004.

Walsh, Sheila, *Extraordinary Faith,* Nashville: Thomas Nelson, Inc., 2005.

————, *Honestly*, Grand Rapids, MI: Zondervan, 1996.

————, *The Heartache No One Sees*, Nashville: Thomas Nelson, Inc., 2004.

————, *Unexpected Grace*, Nashville: Thomas Nelson, Inc., 2002.

Wagner, Holly, *When It Pours He Reigns,* Nashville: Thomas Nelson, Inc., 2004.

Weaver, Joanna, *Having a Mary Heart in a Martha World*, Colorado Springs: Waterbrook Press, 2002.

Notes

PREFACE

1. *Merriam-Webster's Collegiate Dictionary*, 10th ed. (Springfield, MA: Merriam-Webster, Inc., 1998), s.v. "mask."

1—CRYING OUT TO GOD

1. Joanne Lynn, MD, "Transverse, Myelitis: Symptoms, Causes and Diagnosis," *The Transverse Myelitis Association*, http://www.myelitis.org/ (accessed May 22, 2008).

3—THE MASK OF WELLNESS

1. *Dictionary.com Unabridged*, s.v. "hypochondriac," http://dictionary .reference.com/browse/hypochondriac (accessed May 23, 2008).
2. National Institute of Mental Health (NIMH), "Generalized Anxiety Disorder (GAD)," http://www.nimh.nih.gov/health/publications/anxiety -disorders/complete-publication.shtml#pub7 (accessed May 23, 2008).

6—THE MASK OF STRENGTH

1. *Dictionary.com Unabridged*, s.v. "complex," http://dictionary.reference. com/browse/complex (accessed May 23, 2008).
2. Bill Bright, *Moving Beyond Discouragement and Defeat*, (Orlando, FL: New Life Publications, 1994), 30.
3. Ibid., 31–36.
4. Ibid., 32.

8—THE MASK OF DEVOTION

1. Alex Strachan, *The Vancouver Sun*, Wednesday May 10, 2006.
2. Ibid.
3. *Collins Dictionary and Thesaurus Express*, s.v. "devotion."
4. "Heart, How It Works," American Heart Association, http://www .americanheart.org/presenter.jhtml?identifier=4642 (accessed May 26, 2008).
5. *The American Heritage Dictionary of the English Language*, 4th Ed., s.v. "heart."

6. Based on web search on word *heart* in the New International Version, http://www.biblegateway.com/keyword?search=heart&searchtype=all&wholewordsonly=yes&version1=3&bookset=2 (accessed May 26, 2008).

7. James Strong, *Strong's Exhaustive Concordance to the Bible*, electronic ed. (2006), s.v. "yirah," 3374.

8. W. E. Vine, F. M. Unger, and W. White, *Vine's Complete Expository Dictionary of Old and New Testament Words,* (Nashville: Thomas Nelson Publishers, 1996), s.v. "jealous."

9. Quote from *The Lord of the Rings: The Two Towers*, directed by Peter Jackson, 2nd in the trilogy of films based on J. R. R. Tolkien's novel *The Lord of the Rings*, (Los Angeles: New Line Productions, Inc., 2002), http://www.imdb.com/title/tt0167261/quotes (accessed May 26, 2008).

10. Quote from *The Lord of the Rings: The Fellowship of the Ring*, directed by Peter Jackson, 1st in the trilogy of films based on J. R. R. Tolkien's novel *The Lord of the Rings*, (Los Angeles: New Line Productions, Inc., 2001), http://thinkexist.com/quotation/but-the-hearts-of-men-are-easily-corrupted-and/348999.html (accessed May 26, 2008).

11. Billy Graham, *The Holy Spirit*, (Dallas, TX: Word Publishing, 1988), 92–93.

11—The Mask of Satisfaction and Happiness

1. Quote from *Ladder 49*, directed by Jay Russell (Burbank, CA: Touchtone Pictures, 2004), http://en.wikiquote.org/wiki/Ladder_49 (accessed May 27, 2008).

12—The Mask of Optimism

1. Holly Wagner, *When It Pours He Reigns*, (Nashville: Thomas Nelson, Inc., 2004).

2. Quote from *The Lord of the Rings: Return of the King*, directed by Peter Jackson, 3rd in the trilogy of films based on J. R. R. Tolkien's novel *The Lord of the Rings*, (Los Angeles: New Line Productions, Inc., 2003), http://www.imdb.com/title/tt0167260/quotes (accessed May 27, 2008).

3. Quote by Babatunde Olatunji, http://www.quotegarden.com/live-now.html (accessed May 27, 2008).

13—The Mask of Sociability

1. *Dictionary.com Unabridged*, s.v. "social butterfly," http://dictionary.reference.com/browse/social%20butterfly (accessed May 26, 2008).

2. Ibid., s.v. "social," http://dictionary.reference.com/browse/social (accessed May 27, 2008).

14—The Mask of Sincerity and Righteousness

1. Barbara Johnson, *Fresh Elastic for Stretched-Out Moms* (Grand Rapids, MI: Fleming H. Revell, 2003), 103.

2. Stuart Hample, *My Mom's the Best Mom,* (New York: Workman Publishing Company, Inc., 2000).

15—We Find Ourselves at War

1. John Eldredge, *Waking the Dead,* (Nashville: Thomas Nelson Inc., 2003), 26.

2. Steve Russo, *Halloween,* (Eugene, OR: Harvest House Publishers, 1998), 70–71.

16—We Put On the Armor of God

1. E. D. Radmacher, R. B. Allen, and H. W. House, *The Nelson Study Bible: New King James Version,* (Nashville: T. Nelson Publishers, 1997).

2. Sheila Walsh, *The Heartache No One Sees,* (Nashville: Thomas Nelson Inc., 2004), 128–129.

3. Max Anders, *New Christian's Handbook,* (Nashville: Thomas Nelson, Inc., 1999), 135.

4. *Cards Eh!* (Richmond, BC, Canada: JK Productions, 2005). For orders or info: (604) 277-4908.

5. *Canadian Encyclopedia,* "A Mari usque ad Mare," by W. Kay Lamb, http://www.thecanadianencyclopedia.com/index.cfm?PgNm=TCE&Params=A1ARTA0000001 (accessed May 28, 2008).

Conclusion

1. Hans Christian Andersen, "The Emperor's New Clothes," in *Children's Classic Stories,* (Bardfield Center, Essex: Miles Kelly Publishing Ltd., 2004), 271.

2. Eldredge, 75.

3. Ibid., 82.

4. Ibid., 83.

5. Ibid., 87.

6. Ibid., 88.

7. *Herbie: Fully Loaded,* directed by Angela Robinson, (Burbank, CA: Buena Vista Pictures, 2005).

8. *The Love Bug,* directed by Robert Stevenson, (Burbank, CA: Walt Disney Productions, 1968).

9. Graham, 139.

10. Bruce Bickel and Stan Jantz, *Bruce & Stan's Guide to God,* (Eugene, OR: Harvest House Publishers, 1997), 98.

11. Graham, 103.

12. Ibid., 151.

13. Ibid., 99.